Beyond Political Correctness
Toward the Inclusive University

The term 'political correctness' has lately been transformed into a weapon of neoconservatism. Once used to poke fun at social movements and civil-rights groups for occasional lapses into rigidity, it has since become a popular handle for the neoconservative critique of higher education. Aimed at anti-racist and anti-sexist initiatives within universities, colleges, and other major social institutions, the term is used to discredit such innovations as employment equity, selective recruitment of students from groups that have suffered systemic discrimination, sexual harassment policies, and women's studies programs, casting these as forms of tyranny that destroy academic freedom and merit.

This anthology is the first sociological analysis of political correctness and the first study of the phenomenon in Canada. Contributors argue on behalf of an inclusive university, showing that recent reforms not only work toward broadening human rights, but provide a welcome reorganization of knowledge. All but two papers have been written specifically for this text.

Part One explores the history and social organization of the discourse, with the accent on Canadian material. The essays explore what the term has signified to different groups and to what ends they have used it. This section moves from an overview of political-correctness discourse to its explicit manifestation within universities in debates concerning academic ideals. Part Two looks at the classroom, a major site for building the inclusive university. Here, contributors explore feminist and anti-racist teaching and the limitations to such teaching imposed by the economic and political contexts of contemporary universities.

As these scholars trenchantly reveal, the political-correctness debate will ultimately affect the lives of everyone. This book offers insight into the values, ideals, and motives of both sides.

Stephen Richer is a professor in the Department of Sociology and Anthropology, Carleton University. Lorna Weir is an associate professor in the Department of Sociology, York University.

Beyond Political Correctness

Toward the Inclusive University

Edited by
Stephen Richer and Lorna Weir

UNIVERSITY OF TORONTO PRESS
Toronto Buffalo London

Toronto Buffalo London
Printed in Canada

ISBN 0-8020-5025-5 (cloth)
ISBN 0-8020-7748-X (paper)

Printed on acid-free paper

Canadian Cataloguing in Publication Data

Main entry under title:

Beyond political correctness : toward the inclusive university

ISBN 0-8020-5025-5 (bound) ISBN 0-8020-7748-X (pbk.)

1. Discrimination in higher education.
2. Political correctness. I. Richer, Stephen, 1941– . II. Weir, Lorna, 1952– .

LC212.4.B48 1995 370.19'34 C95-930023-6

University of Toronto Press acknowledges the financial assistance to its publishing program of the Canada Council and the Ontario Arts Council.

Contents

Acknowledgments

We are pleased to acknowledge the generous contributions of the following people: Virgil Duff, Executive Editor, University of Toronto Press, for his patience and advice; James Leahy for his fine copy-editing; Imelda Mulvihill, Director of Planning Analysis and Statistics, Carleton University, Ottawa, for her timely provision of missing values; Jennifer Quaile for her editorial and technical work; Graham Lowe for his good leads; Mervin Taylor for his excellent work as research assistant; and Carleton University for its enabling financial support.

Contributors

Jennifer Bankier	Dalhousie Law School, Dalhousie University
Himani Bannerji	Department of Sociology, York University
Janice Drakich	Department of Sociology, University of Windsor
bell hooks	Distinguished Professor of English, City University of New York
Tim McCaskell	Equal Opportunity Office, Toronto Board of Education
Geraldine Moriba-Meadows	Journalist living in New York
Stephen Richer	Department of Sociology and Anthropology, Carleton University
Victor Shea	Division of Humanities, York University
Dorothy E. Smith	Department of Sociology in Education, The Ontario Institute for Studies in Education
Daiva K. Stasiulis	Department of Sociology and Anthropology, Carleton University

Marilyn Taylor	Department of Applied Social Science, Concordia University
Jennifer Dale Tiller	Equity Communications Consultant, Ottawa
Jo-Ann Wallace	Department of English, University of Alberta
Lorna Weir	Department of Sociology, York University

BEYOND POLITICAL CORRECTNESS

Introduction: Political Correctness and the Inclusive University

STEPHEN RICHER AND LORNA WEIR

A neoconservative-driven news media wave carried the phrase 'political correctness' (PC) into North American homes beginning in October 1990, and by May 1991 the English-Canadian media were busily adapting PC to Canadian reference points.[1] Although PC had a long prior history in social movements and news media during the 1980s (see Weir, this volume), the neoconservative use of PC was distinctive. Neoconservative appropriations of PC initially targeted anti-racist and feminist initiatives within universities, casting these as forms of tyranny that destroyed academic freedom and merit. Unlike previous uses of PC that had poked fun at leftist and social movement politics for occasional lapses into overzealous rigidity, neoconservative PC is an ideological move aimed at halting these movements: 'political correctness' thus ostensibly operates as a successor to communism. Recycling hyperbolic anti-communist rhetoric, neoconservatives dismiss human rights initiatives as forms of intolerant fanaticism and oppression.

PC and Canadian Universities

Within Canadian universities, PC discourse has combined with, and transformed, older forms of conservative educational ideology, as can be seen from an examination of two well-known conservative texts on higher education: *The Great Brain Robbery* and *The Closing of the American Mind.* Bercuson, Bothwell, and Granatstein's *The Great Brain Robbery* (1984) was concerned with a purported decline in the quality of higher education, which the authors believed was the result of university expansion during the 1960s and 1970s. Their argument for a core curriculum was directed against both the tenure system and Canadian studies courses. Bloom's

The Closing of the American Mind (1987), a book much read and respected at the University of Toronto, where Bloom had once taught, was a critique of relativism and its influence on education. His argument centred on 'the' moral goal of education, the ideal of the educated person, and the defence of the humanities. For Bloom, undergraduate education offered a crucial opportunity: 'The importance of these years for an American cannot be overestimated. They are civilization's only chance to get to him' (Bloom 1987, 336). Curious the universality, neutrality, and transcendence of 'civilization'; strange the overspecificity of the masculine 'him'; and odd the restrictive 'only' in these two sentences.

These earlier conservative works lack many of the distinctive offensive moves of PC discourse, which specialize in attacks on employment equity; selective recruitment of students from social groups that have suffered systemic discrimination; pedagogy and curriculum integration; and anti-sexist and anti-racist policies. It is, of course, the case that there have been fierce struggles in Canadian universities and colleges around the creation of sexual harassment officers and policies, resistance to the employment equity provisions in hiring required under the federal Employment Equity Act, and a distinct lack of joy in certain quarters around the creation of women's studies programs. Various bulletins and newspapers have transmitted the laments of protesters on these issues from at least the mid-1980s. In the United States, affirmative action, educational equity, and curriculum integration were criticized during the 1980s in neoconservative journals such as *Commentary* and *The New Criterion* years before the term 'politically correct' appeared in their pages. Nonetheless, PC added a new dimension to the neoconservative critique of higher education. The 'political correctness' formulation enabled neoconservatives to fashion a single enemy from disparate institutional initiatives within universities. Proponents of PC discourse take a range of equity-related concerns and conveniently reify them, facilitating counter-mobilization. The marked success of PC as a news theme eventually gave immense popularity to the neoconservative campaign against what has come to be known as 'the inclusive university.'

The neoconservative campaign against political correctness occurs in the context of massive social change taking place within Canadian universities and colleges. It has been well documented that the expansion of universities and colleges since the 1960s resulted in the increased inclusion of people who were working class and lower middle class in origin. In tandem with the expansion of the social-class basis of Canadian universities and colleges, a gender transformation has also occurred. Over the past generation, the proportion of women registered full-time at the undergraduate level has risen from 38.5 per cent in 1972–3 (Association of Universities and Colleges of Canada [AUCC] 1990, 18) to 54 per cent in 1992–3 (Human Resources Development Canada 1994, 8). Women formed 46 per cent of Master's students in 1992–3 (Human Resources Development Canada 1994, 8), up from 27.1 per cent in 1972–3 (AUCC 1990, 18). At the faculty level, in 1990 women comprised 20 per cent of the total (Human Resources Development Canada 1994, 20), rising from 14.4 per cent in 1976 (AUCC 1991). Occupational segregation remains firmly in place among support staff although there has been gradual change in administration at the lower- to mid-management level.

Unfortunately, while most universities and colleges have been gathering figures related to the gender composition of students and employees since the early 1970s, equivalent time series are not availabile for people with disabilities, aboriginal peoples, and racialized groups. It has only been since the late 1980s, in response to the Federal Contractors Program, that universities and colleges began to gather information on the racial composition of their employees. But there are still no available national data regarding the racial–ethnic composition of employees in Canadian universities. This is due both to uneven participation in the Federal Contractors Program and to the variation among universities in the initial year of involvement. The situation with respect to students is worse, in that few universities have educational equity policies, and surveys related to the racial–ethnic demographics of students have yet to take place. The extent to which Canadian universities have or have not reflected the growth of racialized social groups proportionate to the population as a whole is completely unknown.

Since, from their inception in the European Middle Ages, universities have been institutions for white, male élites,[2] a longer historical view would lead us to find remarkably unsurprising the current gender and racial conflicts on Canadian university campuses.[3] The challenge of building the inclusive university is not simply a matter of adding numbers of women, people of colour, aboriginals, and people with disabilities to universities sufficient to mirror their proportion in the national population. This would be relatively straightforward to accomplish. Far more difficult to remedy are situations in theory classrooms where men are garrulous and women lack the confidence to speak, thereby repeating the historic exclusion of women from the genres and registers in which theory has been developed by and for men. Redefining the field of comparative literature so that it will no longer be confined to the study of Western

European languages, a practice complicit with imperialism and racism, will take time and effort. University and college policies can go far in helping to eliminate sexual and racial harassment at the level of abusive epithets and physical assault on campus, where less than a decade ago nothing was done even for those few cases that were documented by departments and reported to administrative authorities. Such policies cannot, however, address the kinds of cultural problems noted above, problems requiring the resignification of academic disciplines at the level of everyday social practice. At issue in 'the PC debates' are issues of profound cultural change and the normative criteria for public and private policy designed to promote such change.

Given that the attempt to build an inclusive university challenges so much of the daily practice of the academy – from textbooks to the organization of classroom talk to hiring practices – resistance was entirely predictable. If, as Bourdieu (1988) argues, there are 'two antagonistic principles of hierarchization' at work in the university – a cultural hierarchy rewarding intellectual contributions and a social hierarchy serving to reinforce extramural temporal power within academe (48) – we believe that the neoconservative campaign against PC serves to further consolidate the social hierarchy. More precisely, the anti-PC campaign uses the universalistic values justifying the first principle against attempts to intervene in the second. The specific campaign against PC may fade, but the struggles around academic culture and policy will continue under differing guises into the foreseeable future.

One can see this ideological adaptability in the Society for Academic Freedom and Scholarship, a Canadian neoconservative organization, and close kin to the National Organization of Scholars in the United States, the work of which the Society commends in its *Newsletter*. References to 'PC' are often made in the *Newsletter* of the Society for Academic Freedom and Scholarship – for example, 'Canadian Philosophic Association Becomes PC' (Brown and Wubnig 1992, 6) and 'John Furedy,[4] University of Toronto, Talked about How an Iron Curtain of Political Correctness Is Falling in North American Universities' (Wubnig 1993, 1). The stated purposes of the Society for Academic Freedom and Scholarship, however, rest on long-term goals not tied to the transiency of PC:

1. To resist the ideological misuse of teaching and scholarship.
2. To support rigorous standards in research and teaching in university hiring practices.
3. To preserve academic freedom and the free exchange of ideas, regardless of popular doctrine.[5]

The embarrassing lapse of rigorous grammar that reduces purpose (2) to nonsense is of little moment here: one gets the general drift.

What one sees in the goals of the Society for Academic Freedom and Scholarship is a tactic that poses the inclusive university in *opposition* to academic freedom and merit.[6] It is either affirmative action *or* merit, either human rights *or* academic freedom. The leaflet advertising their March 1993 conference, The University in Jeopardy, illustrates this antithesis:

> This conference will explore ... the threats to academic freedom and to the quality of university teaching and research, arising from the institutionalizing of influences extraneous to the basic function of a university. Such influences include a myriad of social-policy regulations and bureaus, such as employment equity offices, and sexual harassment and race relations tribunals.[7]

Similarly, in April 1992, the Faculty Association at the University of Western Ontario requested a review of that university's race relations policy. The president of the Faculty Association, Ted Medzon, was quoted counterposing racial harassment policies to academic freedom:

> All of us agree that overt racism and harassment should be removed from university life ... the problem is that the number of programs and policies that faculty have to follow lead to an incremental loss of academic freedom. (Medzon quoted in Chiose 1993, 9)

Tangentially, the above would be open to the reading that *covert* racism and harassment are quite acceptable in university life. In any case, Medzon's objection lies not in the specifics of policy at the University of Western Ontario, but to anti-harassment codes in general.

In Ontario the most recent example of the broad use of academic freedom to oppose human rights occurred in early 1994 subsequent to the October 1993 release by the Ministry of Education and Training of the 'Framework Regarding Prevention of Harassment and Discrimination in Ontario Colleges' – popularly known as the 'zero tolerance' (to harassment and discrimination) framework. The Framework aimed to set up a series of internal policies and programs in all Ontario universities and colleges that would enforce the Ontario Human Rights Code, thereby expanding the enforcement mechanisms for human rights legislation beyond the limited capabilities of the Ontario Human Rights Commission. The Framework document laid down criteria for the development of policy at all universities and colleges – 'The policy will include coverage of (1) harassment; (2) sexual harassment; (3) discrimination; (4) negative environment or climate' – but did not specify the precise content of local policy and procedures. Several months after the initiative had first been announced in October 1993, a great cry was heard from several universities regarding loss of academic freedom.

While we believe that there were major problems with the drafting of the Framework, including the choice of 'zero tolerance' as a code name (a phrase dating to Ronald Reagan's 'war on drugs'),[8] of particular interest here are the ways in which the political debate took place. Those opposed to the Ministry initiative sought to discredit it as an instance of 'political correctness,' placing it in opposition to 'academic freedom.' They feared that the initiative would impose 'politically correct canons of criticism' (Wright 1994) that would lead to self-censorship by minority figures, perchance Nietzsche, 'who did not have the benefit of being enlightened by the politically correct' (Cook 1994). The lead sentence of an article on the controversy in *The Manchester Guardian Weekly* likewise framed the debate in terms of PC: 'There are fears in Canada that political correctness is going too far' (Trevena 1994, 3).

The Faculty Board and Faculty Council at Trent University responded to the Ministry with a tough statement, later endorsed by the McMaster Univesity Faculty Association, that staked out the Framework as an attack on academic freedom:

> We defend, therefore, the right to certain types of speech and academic expression which, in fact, we do not condone, and in some cases deplore. This includes the right to offend one another. It includes the right to express – and the right of access to intellectual materials which express – racially, ethnically, or sexually discriminatory ideas, opinion, or feelings, just as it includes the right to expressions that favour inequality of incomes or benefits. It also includes the right to make others uncomfortable, to injure, by expression, anyone's self-esteem, and to create, by expression, atmospheres in which some may not feel welcome or accepted. (McMaster University Faculty Association 1994, 4)

The passage captures the sense of truculent entitlement that some academics bring to the question of harassment and discrimination at universities and colleges, coupled with conspicuous insensitivity to the question of human rights.

Others responded more positively to the Framework and directly criticized the dichotomy being constructed between academic freedom and anti-harassment measures. The Faculty Association of Waterloo passed a motion noting that, 'the University is free to develop its own policy in its own words, one that recognizes that the relationship between academic freedom and freedom from harassment and discrimination is not an oppositional one' (OCUFA Forum 1994, 4).

Human rights are becoming institutional rights[9] in Canadian universities and colleges. Less than a decade ago there were no sexual harassment offices in Canadian universities and colleges. Individuals – overwhelmingly women – had no de facto recourse when they were subjected to this form of harassment other than to rely on the misogyny of the criminal justice system. The precedents set by feminists fighting gender inequality in the academy are now being entrenched across the gamut of human rights needs that characterize the inclusive university so that racialized groups, sexual minorities, people with disabilities, and others can likewise have institutional recourse; this is the advantage of having institutional rights linked to complaint procedures. This institutional vesting of rights is being done now on many Canadian campuses. The neoconservative appropriation of PC is in part a move to halt this human rights aspect of building the inclusive university.

A recent statement by the Canadian Association of University Teachers (CAUT) demonstrates that classrooms fall within the jurisdiction of the Ontario Human Rights Code under the section guaranteeing equal treatment for all citizens with respect to services (CAUT 1994, 7–9). Persistent comments or behaviour in the classroom that are offensive, intimidating, hostile, or unwelcome on the basis of race, ancestry, place of origin, colour, ethnic origin, citizenship, creed, sex, sexual orientation, disability, age, marital status, family status, receipt of public assistance, record of provincial offences or pardoned federal offences constitute human rights violations in the province of Ontario. Such comments and behaviours fall outside the bounds of academic freedom in teaching, although to this point they have not been subject to much in the way of institutional control. Harassment and discrimination prevention policies open up the classroom to external accountability where heretofore teaching has been culturally understood by faculty as a licence to say well nigh anything in the classroom or office. Such accountability in turn provokes resistance draped in the mantle of academic freedom and resistance to PC.

Misgivings about the entrenchment of human rights within the operating practices of universities and colleges run across the political spectrum.[10] PC can be seen as a discourse device to ally disparate elements ranging from the liberal to the neoconservative and sometimes, on a bad day, the left. Many faculty fear human rights complaints and resent that their behaviour may increasingly be challenged. In fact, human rights legislation likely does have power effects that limit autocratic authority.

In our dealings with other academics we have found people worried about 'frivolous' and 'false' accusations of human rights abuses or the creation of a general climate of intimidation hobbling vigorous debate. The fears are similar to those in circulation about sexual harassment, and the concerns are by no means confined to neoconservatives. In point of fact, however, formal complaints of sexual harassment are few, so few that the policies are often cynically dismissed as toothless. At Carleton University, for instance, during the two years 1991–3, formal complaints numbered a grand total of eight. There is no evidence that false accusations of sexual harassment are greater in number than false accusations of any offence found in the Criminal Code of Canada, and few would argue that the Criminal Code should be abolished, though that argument is often made about sexual harassment policies. Academic freedom has not fallen victim to sexual harassment complaints, and there is no reason to believe that it would expire in the face of institutionally based human rights enforcement.

Given the specifics of organizational culture of research universities, human rights policies and programs will have to be specifically adapted to fit the institutional location. Additional 'interpretation and application' guidelines should be developed adumbrating those that already exist in human rights codes. Academic freedom must be secured within a human rights context.

Whereas academic freedom has been used to impede human rights policies, the merit principle has been invoked to resist affirmative-action and other equity-driven policies. Indeed, even hiring practices not done under such policies are open to charges of violating the merit principle (see Wallace, this volume).

One way to begin analysing the false dichotomy of merit and affirmative action is to problematize the concept of merit itself. One need not be a feminist to acknowledge the intellectual dominance of male academics historically. Monitoring the institutional presence of the groups designated in the Federal Contractors Program (women, aboriginal peoples, members of visible minorities, and persons with disabilities) explicitly recognizes the importance of demographic factors in status allocation. It suggests that non-members of the designated groups, white males in particular, have enjoyed privileges in the past *because* of their background. While merit discourse posits the socially unattached individual as subject, the reality of monitoring necessarily shifts the focus to demographic categories, explicitly revealing the contradiction.

What must be emphasized, however, is that one does not redistribute access as an end in itself. Says professor of English, David Miall (1991):

> For some positions it seems appropriate that merit be redefined so that experience, background, culture or gender are given as much weight in assessing the qualifications of candidates as publication records. The issue here, of course, is not (say) culture as such, which would be meaningless, but what specific insights a candidate of a given cultural origin can offer which is due to that background. (5)

Such 'insights' might include different conceptions of 'curriculum,' epistemology, and pedagogy.

The practice of appealing to academic freedom and merit – fundamental values of the research university – in order to resist anti-sexist, anti-racist, and other equity-based measures is an anti-PC strategy aimed at forming a broader political bloc under neoconservative leadership. Contesting the neoconservative antitheses is essential for maintaining the credibility of human rights and affirmative-action policies, especially in light of the neoconservative ability to successfully market the antitheses in the popular media.

For us, such contestation involves three related processes: revealing PC as an ideological code, tracing its emergence historically (focusing particularly on the media's role in inserting 'political correctness' into popular consciousness), and explicitly undoing the construction of human rights and affirmative action policies as oppositional to principles of academic freedom and merit.

Organization of the Text

The text is divided into two sections. Part One takes up the three processes listed above by examining the history and social organization of PC discourse with a focus on Canadian material. The articles are concerned with what PC has signified, the mode of its operation, and what it has been used to mean – by whom and to what ends. We move in this section from a general contextualizing of PC discourse to its explicit manifestation within the university in debates around academic freedom and merit. Part Two extends the discussion to the university classroom itself, where struggles over PC issues are part of the ongoing process of teaching and learning.

Predictably, and well documented in the chapters by Smith, Weir, Shea, and Wallace, initiatives around the inclusive university have met with considerable resistance. As we argue in this text, the most recent wave of resistance has largely been manifested in the construction of PC discourse, an ideological code designed to delegitimize the claims made upon universities and colleges by subordinated social groups. As part of this discourse, PC is constructed as a homogeneous social movement aimed at undermining traditional, and ostensibly universal, educational precepts (particularly academic freedom and merit). Yet the term PC is a reification or a blanket term given to a range of equity-related concerns arising from demographic change and political challenges.

The chapters in Part One seek less to rebut the anti-PC campaign than to examine it as a social phenomenon, an offensive rather than a defensive strategy. Smith, Weir, and Shea analyse the news media as a site for the dissemination of neoconservative versions of PC, while Drakich et al. and Wallace examine its manifestation in Canadian universities.

In Smith's chapter we get an insight into how PC is incorporated into our everyday practices. It does this by operating as an ideological code, as a generator of procedures for 'appropriately' interpreting discourse, positioning subjects in discourse, and even for selecting appropriate words and phrases in given contexts.

Such codes are 'designed' in the sense that they are explicitly constructed for media use to achieve desired political ends. An early example is the notion of 'commie,' deployed by Joseph McCarthy and the House Un-American Activities Committee. As a designer code, the term functioned to define as 'unpatriotic' anyone who challenged establishment precepts. Similarly, PC, operating largely through the mass media, functions to delegitimize equity and related claims of marginalized groups by stripping them of authority in the public domain. Once the code has been learned it is taken up as a matter of common sense and is reproduced in everyday interaction. Smith's analysis of a CBC 'Sunday Morning' program on political correctness serves to illustrate in detail how ideological codes work.

Weir's chapter analyses PC as a sign that has, over the course of its history, been reaccented by different social groups. Her account is a history of PC as a discourse phenomenon. She documents three main phases in its history: a social movement use, a mass media rearticulation of social movement meanings, and a neoconservative appropriation of PC. She characterizes its initial phase in the 1960s and 1970s as an internal critique of social movement culture, a critique marking a contested boundary between the cultural forms of social movements and dominant cultural forms. The second phase of PC, she argues, occurred in mass circulation newspapers of the 1980s mainly in arts and entertainment coverage, secondarily in news coverage. These news articles had a hybrid voicing, poking fun at the new cultural forms associated with social movements, but operating from a standpoint outside the movements. Through a close reading of two key neoconservative PC texts, Weir shows how PC came to be part of a pattern of contrastive rhetoric about civic virtue and vice, with PC located in the semantic field of tyranny, and the consumers of the mass media trained in a series of new meaning entailments for PC. These globally associated PC with a variety of democratic movements present in universities and colleges. Weir's article shows in detail how, at the level of discourse, PC was produced as a reified category within neoconservatism.

Victor Shea establishes how deeply embedded within the Canadian news media is the Arnoldian concept of culture as the best of the West (where 'West' and 'world' are treated as equivalents). His case study of the deployment of PC against the New Democratic Party and community groups in the debate over public funding to the Art Gallery of Ontario (AGO) clearly displays the class location of PC: the high culture of the refined Art Gallery of Ontario vs. the popular culture of uncouth social democrats. We see in the conflicts around the AGO the local operation of PC as an ideological code deployed to rescue canonicity and the autonomy of the aesthetic from a variety of encroachers, including living local artists and feminists.

The ensuing two chapters take up elements of the PC debate particular to universities: academic freedom and merit. In their chapter, Drakich, Taylor, and Bankier reject the binary opposition between academic freedom and equity that is embedded in PC discourse. Rather, they develop a different conception of academic freedom, one that is consistent with, and indeed, supportive of, the inclusive university. Such a conception emphasizes social context and relationships, and especially the affective dimension of relationships. The authors argue that a foundation for their view of academic freedom is already present in the policy of the Canadian Association of University Teachers (CAUT) and in the Charter of Rights and Freedoms. Reciprocal rights and obligations, rather than protecting individual autonomy, are the hallmarks of their reworked notion. Necessarily, then, academic freedom must be expanded to include librarians, staff, and students.

In 1989 the Department of English at the University of Alberta hired five women in tenure-stream positions. Jo-Ann Wallace describes the tactics used to discredit their appointments, tactics that cast equity as the antithesis of merit. The social process of undermining women, people of colour, and people with disabilities by interpreting their hirings as token appointments is now a systemic problem in Canada. We speculate that this form of resistance to occupational desegregation is widespread outside academic institutions as well. Wallace interprets the Alberta case as drawing on the neoconservative ideological repertoire of PC: merit and literary canonicity. One possible response to such attacks is, as suggested earlier, to provide historical analyses of the social construction of merit, revealing its connection to particular times, places, and interest groups. This would open the door to a reconceptualization of the relationship between 'merit' and equity-based practices.

The above chapters set the wider context for the ensuing section on pedagogy. Smith, Weir, and Shea have examined one extra-university site – the news media – for the production and reproduction of PC discourse. Drakich, Taylor, and Bankier, and Wallace move us inside the university in their specific focus on academic freedom and hiring practices.

In Part Two of the book we zero in on the classroom itself – a central site for building the inclusive university. Struggles over the canon, voice, academic freedom, the demographic backgrounds of faculty and students – raised more generally in Part One – emerge on a daily basis in the give and take of classroom interaction. The inclusive university demands a creative, critical pedagogy. A classroom embodying such a pedagogy is necessarily a microcosm of the dynamics of change and resistance played out at other levels. The five chapters that follow examine these dynamics. The facile gloss of the PC caricature is revealed in these works; their thoughtfulness and disparateness belie the rigid orthodoxy often attributed to the 'politically correct.'

Daiva Stasiulis points to the constraints on the development of critical pedagogical practice, an issue that has been relatively ignored in favour of utopian constructions of the ideal critical classroom. Some of these constraints emerge from the difficulty of the mission itself, which involves the desire to validate student voices and various forms of oppression in the face of the 'multiple, partial, and contradictory' reality of human subjectivity. How do we reflect this complexity both in our analysis of societal life and in our teaching practices? How do we develop adequately nuanced analysis without at the same time inducing theoretical and political paralysis? And what does the focus on student voice and experience imply for the place of scholarly knowledge – and hence for the role of the academic – in the educational process? Stasiulis stresses the importance of legitimizing both types of knowledge, and the delicate pedagogical balancing act this entails.

Also impinging on teaching practice are a set of wider forces that put real material, institutional, and cultural limits on what one can reasonably accomplish. These include the changing university – labour market connection, the devaluation of teaching in promotion and tenure decisions, the current fiscal crisis in postsecondary education, and the particular demands placed on female and feminist teachers. The central message conveyed by Stasiulis is that discussions of critical pedagagy must be grounded in these realities of contemporary university life.

The next three chapters further address the issue of diversity, with a particular focus on professor–student and student–student dynamics. Richer attends to the dynamics of classroom gender and age composition in the context of feminist teaching. He recounts his three years of experience introducing a feminist perspective in an introductory sociology course, analysing the extent of acceptance and resistance among various age/gender categories of students. His own gender is shown to be a primary factor in the dynamic, evoking different responses and readings depending on students' own backgrounds and experiences. These in turn force the critical pedagogue to reflect on and modify his or her own teaching objectives and practices.

Some strategies are offered to reach male students, an objective the author posits as the major role male academics can play in relation to the feminist movement. Such strategies include explicitly positioning oneself as a masculine subject, contextualizing patriarchy both historically and structurally, adopting a non-essentialist position on the reproduction of patriarchy, and reconstructing one's own discovery of the legitimacy of feminist analysis.

While Richer explores the dynamics of a male teaching feminism, the next two chapters explore the confluence of gender and race. In an experiential piece, Bannerji graphically conveys the stresses inherent in being a non-white woman teaching in a predominantly white setting. She describes how in teaching courses that provide a critical perspective on race, class, and gender organization, her own physical presence becomes a pedagogical tool: 'my body is offered up to them to learn from.' Teaching and learning thus become relations of symbolic violence as student racism is projected onto the person at the front of the class. For Bannerji this necessitates a dissociation, a severance of her emotions and public performance, so that some modicum of self is retained in reserve. That she finds such dissociation necessary as well to deal with the defensiveness/offensiveness of white colleagues, forces reflection on everyday racism present among faculty.

Bannerji's chapter contrasts pointedly with the neoconservative stories of PC in the classroom: harassment of white teachers by groups of socially marginalized challengers. She speaks from a standpoint outside these neoconservative parables. The standpoint reveals a position of both vulnerability and everyday courage in the face of relentless invalidation.

Moriba-Meadows and Tiller were students at the University of Western Ontario – Moriba-Meadows an African Canadian and Tiller a European Canadian. Their chapter is an introspective description of their joint encounter with African-American feminist, bell hooks. The two authors recount their separate readings of the encounter, exposing the way in which student expectations, rooted at least partially in social background, influence the teaching and learning process. The paper is multifaceted and open to many different readings. We see its contribution to the inclusive university as twofold. First, the paper can be assigned in a variety of courses to illuminate the complexity of the race–gender couplet. As Stasiulis has argued, 'case studies examining particular women's conditions or representations in particular sites' have been a fruitful way of beginning to comprehend the intersection of gender, race, and class. The presentation of Moriba-Meadows and Tiller is an especially good example, we think, of such a case.

Second, it is a model for critical pedagogical practice in that it manifests both collaborative learning and the validation of personal experience. Further, keeping separate journals on the same event and then bringing them together to reflect on differences in feelings and perception is a potentially powerful tool for building 'understanding and solidarity.' As bell hooks points out in her postscript, such work allows for the development of empathy among white women regarding the typical marginalization of black women in feminist circles. The dialogue manifested in the paper 'enables us to bear witness to a feminist process of interaction where different perspectives, disagreements, and emotionalities ... can be acknowledged ... The more concrete examples we have of this process the more confident feminist women will be that there is hope for a mass-based feminist movement.'

While the authors focus on gender and race, the learning process exemplified in the chapter can be usefully applied to any situation where exploring social difference is of concern.

The final chapter by McCaskell is the only one in the text set in the public school system. We include his paper for two reasons. First, there are insights here regarding anti-racist education that might well apply to university teaching. For example, the notion of active community involvement as a fundamental premise of such education raises the question of the extent and nature of such involvement possible in a university. Although the university 'community' is not so easily demarcated compared with that of a public school, the idea of soliciting wider input into university curriculum and pedagogy is an interesting one.

Second, extending the analysis to public schools enables a heuristic comparative analysis of the conditions under which PC discourse is likely to emerge. In effect, McCaskell shows that one such condition is an entrenched valuing of free speech and the exchange of ideas (typically couched in terms of academic freedom). In such a system, claiming to have been 'silenced' by the tyranny of PC strongly resonates and confers victim status. As the 'marketplace of ideas' is not institutionalized in the public system, however, resistance to equity-related changes takes a different form than PC discourse. As the author argues, because of the nature of public schools, the loss of control over students rather than the loss of free speech, is the major spectre roused in the effort to impede democratization.

McCaskell thus brings us full circle to an analysis of PC discourse itself, and raises some hypotheses regarding the conditions for its emergence as a strategy of resistance.

As a concluding note, we would like to point out that the neoconservative position of delegitimizing moves to build an inclusive university often polarizes debate, leading to little public critical reflection about the strategies, policies, and procedures that are recommended by those who do want to foster egalitarian difference within the academy. An example of this occurred during the debate on the Ontario government initiative discussed above. Those of us who are committed to an inclusive university need to create forums where we can challenge each other rather than endlessly defend ourselves against those who would undermine our legitimacy with the charge of PC. There is, for instance, a range of opinion about speech codes that has not yet been heard in Canada among those who side with language reform against sexism and racism.[11] A general discussion about positive work relationships and revisions to professional codes in the inclusive university will likely ensue over the next few years; no one has the answer yet (and of course there will be no single answer), but surely discussion should include a gender-sensitive analysis of the different problems faced by women and men in handling status boundaries even if the professional guidelines themselves are gender neutral. The way forward here is not pregiven. Clearly, part of the challenge is to change the institutional culture of academia, to encourage people to speak, write, and interact in new ways; educational programs rather than sanctions will be more effective in accomplishing this change, though, let us not be naïve, sanctions with due process will have a continuing role to play. The issues are complex and the morally righteous, cynical about historical precedents, are not always wise about the finer points of institutional procedures, tending to cleave to immediate interest, and to manifest little patience with designing institutional structures valid in the longer term (Yeatman 1993). Building the inclusive university is not for the faint of heart.

Notes

1 Interestingly, PC was an exclusively English-Canadian phenomenon, with no corresponding term in French and no mass media publicity in Quebec.

2 The partial exception here would be the growth of women's colleges during the second half of the nineteenth century.

3 We concentrate on gender and race, these being the two major social cleavages around which Canadian neoconservative use of PC is mobilized. Unlike the situation in the United States, gay and lesbian studies are weakly institutionalized in Canada and thus have only rarely been attacked by neoconservatives. Neither disability nor environmental politics has been the object of a concerted neoconservative attack under the PC rubric.

4 John Furedy, Professor of Psychology at the University of Toronto, was, during 1993, a member of the Board of Directors at the Society for Academic Freedom and Scholarship. The citation in the text refers to his presentation before a conference, The University in Jeopardy, organized by the Society for Academic Freedom and Scholarship and The Fraser Institute in Toronto, during March 1993.

5 The statement of purposes is found on page one of each issue of the *Newsletter* of the Society for Academic Freedom and Scholarship.

6 For a critique of academic freedom and merit as transcendent values, see Fish (1994, 31–50).

7 Advertising flyer for The University in Jeopardy conference (see note 4).

8 Ministry of Education and Training (Ontario) (1993), 4. There was widespread consensus against the Framework document. Both the Canadian Association of University Teachers and the Ontario Confederation of University Faculty Associations requested the Ministry of Education and Training to withdraw the document.

9 See Hunt (1990, 321), for a discussion of the concept of institutional rights.

10 Companies such as Bell Northern Research and Imperial Oil have also

passed anti-discrimination policies, but these have not been subject to the same degree of internal or public resistance as has occurred in the educational sector. We note that universities and colleges are not unique in concerns about the intra-institutional enforcement of human rights.

11 For an anti-racist African-American position critical of speech codes, see Gates (1993).

References

Abbott, Frank. 1983–4. 'Academic Freedom and Social Criticism in the 1930s.' *Interchange* 14(4) & 15(1): 107–23

Association of Universities and Colleges of Canada (AUCC). 1990, 1991. *Trends: The Canadian University in Profile.* Ottawa: AUCC

Bercuson, David J., Robert Bothwell, and J.L. Granatstein. 1984. *The Great Brain Robbery.* Toronto: McClelland and Stewart

Bloom, Allan. 1987. *The Closing of the American Mind.* New York: Simon and Schuster

Bourdieu, Pierre. 1988. *Homo Academicus.* Trans. Patrick Collier. Stanford: Stanford University Press

Brown, Grant A., and Judy Wubnig. 1992. 'Canadian Philosophic Association Becomes PC.' Society for Academic Freedom & Scholarship *Newsletter* 2 (November): 6–7

Canadian Association of University Teachers (CAUT). 1994. 'Reply to the Ontario Government: Academic Staff and the Ontario Government's Framework Document' (April)

Chiose, Simona. 1993. 'Code of Silence.' *The Varsity* 18 (Jan.): 9–10

Cook, Deborah. 1994. 'Freedom of Speech Getting Lost in Shuffle.' *The Windsor Star* (8 March)

Ede, Andrew. 1991. Letter to *Folio* (Fall)

Fish, Stanley. 1994. *There's No Such Thing as Free Speech and It's a Good Thing Too.* New York: Oxford University Press

Gates, Henry Louis, Jr. 1993. 'Let Them Talk: Why Civil Liberties Pose No Threat to Civil Rights.' *The New Republic* (20 and 27 Sept.): 37–49

Human Resources Development Canada. 1994. *Profile of Post-Secondary Education in Canada.* Ottawa: Minister of Supply and Services

Hunt, Alan. 1990. 'Rights and Social Movements: Counter-Hegemonic Strategies.' *Journal of Law and Society* 17(3): 309–28

McMaster University Faculty Assoc. Newsletter. 1994. Vol. 20, #5, pp. 4–5, Hamilton, Ont.

Miall, David. 1991. Letter to *Folio* (Fall)

Ministry of Education and Training (Ontario). 1993. 'Framework Regarding Prevention of Harassment and Discrimination in Ontario Colleges' (Oct.)

Monahan, Ed. 1983–4. 'Tenure and Academic Freedom in Canadian Universities.' *Interchange* 14(4) & 15(1): 94–106

OCUFA Forum. 1994. 'Faculty Consider Harassment Guidelines.' 9(4)(March/April): 4

Statistics Canada. 1991. *Universities: Enrolment and Degrees.* Ottawa: Ministry of Supply and Services

Trent University. 1994. 'Statement on Free Inquiry and Free Expression.' Reprinted in *McMaster University Faculty Association Newsletter* 20(5)(Feb.): 3–4

Trevena, Claire. 1994. 'Campus PC Offends Spiky Ontario Dons.' *The Manchester Guardian Weekly* (20 Feb.): 3

Wright, John P. 1994. 'Freedom to Discuss the Unthinkable.' *The Windsor Star* (31 March): A2

Wubnig, Judy. 1993. 'The University in Jeopardy: Toronto Conference, March 12, 1993.' Society for Academic Freedom and Scholarship *Newsletter* (3 April): 1–3

Yeatman, Anna. 1993. 'Voice and Representation in the Politics of Difference.' In Sneja Gunew and Anna Yeatman, eds, *Feminism and the Politics of Difference,* 228–45. Halifax, NS: Fernwood

PART ONE

PC: The Social Organization of a Right-Wing Offensive

'Politically Correct': An Ideological Code

DOROTHY E. SMITH

Repossessing the Relations of Ruling: Ideological Codes at Work

We cannot understand what is happening to us today without understanding the distinctive ways in which society is organized as text-based or mediated relations. I use the word 'text' here to collect all the material forms – print, film, tape, video, computer monitor or printout, etc. – that link us as we are in the local settings of our lives into relations organized extra-locally. State, bureaucracy, management, mass media, professions, discourse, and the like,[1] are text-based; their complex interrelations are text-mediated. Texts are 'active' in their organization, coordinating the multiple local sites of people's lives and work. I use the term 'relations of ruling' for this complex of relations to reflect the expropriation of organization from local and particular relationships and its functional refinement and elaboration in technically specialized forms – a development analogous to the abstracting of what Marx (1976) described as relations of dependence from the localized and personal relationships of pre-capitalist societies to relations mediated by the exchange of money and commodities that we call the economy.

Marx and Engels (1976) wrote of social consciousness as material because it is in language; but in the text-mediated relations of ruling, social consciousness has been objectified as organization and relations grounded in increasingly sophisticated technologies. Rather than being processes of individual minds, the activities of judgment, knowledge, decision-making, and the like, become properties of organization, now increasingly vested in the hard- and software of computers. The objectification of these forms of social consciousness does not mean that they operate wholly automatically. We are not entirely inert lumps in these relations (though we are being increasingly displaced by computer software). Complex educational processes trained us, particularly those of us who participate as members of an intelligentsia, in its methods of thinking and its organizing concepts, ideology, theories, etc.

Traditional social science has viewed this complex as discrete forms or units of organization – state, bureaucracy, formal organization, mass communications, science, popular culture, etc. But its evolution has produced an increasingly coordinated complex forming a system or field of relations occupying no particular place, but organizing local sites articulated to it. The relations of this complex are based in and mediated by texts. Whether in writing, in print, or on computer, texts are essential to their organization and indeed to the existence of the complex. Important functions of coordination are therefore performed by ideologies, concepts, theories, etc. that insert their ordering capacity into specialized sites operating otherwise independently. Ideologies, concepts, and theories generate texts and constitute their internal organization, structure intertextuality, and interpret texts at sites of reading. Texts generated in different settings – for example, government systems of collecting statistics, social scientific research in universities and think-tanks, policy-making in government, and mass media – are coordinated conceptually, producing an internally consistent picture of the world and providing the terms of policy-talk and decisions (Smith 1993).

A recent article in the *New York Times* (Uchitelle 1993) provides an example of this effect: The current theory that national economies are revived by reducing the deficit, hence promoting the lower interest rates that encourage investment, has come to operate in this way. According to the article, evidence for the theory is lacking; some leading economists, including Nobel Prize winners, dissent from it; yet it coordinates the terms of the debate, locking in even those who do not agree with it. 'Nowhere has deficit reduction been embraced more militantly than in the [U.S.] budget debate. Virtually no one in either party any longer challenges the proposition that deficit reduction will eventually be good for the economy.' The theory is established as *organizer* of the public discourse, and dissenting views must operate on its terms.

Ideologies, concepts, and theories, etc. are particularly powerful in regulating public text-mediated discourse. By public text-mediated discourse I mean those relations of discourse to which, in principle, access is unrestricted within a given national population. Notice that in this approach, discourse is a field of relations and not only of statements (as in Michel Foucault's [1972] thinking). Discourse is a form of social act and therefore has social organization. Ideologies, concepts, theories, etc. are among the organizers of its relations and process, whatever function they may be understood to have when addressed from other analytic stances.

Public text-mediated discourse consists of those relations that have evolved historically, under conditions of contemporary mass communication, from the 'public sphere' that Jurgen Habermas (1989) analyses in his early study. In making its text mediating integral to a definition, I do not mean to suggest that it exists only in texts. It includes the mass media in all its forms as well as the talk that goes on around and about media: political talk and writing, academic discourse, both in print and talk, and so on. Imagine the field of public text-mediated discourse as many ongoing conversations carried in part in print, or as broadcast talk, or as images on television or film, and in part in the many everyday settings of talk among people that take up, take off from, or otherwise incorporate ideas or substance from public discourse. They are conversations among people who do not necessarily know one another except through that medium. They are situated in many different places. Some are only readers or watchers, while others – writers, actors, celebrities, politicians, and so on – appear in the parts they play in print and on screen, split off from the actualities of their own lives; yet others are writers, film directors, camera people, technicians, publishers, and others at work in the vast industrial basis of the text-mediated and -based relations of public discourse. The textuality of public text-mediated discourse is essential to its peculiar temporal and spatial properties of ubiquity and constancy of replication across multiple and various actual situations of watching, reading, or hearing.

Controlling ideologies, concepts, and theories and their dissemination in public text-mediated discourse is an important source of power in a society organized by text-mediated relations. Indeed, the complex of text-mediated relations is itself an organization of power. Michel Foucault (1980) writes of it as 'power/knowledge,' envisaging it as a decentred form of power, distributed over a complex of discursive sites. This has been largely true. Creating and reproducing ideologies, concepts, knowledge, theories, etc. have been largely the business of an intelligentsia, carried on in multiple sites and in a variety of media, but participating in the same, loosely coordinated, complex of relations that Foucault called 'discourse.' New conceptualizations and knowledge did not proceed from a determinate source and spread into discourse as its organizers. Rather, the creative sources of change operated in a field of relations from multiple sites of interplay with going discursive concerns. No one position could command. But envisage now this complex of text-mediated relations as lending itself to control from a centre that works with precisely the dispersal of discursive sites, and, importantly, through a command of the concept-, ideology-, and theory-making that organize the production, 'operation,' and reading/watching/hearing of texts!

We have reason to think that such a process is happening now in the United States and is being extended to Canada. Ellen Messer-Davidow (1992), in her remarkable paper, 'Manufacturing the Attack on Liberalized Higher Education,' describes an ideological campaign waged by the right wing in the United States. Her paper is based on field-research of the think-tanks, institutes, and foundations that are forming an apparatus aimed at securing control of the concepts, ideologies, and theories that operate to coordinate multiple sites of power/knowledge generated by the relations of ruling. The right wing, representing a powerful section of the capitalist class in the United States, has created information and policy-generating think-tanks, an institute for training journalists as recruits to replace the predominantly liberal professional journalists of today, and a multi-headed attack on liberal higher education, particularly on 'multiculturalism' and on the gender and ethnic diversification of the university curriculum. Right-wing control of public discourse through command of ideologies, concepts, and theories has been an objective of right-wing intellectuals and ideologues since the 1960s, and the great fear was that liberals or, worse, the left, had been successful in securing the ideological heights (Blumenthal 1986). Ideological/conceptual/theoretical command of the field of text-mediated relations is immensely powerful, the more so as it is *largely invisible* as power, and, the right wing, or perhaps more realistically, the U.S. capitalist class, aims at and is increasingly effective in securing it.

I use the term 'ideological code' here to identify a particular ideological function that travels in the peculiar space-no-space of text-mediated relations, reproducing its distinctive organization in the multiple sites articulated to them, and both in text and in talk about and on the way to text. My model is the genetic code and the replicating capacity of a DNA molecule, which produces copies identical to itself, passing on its genetic information and its ability to replicate. This reverberative reproducing is exactly the property of ideological codes that I want to capture. An ideological code such as 'political correctness' operates in the field of public discourse to structure text or talk, and each instance of its functioning is capable of generating new instances. Reproduction occurs, of course, as people 'pick up' its organization from reading it or about it or hearing it used, and using it themselves, hence passing it on to readers or hearers (I doubt that it is a device that is effectively transmitted by or an effective organizer of visual media).

The formal openness of the relations of public discourse has been established against the state's crude efforts to regulate it. In the liberal state, constitutions protect against those in positions of power from limiting people's right to speak and to hear others speak in their interests. Freedom of speech has been a principle limiting the powers of the state to repress its citizens and restrict the openness of public discourse. Censorship has traditionally been an issue of governments' attempts to impair that openness. But constitutions do not protect the openness of public discourse against those positioned to regulate public discourse, for example, through control of the mass media. They do not protect against controls through the conscious creation and seeding of ideological codes independently of the state. Ideological codes do not appear directly as they do in an act of censorship; no one seems to be imposing anything on anybody else. People pick up an ideological code from reading, hearing, or watching, and replicate it in their own talk or writing. They pass it along. Once ideological codes are established, they are self-reproducing.

Thus ideological codes operate as a free-floating form of control in the relations of public discourse. They can replicate anywhere. They organize talk, thinking, writing, and the kinds of images and stories produced on film and television. I want to make clear that an 'ideological code' in this sense is not a definite category or concept. Nor is it a formula or a definite form of words. Rather, it is a constant generator of procedures for selecting syntax, categories, vocabulary in writing and speaking, for interpreting what is written and spoken, and for positioning and relating discursive subjects. It is not as such social organization, but it is a social organizer.

'Ideological codes' may be, and perhaps often are, components of ideological 'master frames.' They operate as 'outriders' of that frame, carrying it into discursive sites where the ideology itself might be unassimilable. Characteristically, they operate pretty independently as devices, carrying the effects but not the body of the master frame that governed their design. This is their power as discursive devices; this is their utility to the right-wing industries of ideology described by Messer-Davidow and others. People pick them up and use them without realizing the source and the efficacy of meaning they carry with them into the settings of their use; they become an active currency of ruling operating in the interests of those who set them afloat and may have designed them, but their provenance and ideological 'intention' are not apparent in them.

They do not appear as regulatory measures; they are not forms of censorship by the state. Indeed, characteristically, they are 'spontaneously' adopted and reproduced.

A Somewhat Marxist Theory of Ideology

Rather than adopt the traditional opposition of theory versus practice or reality, I understand ideologies, concepts, or theories themselves as people's actual practices. My problem here is to preserve the linkages with a Marxist tradition of thought and politics and its uses of the term ideology while inserting it into a method of inquiry into the social that differs radically from contemporary Marxism and contemporary cultural theory – though it is not, I claim, that distant from Marx himself. My problem is how to demarcate a usage of the concept of ideology that locates it in people's actual practices of conceptualizing and theorizing, from the usage characteristic of the reductive 'flatlands' of standard Marxism and of cultural theory.

In the longer version of *The German Ideology* (1976), which contains Marx's detailed and acerbic comments on the German ideology, his critical method identifies ideology as a method of thinking, distinctively circular in its relation to the world of people's actual activities in which his own conception of a 'positive' science is to be grounded. His treatment of ideology as a practice of reasoning about society and history is clearly in keeping with his social ontology, but it is never incorporated theoretically. This implicit theory of ideology assimilates it to the same ontological ground as other activities.

Thus, rather than a component of a superstructure, or the ideas or beliefs of a ruling class, I've taken ideology to indicate ideas, concepts, theories, and so on, as they enter into the practices and organization of ruling. Ideology and ideological practices govern and coordinate the multiple specialized sites of ruling in and beyond the state, in the professions and professional discourse, in management, and in the mass media and other more specialized forms of discourse. A view of ideology as a system of beliefs or ideas legitimating practices of ruling vastly underestimates its significance. Here the concept of ideology identifies theoretical and conceptual practices coordinating at different levels and recursively[2] the multiple sites of ruling in contemporary capitalism.

This approach also diverges significantly from 'cultural theory' in repudiating its peculiar ontology of signification or meaning without people. Instead, I develop, here and elsewhere (Smith 1990a, b, 1992, 1993), a method of inquiry into society's objectified forms of consciousness that, unlike cultural theory or neo-Marxist versions of ideology, does not take objectification for granted. Rather, this method of inquiry works in and from the same world that it investigates. It does not begin by assuming discursive frameworks and discursively designed subject-positions. It assumes that inquiry begins in life, in living, and that the social relations and organization that objectify consciousness are concertings of people's ongoing activities. Concepts, theories, ideas, and so forth, are also activities as people bring them into the coordinative process as local practices.

That is what has interested me. I have wanted to be able to address knowledge, concepts, theory, ideology, and so on as people's actual practices, 'occurring' in time and place, and as significant in the ongoing organization of social relations. The analysis in this paper builds on this method of thinking about the social. My interest is in making visible how the ideological code 'politically correct' enters as a method or practice of interpretation into public text-mediated discourse as people's practices, including our own. This means explicating our own practices of ordering and interpreting textual materials. That we 'know how to do it' is a major resource in the analysis that follows.

Michel Foucault (1972, 41) provides an account of the formation of objects within a discourse that calls first for a mapping of the *surfaces* of the emergence. This paper aims to map the *surfaces* of 'political correctness' as an object formed within public discourse. However, Foucault's formulation presupposes – and occludes as part of a conscious theoretical strategy – the interplay of actual practices among people that, within a discourse, constitutes the object. His mapping of the emergence of objects is at the level of statements and concepts, and though he writes of 'formation,' his account is peculiarly static. Working with a conception of discourse as social relations actively produced by people situated as they are and must be in the local actualities of their living calls for a formulation of 'object formation' as an active, and *social,* process. George Herbert Mead's (1947) account of the capacity of symbolization to bring objects into being within the social act is congenial here. For Mead, the existence of objects for a group is accomplished in a social act, and language 'does not simply symbolize a situation or object which is already there in advance; it makes possible the existence' (Mead 1947, 78) of that object for those active in the social act. Here the social act is discursive; the object brought into being, 'political correctness,' comes into discursive existence in people's textual practices. 'Political correctness' is the symbolization that brings into being within the social processes of discourse objects that are there for any of us, regardless of our political views.

In analysing 'political correctness' as an ideological code, I am analysing how it operates or might be entered into the organization of a text in its writing, or as a 'knowing how' to 'read' a text it has organized. My use of the quotes around 'read' is intended to locate the reader's deployment of concepts, schemata, and the like that catch up the conceptual or schematic organization that the text intends. This is a level of interpretation that occurs before we bring what we have read (heard or seen) to other settings in which we might be writing or talking about what we have read. I have analysed this relation of reading in an analysis of an account of someone becoming mentally ill (Smith 1990b), in which I show how the structuring of instances making up the account 'fits' a reading of mental illness and can be read by that concept. Hence the reader can find in the text what it has told her to look for. In the analysis that follows, I have followed a similar procedure. A CBC program is analysed for how it both instructs the listener in the ideological code of 'political correctness' and then provides a series of stories that the code will read. The stories are of episodes that both express and expand the listener's ability to reproduce the code. In this social act of text-mediated discourse, 'political correctness' is constituted as a discursive object.

'Political Correctness' – A Right-Wing Incursion into Public Discourse

The PC code regulates the social organization of authorized speech in public, text-mediated discourse. Mikhail Bakhtin (1981) theorizes the novel as a dialogue woven out of the multiple and diverse speech genres of a heteroglossic society. But though public discourse appears formally open, in fact speaker participation in it has been and is quite powerfully controlled by devices that regulate the authority of speakers. 'Authority is a form of power that is a distinctive capacity to get things done in words. What is said or written merely means what the words mean, until and unless it is given force by the authority attributed to its "author" ' (Smith 1987, 29–30). Public discourse is also a social organization of authority, regulating whose voices will count in the making of its topics, themes, concepts, relevances, etc. Men, as participants in public discourse, have been 'those whose words count both for each other and for those who are not members of this category' (Smith 1987, 30) and they have been those who therefore could speak from their experience and express their interests as men. The authority to speak for themselves as women has been denied to women, and major struggles in the women's movement have focused on gaining entry for women to speak as women in the public discourse. Similarly, non-white speakers have been deprived of authority to speak as members of their social category, putting forward their experience and interests as belonging by right to the public sphere. The teaching of the literary canon established for public discourse a standardization of background understandings, language, references, and so forth for its participants. These have been and are currently under attack by marginalized groups.

'Political correctness' as an ideological code is a piece of the counter-establishment's resistance to loss of an exclusive authority founded in gender and imperialism within the sphere of public discourse. Of course, the production and operation of ideological codes is not new, nor is it an exclusively right-wing device. But 'political correctness' is specialized to focus on regulating the authority of participants in public discourse and hence restricting who can be part of the making of its topics and relevances and hence the social forms of consciousness. Its power as a free-floating code is that it can operate independently of the right-wing ideologies that generated it. The code's history, as is told elsewhere in this volume, follows a sequence: It begins with authoritative enunciations, instructing readers in how to operate the code themselves (Richard Bernstein's [1990] role in this respect is interesting); goes through a dissemination phase when it is given more widespread circulation (*Newsweek*, President Bush's 1991 Michigan speech, *Maclean's*, the Canadian Broadcasting Corporation); is brought into more general use in settings of conflict within public, text-mediated discourse; and is finally incorporated into that discourse's anyday vocabulary. We should not suppose, of course, that this means necessarily that there has been a sudden rightward shift in the population – though of course this may have happened. The PC code has 'caught on.' This is the 'power' of the device.

In the context of the political sectarianism of the 1970s and 1980s, the term 'political correctness' was used to extend a political sect's politics to the everyday conduct of its members. It became later a left-wing insider's joke, used ironically. The right-wing 'political correctness' code (the PC code), by contrast, is specialized to operate in the field of public, text-mediated discourse. It is reworked to locate initiatives by or on behalf of those excluded from authoritative participation in public discourse to transform their place and their right to insert the topics and relevances of the groups they represent, particularly into the universities. Its syntax is transformed: rather than as a challenge to bring private behaviour into line with political principle, it operates as a category of deviance; it names the actions it is used to characterize as deviating from principles of freedom of speech. It operates to reaffirm the authority of the established and to discredit the voices of those attempting change.

The CBC Joins the 'Political Correctness' Campaign: Analysis of a Documentary

A CBC 'Sunday Morning' program on political correctness was broadcast on 28 July 1991.[3] It was a documentary bringing to the listener an account of episodes identified as instances of 'political correctness' using commentary and passages from interviews to tell the story. The documentary form is essentially dialogic in ways that lend themselves to analysis following Bakhtin's (1981) conception of the dialogic structure of the novel. According to Bakhtin, it is the novelist's art to bring different genres of speech into active, though not necessarily equal, dialogue with one another. In the documentary, the radio reporter or the filmmaker creates a dialogic structure of voices or (in film) images originating in actual events and claiming to represent them to an audience. Thus, unlike the novel, the documentary claims to represent a world beyond its textuality. Its internal dialogic organization relates the listener/watcher to the world it posits beyond itself. V.N. Volosinov's formulation of the dialogic of reported speech applies here – 'Reported speech is speech within speech, utterance within utterance, and at the same time also *speech about speech, utterance about utterance*' (Volosinov 1973, 115). As we shall see, the ideological code of 'political correctness' is both topic and regulator of the dialogic organization of the CBC program. In a sense, the program instructs the listener how to operate the code.

Hooking the Intra-Institutional into Public Discourse

I have imagined the dialogic organization of the documentary as a set of layered transparencies relating listeners who participate in the public discourse of radio to a series of events or episodes in postsecondary institutions or, in one case, a museum. The layers are a structuring of reported speech: Each inscribes messages that overlay those on lower layers; what comes through from lower layers (and hence from the original events) is what subsequent layers allow to surface. The top layer is that of public discourse, where listeners interface with the documentary in the radio program; at the bottom are the original events, only accessible as they are inscribed in and 'written over' at subsequent layers. The original events or the original controversy do not appear directly. They are 'represented' to listeners as mediated by a lamination of layers and their top-down dialogic regulation. Listeners hear of the original events only through what participants have to say 'directly,' or in their reported speech, or as the events are described by others (a concealed form of reported speech, relying, as such description must, on a telling of original events by participants).

The image of layered transparencies corresponds to the layering of the dialogic of reported speech in the documentary. The original events become accessible to listeners through the 'series' of layers and their one-way dialogic. Higher layers comment on and regulate lower layers; lower layers do not comment on or interpret upper layers. The first and topmost layer (layer I) is the 'surface' of the documentary, located in and setting the social relational framework of public discourse through an introduction by 'Sunday Morning's' 'host' Mary Lou Finlay. This introduction sets up the governing framework for listeners participating in the program as follows:

1. The documentary is identified, and thus authorized, as part of the 'Sunday Morning' program.

2. Finlay introduces the reporter as ' "Sunday Morning's" Mary O'Connell,' delegating to her the authority of voice that she holds as host of the CBC program. She thereby authorizes the reporter's control of the dialogic of the documentary. This sequence also establishes Mary O'Connell as the connecting link between original and intra-institutional events and the moment of public discourse by telling us that O'Connell has been visiting universities in Canada exploring 'the world of the "politically correct." '

3. Third, and perhaps most important, Finlay establishes the narrative theme of the documentary, introducing the concept of PC and a schema that will interpret the stories of what happened and find the coherence of the layering and sequencing of reported speech in the documentary. The schema is set up in two steps. First a question is posed: Is political correctness 'the new enlightenment or the new tyranny?', then the apparent openness of the question is foreclosed by describing O'Connell's investigations as aimed at discovering 'how enlightenment "crosses over" into tyranny.'

Layer II is wholly the reporter's. She comments on what other speakers say, assigns or withdraws credibility, and ensures narrative coherence by, for example, adding supplementary descriptive material. She produces the overall coherence of the documentary both as narrative but also by locating its different pieces as expressions or instances of the 'crossing over' of 'enlightenment into tyranny' that is the effect of 'political correctness.' At layer III, participants in the original events speak *about* them. They do not, of course, regulate their own speech. It is an artful selection managed by the reporter, who functions as a filter selecting passages that will intend (or fit) interpretations of layers II and I. The reporter's voice is also heard at this level in extracts from interviews with speakers from the original events.

In the overall dialogic organization of the documentary, high layers filter and control the interpretation of speakers appearing on lower layers. In so doing, the original events become expressions of the overall interpretive framework, established first at the level of public discourse (layer I). The documentary as a whole transposes local events arising in specific institutional contexts within their organization of power, authority, and communication, into the arena of public discourse with an entirely different organization of power, authority, and communication. Listeners, lacking access to the original site or the original events, are committed, as a course of listening, to the palimpsest of the layered reported speech and its one-way dialogic.

The series of layers structures the telling of a series of episodes in which challenges to the 'normal' (taken-for-granted) course of institutional affairs have been made. Here is a summary of them:

- Members of the Student Union at the Ryerson Polytechnic Institute in Toronto complain about racist and sexist content in a student union entertainment, and a self-declared schizophrenic demonstrates against the title, 'Loonie Bin,' of a comedy night on the grounds that it demeans people who are mentally ill.

- A complaint of sexism against a rock group made by a woman from the Queen's University Women's Centre results in Queen's Student Council cancelling the group's invitation to perform at the University.

- The University of Toronto student newspaper, *The Varsity*, has an editorial policy that would refuse publication to material inciting violence or hatred toward people particularly on the basis of their membership of a disadvantaged group.

- A small group of students at the University of Toronto demonstrate against the possibility that courses in the African studies program may be cut.

- An Afro-Canadian activist argues that African history should be taught by Africans or people of African origin.

- Afro-Canadians demonstrate against the Royal Ontario Museum's exhibit 'Into the Heart of Africa' and later harass Jeanne Cannizzo, an Africanist associated with the design of the exhibit, while she is giving a course at the Erindale campus of the University of Toronto.

What is at dispute? On college and university campuses students and faculty are going about their 'normal' business: putting on comedy shows, arranging for rock performances, publishing student newspapers, giving lectures in anthropology, arranging museum exhibits, and the like. In so doing, the taken-for-granted, 'normal' forms of discourse or performance, embedding the 'normal' gender and imperialist presuppositions, are reproduced.

These normal forms are subjected to critical challenges by (or on behalf of) members of social groups who see them as reproducing the forms of domination that marginalize and subordinate them. In this collection of episodes, challenge takes the form, severally, of appealing to college authorities, action by an elected body, picketing, and direct confrontation in the classroom. In several episodes there is a reversal of established institutional power relations: a former mental patient demonstrates against a college-sponsored entertainment; a group of students protest threatened cuts to an African studies program; an unnamed group of Afro-Canadians demonstrates against a museum exhibit; students in a class harass a professor. Other than actions by student unions, the initiatives described are from those who lack access to the institutional processes of regulation and change.

The Layering of Dialogue in the Episodes

In ways that are perhaps characteristic of radio documentary reporting, listeners are placed in a relation of overhearing comparable to the 'voyeuristic' structure of film. In some instances extracts from original interviews have been edited to represent direct speech to the listeners. The structuring role of the reporter is concealed, backstage. Thus, those who were active as participants in the original controversies seem to speak, but they are no longer independent subjects, speaking for themselves. Fragments of their talk are used by the reporter to constitute them as subjects, subordinated to her script. They are her fabrications and do her will.

The dialogic of each episode has two layers: At layer II, the reporter's narrative and commentary directly address the radio listener. For example, in the Ryerson vignette, the reporter narrates the original events and comments on what speakers who were participants in those events say, assigning value and credibility to those speakers or what they had to say; at level III segments of speech by participants in the original events appear in two modes of reported speech.

1. Segments of original participants' speech are inserted into a two-level dialogue (layers II and III) with segments of the reporter's commentary – a kind of mock dialogue that hops back and forth between layer II where the reporter addresses listeners and layer III of original participants' speech produced in an interview with the reporter. For example, in the episode of the University of Toronto *Varsity*, the reporter comments on how freedom of speech is coming on university campuses to mean 'freedom to censor.' This is followed by a segment of speech from the *Varsity* editor stating the *Varsity*'s policy. It is structured as if the latter were a response to the former. But in fact they are at different dialogic levels, the reporter's 'editorial' comments overlaying the *Varisty* editor's statement. The latter has presumably been extracted from an original interview. Who knows what its context was in the original?

2. Layer II consists of snatches of interviews in which the reporter questions or comments and the speaker from the original events responds or makes a statement. In the *Varsity* episode, the two-level dialogue is followed by a direct interchange in which a statement by the *Varsity* editor is followed by a question from the reporter and a response to it from the *Varsity* editor.

The Events as Expressions of PC

The stories of the episodes float the intra-institutional events free of their institutional context and shape them up to operate as expressions or instances of the overall theme. Exemplification is a powerful device: On the one hand, a schema – in this case of the passage from enlightenment to tyranny – and on the other, a collection of episodes. The schema is empty without its instances; the instances are merely a collection of stories without the schema that interprets them. The PC code structures how the intra-institutional events are told so that they will instantiate the schema it governs. A circular procedure is in operation: Listeners are given instructions for finding each episode as an instance of PC, and the telling of each episode is constructed to correspond to those instructions.

If you listened to these little stories presented without the code as interpreter, you probably would not see them as belonging together. Some PC collections I have listened to on the radio have assembled instances that I have found really strange – for example, a Peter Gzowski panel on this topic included, among more standard representatives, someone speaking on issues of sexual harassment in the university. She was represented as part of the PC movement, not, as might have been conceived, to address sexual harassment as denying women their authority as speakers within the academic community, but as an instance of challenge to institutional authority.

So the episodes do not hang together 'naturally,' that is, without interpretive artifice, out of a simple telling of episodes. The coherence of the collection as a sequence has to be complemented by listeners' application of the code as interpreter. Otherwise the whole thing might fall apart, an effect forestalled by the reiteration of the code for each episode. Coherence is an effect, on the one side, of the structuring of episodes to fit the code as interpreter, and on the other, of the hearer's uses of the code (under instruction) to find how each new episode expresses it. There is a circular process, peculiar to the ideological organization of narratives. The particulars are selected to intend the code as a procedure for making sense of them, and the code finds for the listener or reader just that sense in the particulars.[4]

A variety of strategies are used to 'produce' the episodes as expressions of 'political correctness.' In some, the actions of the challengers are represented as coercive, sometimes as violent and abusive. The culminating story in the CBC program is of the verbal abuse and harassment of Jeanne Canizzo, the anthropologist who designed the Royal Ontario Museum exhibit, the focus of Afro-Canadian protest. It casts its shadow backward on to other incidents, such as that of the solitary former mental patient picketing a students' comedy night, that otherwise might be hard to assimilate to the frame of 'tyranny' or 'totalitarianism.'

In the telling, some of the episodes represent those challenging the taken-for-granted order through its authorities as violent or abusive, as for example in the account of Jean Canizzo's harassment. Other episodes undermine and invalidate the rationality of what is recommended and the principles that justify the critique. For example, the decision of the Student Council at Queen's to cancel a rock group's performance is represented as based on irrational and counter-factual interpretations. The reporter's commentary legitimates those speaking for the 'normal' institutional order and discredits those who challenge.

The PC Code as Regulating the Dialogue between Original Events and Public Discourse

In their reporting, the original events are lifted out of their local historical contexts and reshaped in their reporting to the relevances established for that discourse. The series of levels embedding the intra-institutional events in the relations of public discourse set up a dialogue between the two, but it is a dialogue that is heavily stage-managed: Not everyone identified as a participant is given a speaking part; none get to choose what parts their voices will play. That is the reporter's privilege. Their voices appear only as reported speech, either embedded in the reporter's narrative or as extracts from interviews.

As we have seen, the PC code organizes a telling that selects and reshapes the intra-institutional issue by embedding it in the relevances of public discourse. It has been put in place to govern listeners' interpretive practices. To return to my image of laminated transparencies, it is inscribed at the top layer and is recursively effective in those below. The challenge to the normal course of institutional affairs that each vignette presents *raises issues in terms of principles of human rights*. Those challenging are either subordinate to or outside the institutional structure of authority. Generally they are students, but sometimes they are outsiders altogether, without standing in the institutional process.

In the layered and PC-governed dialogue that brings the challengers' voices forward from the institutional context to the listeners present and on to the terrain of public discourse, this lack of institutional authority to speak is consequential. The authority of their challenge is grounded in principles that are held to have jurisdiction within the institution superordinate to its formal structure of authority. Hence those lacking institutional authority can assume the authority of the principle, in this case, of human rights. This authority, however, is peculiarly vulnerable to the PC code, which, in the one-way dialogue between public and intra-institutional discourse, displaces *principles of human rights and installs 'freedom of speech' as an exclusive principle.* This displacement undermines students' or outsiders' authority to challenge institutional authority and to speak in the institutional context that has been legitimated with reference to principles of human rights. Deprived of the validation of principle, their challenges to the normal course of institutional affairs appear arbitrary and unwarranted. A retroactive fit is thus created between the stories told and the schema of a passage 'from enlightenment to tyranny' introduced in the opening remarks by Mary Lou Finlay.

The various devices of reporting speech in the radio documentary medium operate in the program to subordinate the original speakers to the monologic regime that the PC code sets up in public discourse. The code's structuring of 'reported speech' represses. The voices of those speaking for the 'human rights' issue appear only as expressions or instances of 'political correctness.' Voiding the 'human rights' principle removes authority and credibility from those challenging institutional authority.

Here is a detailed analysis of how this effect operates in the dialogic of reported speech in one episode, that reported of the Ryerson Polytechnic Institute:

- A comedian performing at a Ryerson Polytechnic 'club' ridicules 'political correctness' and 'leftish' students.

- Members of Ryerson's Student Union complain to the entertainment officer about the racism/sexism of a comedian's performance (presumably this is the same comedy show as that at which the comedian ridiculing 'political correctness' appears, but this isn't clearly stated).

- They ask the entertainments office to adopt a policy that will conform with the human rights code.

- The comedy performance, named 'Loonie Bin,' is picketed by an ex-student who claims that its title trivializes mental illness.

Here students pressure for change from the administration. The students' complaint of racism and sexism in the comedian's performance appeals explicitly to principles of human rights as embodied in Canada's human rights legislation. It isn't just a personal matter; it isn't arbitrary. The issue is independent of their particular subjectivities. Reference to 'human rights' principles authorizes their initiative, providing an authority beyond that of the institution itself.

The PC code removes that authorization. At the documentary surface, where the reporter is telling the story (layer II), a dialogue internal to a sentence reduces the students' principled claim to the merely subjective and arbitrary. The reporter's account produces a classic instance of Bakhtin's (1981) hybrid sentence in which two 'utterances' are blended:

> What we are calling a hybrid construction is an utterance that belongs, by its grammatical (syntactic) and compositional markers, to a single speaker, but that actually contains mixed within it two utterances, two speech manners, two styles, two 'languages,' two semantic and axiological belief systems. We repeat, there is no formal – compositional and syntactic – boundary between these utterances, styles, languages, belief systems; the division of voices and languages takes place within the limits of a single syntactic whole, often within the limits of a simple sentence. (Bakhtin 1981, 304)

In this instance, the blending is in fact the overlaying of the reporter's interpretation on to the reported speech of the students, so that her interpretation appears as what they said. Here is the sentence:

> They said a new policy was needed to ensure that the content of entertainment would not violate the human rights code *or their notions of 'politically correct.'* (my emphasis)

The two 'utterances' are both represented as reported speech, as predicates of 'they said.' The duality of language and 'belief system' become visible if we break them out of the hybrid construction. Here they are:

> A new policy is needed to ensure that the content of entertainment will not violate the human rights code.

and

> A new policy is needed to ensure that the content of entertainment will not violate our notions of 'politically correct.'

The first 'utterance' is subordinated to the interpretation in terms of 'political correctness' supplied by the second. The blending is done by treating both as reported speech, what 'they said.' The sentence as a whole does indeed contain two 'belief systems,' to use Bakhtin's conception. But they do not stand in an equal relationship in the dialogue created by the hybrid. The second, incorporating the PC code, is thereby empowered to invalidate the principles enunciated in the first (we see layer III through an inscription at layer II). It introduces definite shifts of meaning to this end. The reference is no longer to an objective human rights code, but to the students' 'notions' of 'politically correct.' Their reported proposal appeals to objective principles embodied in Canada's Constitution; the reporter's interpretation represents them as seeking to impose on policy their own subjective and arbitrary notions of what is 'politically correct.' Again, they begin with 'enlightenment' and conclude in 'tyranny.'[5]

The Ryerson story contains two episodes. The second is the story of the former student, the solitary picketer of Ryerson's comedy night protesting its 'Loonie Bin' title. He pickets because he 'thought that [the title] trivialized mental illness.' He is described by the reporter as a schizophrenic. Here, on layer II of the laminated transparencies, is a powerfully recursive concept suspending the credibility of what is reported of someone involved in the original events. Categorization as mentally ill suspends the attribution of agency and hence of responsibility. So the solitary picketer is represented (through the reported speech of the entertainments officer) as a '*victim* of a "politically correct" way of thinking' (my emphasis). Somehow a 'way of thinking' has fastened itself on to him and taken him over.

Reflections

What puzzled me at first about the program was that in a number of rather obvious ways it departed from what I have come to assume as the canons of good reporting. This was particularly so with respect to how the different positions were represented. Perhaps it was my imperfect assimilation of the PC code that permitted this puzzlement since operating the code establishes one side as what is taken for granted among participants to public discourse.

In the documentary's final sequence, there is some representation of the 'human rights' issues involved, but in portraying the intra-institutional events, no attempt was made to give the other side a voice. The PC code organizes listeners' relationship to the intra-institutional controversy so that while the offensiveness of the protest to those challenged by it may be fully represented, the nature of the offence to those protesting is either not presented at all or presented in a cursory way, sometimes by those who oppose it.

The PC code produces a selective hearing of this dispute. The taken-for-granted forms that have given offence are either not described at all or described only to discredit them. We are not told what the students who complained to the administrator at Ryerson found racist and sexist about the student comedy hour; we are not told what kinds of hate material the University of Toronto student newspaper will not publish; we are not told what is problematic about the built-in perspective of an anthropology of Africa created by anthropologists of European origin; we are not given details of what Afro-Canadians found objectionable about the Royal Ontario Museum's African exhibit. Where we are told, it is only to trivialize or ridicule. The solitary schizophrenic picketing Ryerson's 'Loonie Bin' comedy show is presented without dignity or textual compensation for the established stigmatizing of the mentally ill; the technical rationality of the male spokesperson for the rock group is contrasted with the (female) 'subjectivity' of the grounds on which its performance was cancelled.

A characteristic of the taken for granted is that it is not subject to reflection or reflective revision. Hence, if the listener or reader is not told what is wrong with the normal institutional forms, she or he will not know how to see it. Apart from the devices described above, challenge and protest are trivialized in the absence of such information: they appear to be about nothing in particular, a fuss about nothing. Whereas, of course, from the side of the group demeaned by them, such normal forms incorporate practices that are acutely painful, silencing, and enraging.

The PC code reproduces the social contours of the normal form. It generates its 'deviant category.' As Durkheim has shown us, the social logic of identifying the deviant is to reinforce the sentiments sustaining the normal form. The rule – here, the 'normal' form – does not have to be explicit to be affirmed in the shared repudiation of the deviant; it is affirmed collectively. Hence the significance of the PC code as a device that positions participants in public discourse so that they are at the centre of what everyone knows and takes for granted vis-à-vis which the 'politically correct' are 'other.' We, listening, watching, reading, are drawn into the magic circle defined not by determinate values, but by what it constitutes as other, implicitly, but *not* explicitly, affirming our freedom to continue our taken-for-granted practices of sexism and racism without being subjected to challenge.

Like Theseus entering the labyrinth, listeners are given the thread that will enable them to retrace the maze. We are instructed in the code at the outset (layer I), instructions reinforced as each episode is narrated. The code is thereby established as an interpretive paradigm enabling listeners to find for each episode and for the collection as a whole the lineaments of the transition from 'enlightenment' to 'tyranny.' The listener gets the message. Of course, she doesn't necessarily interpret it in exactly the same way – she may agree or disagree or have a variety of reactions to different episodes – but agreement or disagreement or a variety of reactions presuppose that she has already recognized 'what it's about.' Most important, listeners have acquired a device they can deploy thereafter. The code has been enunciated. In listening, our consciousness has participated in it as a practice. We have heard a collection of instances matched to the 'enlightenment-to-tyranny' schema and hence have been instructed in how to recognize cases to which it applies. We will know how to do it again; we can carry it away for our own future use; we can discover and construct our own PC stories; and we can apply it to situations where we are challenged.

Replicating

Thus the code replicates. Once it is seeded, what came first is not a relevant issue. The listener or reader learns how to operate the code, as teller of a story or as reader/hearer. Recurrent multiple instances for a variety of sources confirm its reality. The narrative structure fitting the schema of tyranny is replicated. The protester or challenger, normally a member or members of a group of relatively low institutional authority, is the initiator; the institutional representative is represented as victim (his/her 'offence' is minimized); a language of violence, force, or coercion is used to describe the protest. For example, *Newsweek*'s article tells of students marching into the classroom of the Berkeley anthropologist Victor Sarich and 'drown[ing] out his lecture with chants of "bullshit." ' The article does refer to a piece Sarich had published in a campus newspaper arguing that the university's affirmative-action program was discriminatory to whites and Asians. The classroom action is not, however, set in the context of information appearing in the following paragraph – that Sarich holds the view that different races have genetically determined differences in intelligence. Presenting the action of students first, and displacing what might have provided a motivational context for that action, represents it as inadequately motivated and arbitrary. It is fitted thereby to the PC code as a method of reading.

Another PC-coded story in the same article tells how 'students forced [the] withdrawal' of a case on the rights of lesbian mothers that had been assigned to the New York University Law School moot court. The dean of the College of Liberal Arts overrode the decision of the curriculum committee to suspend that session of the moot court. The students' action is described as coercive; the dean's is recorded neutrally and without comment. The telling fits the story to the theme of 'tyranny' established in the CBC program described above. Notice that exercise of institutionalized power and authority goes unremarked even when it acts to censor or restrict academic freedom. No issues of McCarthyism, tyranny, or censorship are raised. The same *Newsweek* article reports actions by University of Texas administrators to suspend the use of a text for an undergraduate course. No issues of academic freedom or censorship are raised in the article. The text is described as 'a primer of PC thought' (Adler et al. 1990, 52). The structuring of these narratives fits the PC code as the reader's method of making sense of them. As readers we already have the template; we have only to apply it to find the fit; when we find the fit, there is no experience of incongruity, and no reason therefore to question.

The PC code authorizes representatives of the institutional order to repress and discredit those who challenge it. Characteristically, the device appears in stripped form, without being embedded in a particular ideology and without reference to the conservative political interests from which the device originated. By using descriptive terms that conflate the challenge to the established order with the oppressive use of coercive state power, the code is grafted on to legitimating frames or principles that have public currency, notably the principles of freedom and of 'freedom of speech' in particular. The original ideological provenance of the device is displaced at the surface by using terms from a vocabulary of liberal politics, particularly terms identified with the anti-totalitarian liberalism of the 1950s. Terms such as 'totalitarian,' 'tyranny,' 'McCarthyism,' and 'storm troopers' (with its reference to Nazi Germany) are used. A memorandum circulating in a Canadian university refers in its topic line to 'an apotheosis of tyranny.'

The original liberal critique of totalitarianism was, of course, a critique of the coercive and arbitrary uses of state power. Detaching the terms from their ideological ground takes advantage of the moral valence they have come to carry, excising reference to the practices of repression sustained by the state's command of judicial procedure and its monopoly of the legal use of force. To those of us who remember the McCarthy period (even from a distance, as I do), the conjunction is disorienting. But stripped of their theoretical provenance, and resituated in the PC code, their operation is governed by it. Hence critiques of established powers from those in lower power positions can be described as tyranny or censorship or the like without any sense of strangeness. An exaggerated power is attributed to them. Metaphors of 'force' are brought into play. The actions or effects of protestors' actions are represented as coercive and repressive (Adler et al. 1990) or as terrorist. Genovese (1990) in his *New Republic* article calls for the firing of 'cowardly' administrators who do not stand up to 'terrorism' (32). Thus, the solitary picketer, former student, and ex-mental patient, demonstrating against the 'Loonie Bin' title of Ryerson's comedy night, can be subsumed under the category of 'tyranny' put in place in the introduction to the topic without arousing, at least for the writers of the script, a sense of anomaly.

In the mass-media stories that are doing the work of seeding the concept, terms such as these are often positioned prominently in the introductory material, in titles, and in headlines, functioning to announce the applicability of the PC code even in instances when the story itself does not readily produce a fit. For example, the *Newsweek* issue includes an interview with Stanley Fish. It is headlined: 'Learning to Love the PC Canon.' Fish speaks against the teaching of the literary canon in American universities, opposing the imposition of an orthodoxy, and supporting the enjoyment of difference and diversity. The reader who knows how to apply the PC code will know how to treat the headline as instructions for a selective reading; she or he will search the interview for items that can be interpreted as PC, neglecting those that cannot. Fish's commitment to the enjoyment of difference and diversity in universities can now be seen by the reader as an expression of the 'PC canon,' implying that it imposes a new orthodoxy rather than breaks with the old.

As it appears in multiple media sources, 'political correctness' comes to have a discursively constituted reality; it is represented as a definite movement or group. However heterogeneous the actual bases of protest may be, and they are far from forming even effective political coalitions, the PC code enables them to be represented as a political entity, threatening freedom of speech. As such, the code is even replicated and transmitted by people who would recoil from the right-wing political ideology in which it originated. Timothy Findley (1994), responding to recent accusations of racism in the Canadian literary establishment, identifies the 'politically correct' as a kind of sectarian cult:

> It is distressing to imagine how freedom to read might ultimately be affected by those who believe in what is called political correctness. The politically correct have been so well intentioned, so protective of those whom they saw as defense-

less; soon became infected with paranoia. They threw up walls. They created ghettos. We stay in. You stay out, especially where the written word is concerned.

'They' take on a virtual reality. In some interpretations, 'their' threat to freedom is more than contingently related to good intentions. 'They,' the 'politically correct,' are represented as embracing an actively repressive philosophy: 'PC is, strictly speaking, a totalitarian philosophy,' the *Newsweek* article tells us. The circle is drawn; 'we' are inside; 'they' are the other who threaten 'our' freedom. It is a circle drawn in precisely the same way by Arthur Schlesinger, Jr, speaking in May 1994 to a Manhattan audience, who warns that, 'in a bizarre switch of roles,' First Amendment Rights are endangered by the movement for political correctness in 'our' (U.S.) universities:

The ideologues of multiculturalism would reject the historic American purposes of assimilation and integration. They would have our educational system reinforce, promote and perpetuate separate ethnic communities and do so at the expense of the idea of a common culture and a common national identity. (Honan 1994)

That his argument replicates Findley's so exactly testifies to the operation of the code as more than concept or idea. It is an *organizer* of text-mediated relations. The sentences and language differ from text to text but the social organization that orders and transmits its ordering is recursively reproduced.

Once effectively seeded, the code reproduces the social organization that draws the circle identifying 'us' with established institutions from 'them,' an enemy who threatens freedom of speech by insisting on being heard, and threatens what 'we' have in common by insisting on the validity of diverse cultural traditions. The generative power of the code reproduces this organization in the diverse and multiple sites of its use. Programs such as the CBC's on 'political correctness' or news stories such as that in *Newsweek* have taught us, listeners or readers, the organization generated by the PC code. We know how to take it up, how to practise it. From editorial instructions (introductions, headlines, etc.), and from the stories and their narrative structure, readers/hearers have learned how to apply the code and how to identify PC-type situations. It is now established as a device through which a politics may be entered into texts and talk without politics or ideology ever appearing. Here are two examples from a recent (to the writing of this paper) issue of the *New York Times*

Book Review. The first is from a review of Stephen Birmingham's novel, *Carriage Trade*:

Silas Tarkington has done every merchandising trick in the book to make himself and his store appear Old World Classy. Neither 'Carriage Trade' nor Silas Tarkington is remotely interested in political correctness. (Wasserstein 1993)

The second is from a review of Allan Bloom's *Love and Friendship*:

Nor did Bloom's social observations strike me as sharply observed. He mocks Smith College for urging students to resist 'lookism' (bias in favor of attractive people), an especially silly bit of political correctness, to be sure, but hardly proof that Americans no longer care about beauty. (Pollitt 1993)

These examples show the term 'political correctness' positioning reader and writer within the circle of the 'normal forms' and not among those 'interested in political correctness' or among the 'silly' opposed to bias favouring 'attractive people.'

When people are criticized for how they have spoken or written of non-whites or women, they can turn the tables on criticism by discrediting it as PC. They are thereby magically positioned in an authoritative and legitimating order. Faculty in universities write memoranda identifying pressures felt in the classroom as 'political correctness'; students ward off challenges to racist or sexist language; emblematic stories travel as a media-mediated form of gossip and crop up in characteristically formulaic forms in meetings as accusations against progressive spokespeople or as supportive evidence or comments for right-wing speakers; a newspaper columnist identifies a university dean and vice-president with 'feminist/politically correct forces' because they sought to establish a teaching evaluation that asked whether instructors used demeaning sexist and racist language in the classroom;[6] even progressive people, finding themselves under attack for racist and sexist practices built into the normal forms they have taken for granted, avail themselves of the PC code.[7] Thus the PC code, as regulator of the social relations of public discourse, sets up a discursive order locating the reading/listening subject within the circle that preserves the 'normal forms' and exclusions against initiatives for change from those the circle marginalizes. It redraws the time-dishonoured boundaries constituting the centrality of white masculinity to the relations of ruling and the otherness of those who challenge that hegemony.

Notes

A number of people have helped me, particularly by introducing me to sources and examples. I am indebted to Andree Stock and to Barbara Pope in this respect. I am also generally indebted to members of my Social Organization of Knowledge course in 1991 whose discussions of the CBC program on political correctness analysed in the paper were invaluable in the development of my thinking. Ellen Messer-Davidow provided valuable critical comments.

1 Here these terms are used together, with an 'etc.' to collect types of function in text-mediated social relations and organization, without claiming to be exhaustive. My procedure is that further specification of terms follows as part of the course of investigation. This is how I've worked with the concept of ideology elsewhere (Smith 1990a). I have also some work in progress on the operation of 'theory.' Their operations are just exactly what we, members of society and participants in these relations, know how to do, where knowing how means taking up the concepts, ideology, theories, etc. as our own methods of thinking and knowing and, of course, speaking and writing. They are our own methods of producing talk and texts.

2 I am very much indebted to George Smith's development of the concept of recursivity in this connection. See his unpublished paper on this topic, Department of Sociology, Ontario Institute for Studies in Education, no date.

3 All references in this section are to 'Politically Correct,' 'CBC Sunday Morning,' 28 July 1991.

4 I have made a detailed analysis of ideologically generated accounts in chapters 6 and 7 of *The Conceptual Practices of Power* (Smith 1990a).

5 The course of hearing is more powerful in its effects than the course of reading. In the latter, both statements appear as alternatives so that the substitution of the second for the first is weakened. But in the hearing the second simply supersedes the first; the first doesn't hang around for comparison with the alternative version that follows it.

6 The example refers to a column by Trevor Lautens in the *Vancouver Sun* of 29 March 1994. His opening remarks (characteristically for this type of writing) set the PC frame. 'What's the tamest word? Rebuke. The University of B.C. administration, specifically the feminist/"politically correct" forces widely identified with dean of arts Patricia Marchak and academic vice-president Dan Birch, has been rebuked.' The effect of the PC code as organizer of the story he goes on to tell is substantial. When I first read the column I assumed that dean and vice-president had been 'rebuked' by those higher in the administration than they. In fact the dean and vice-president had been criticized

by some faculty members for the inclusion of the items in question in the proposed teaching evaluation. It is the PC code that transforms 'criticism' into 'rebuke' by according the critics overriding institutional authority.

7 Or members of the related complex of terms that the PC code appears to have drawn into play along with it, such as 'McCarthyism.' My impression is that that epithet came into play in this new form (detached from any reference to state censorship) attached to and as an elaboration of 'political correctness.'

References

Adler, Jerry, with Mark Starr, Farai Chideya, Lynda Wright, Pat Wingert, Linda Haac. 1990. 'Taking Offense: Is This the New Enlightenment on Campus or the New McCarthyism?' *Newsweek* (24 Dec.): 48–55

Bakhtin, Mikhail. 1981. *The Dialogic Imagination: Essays*. Austin, TX: University of Texas Press

Bernstein, Richard. 1990. 'The Rising Hegemony of the Politically Correct.' *New York Times* (28 Oct.): 1

Blumenthal, Sidney. 1986. *The Rise of the Counter-Establishment: From Conservative Ideology to Political Power*. New York: Times Books

Findley, Timothy. 1994. 'Daring to Wake Up at the Gates of the Politically Correct.' *Vancouver Sun* (11 March): A19

Foucault, Michel. 1972. The Archaeology of Knowledge and the Discourse on Language. New York: Pantheon Books.

– 1980. *Power/Knowledge: Selected Interviews and Other Writings, 1972–1977*. New York: Pantheon Books

Genovese, Eugene D. 1991. 'Heresy, Yes – Sensitivity, No: An Argument for Counterterrorism in the Academic.' *The New Republic* (15 April): 30–5

Habermas, Jurgen. 1989. *The Structural Transformation of the Public Sphere: An Inquiry into a Category of Bourgeois Society*. Cambridge, MA: The MIT Press

Honan, William H. 1994. 'Arthur Schlesinger Jr Assails Campus Speech Codes: A Historian Denounces "Ideologues." ' New York Times (27 May)

Lautens, Trevor. 1994. 'Fair and Square: Profs. Fire Rebuke at Dean.' *Vancouver Sun* (29 March): A15

Marx, Karl. 1976. *Grundrisse: Foundations of the Critique of Political Economy*. New York: Random House

Marx, Karl, and Friedrich Engels. 1976. *The German Ideology*. Moscow: Progress Publishers

Mead, George Herbert. 1947. *Mind, Self and Society: From the Perspective of a Social Behaviorist*. Ed. Charles W. Morris. Chicago: University of Chicago Press

Messer-Davidow, Ellen. 1992. 'Manufacturing the Attack on Liberalized Higher Education.' Paper presented at the conference on 'Rethinking Marxism.' University of Massachusetts, Amherst (Nov.). Forthcoming in *Social Text.*

Pollitt, Katha. 1993. 'This Just In: We're Not as Wise as Plato: Allan Bloom Has Departed, Leaving Behind His Indictment of American Cultural Life.' A review of Allan Bloom's *Love and Friendship. New York Times Book Review* (8 Aug.): 9

Smith, Dorothy E. 1987. *The Everyday World as Problematic: A Feminist Sociology.* Toronto: University of Toronto Press

– 1990a. *The Conceptual Practices of Power: A Feminist Sociology of Knowledge.* Toronto: University of Toronto Press

– 1990b. *Texts, Facts, and Femininity: Exploring the Relations of Ruling.* London, New York: Routledge

– 1992. 'The Out-of-Body Subject: Contradictions for Feminism.' Paper presented at the meetings of the American Sociological Association, Cincinnati

– 1993. 'The Standard North American Family: SNAF as an Ideological Code.' *The Journal of Family Issues* 14(1) (March): 50–65

Uchitelle, Louis. 1993. 'How Clinton's Economic Strategy Ended Up Looking Like Bush's: A Theory of Growth That Has Never Worked Is Now the Sacred Text,' *New York Times* (1 Aug.): 1, 4.

Volosinov, V.N. 1973. *Marxism and the Philosophy of Language.* New York: Seminar Press

Wasserstein, Wendy. 1993. 'I Can Get It for You Retail: Murder, Mystery, and Romance, in a Novel about a High-Profile, High-Fashion Department Store.' A review of Stephen Birmingham's *Carriage Trade. New York Times Book Review* (8 Aug.): 8

PC Then and Now: Resignifying Political Correctness

LORNA WEIR

The United States plays a defining role in the World.

George Bush, remarks at the University of Michigan commencement ceremony at Ann Arbor, 4 May 1991

During his speech, the captain kept saying his government was democratic and gave us everything ... the captain gave a panoramic description of all the power they had, the capacity they had ... This was really being said to strike terror into the people and to stop anyone from speaking.

Rigoberta Menchu, *I, Rigoberta Menchu*

During the late 1960s and early 1970s, the phrase 'politically correct' circulated in the everyday speech of social movement activists. Since its appropriation and dissemination through the mass media by neoconservatives in the early 1990s, 'politically correct/political correctness' has spread to become a household word among anglophone[1] Canadians of all social classes. Over the course of this trajectory, 'politically correct/ political correctness' (hereinafter abbreviated 'PC') has come to be resignified, and the course of its resignification is a history of how differing social groups, institutions, and politics have inscribed their own distinctions on the phrase. The intent of the present paper is to write this history and to demonstrate the political significance of its constant changes in accent.

In reply to the question, 'What is PC?', one may respond that PC is what it has been used to mean, and that there are claims and social actions that have been enabled by these meanings. Thus, I do not here examine substantive areas like speech codes or employment equity because I am interested in how PC came to be connected with these issues when its earlier usage had nothing to do with them. This process involved a neoconservative reaccentuation of PC through the mass media that was, I would agree with Dinesh D'Souza, remarkably successful. This article explores some of the reasons for this success in order to help prepare liberals and leftists for future political contests of meanings and actions, for, as D'Souza has also pointed out, 'the fight on the ground has barely begun' (D'Souza 1991a, 46). However, this article is a sociology of PC rather than a normative political critique.

I am not inclined to reduce politics to a discourse phenomenon, but do maintain that politics is socially organized in part through discourse, which thus merits its own level of analysis. Durkheim and Mauss, at the beginning of this century, argued that collective representations – representations of social life – are made through signs (Durkheim and Maus [1903] 1963). Morever, Gardin and Marcellesi (1974) have argued, the political text operates to impose its own dictionary on politics and to undermine those of adversaries; political discourse is thus a kind of struggle to modify discourse semantics and impose its own set of meanings. In advanced capitalist societies collective representations are deeply contested, with the mass media being one of the institutional sites for this contestation, a political struggle organized through signs. Discourse and discoursal change are thus clearly important to understanding the influence of the mass media, the channel through which neoconservative uses of PC have been propagated. The media disseminate new meaning potentials that are available for use in local settings – meetings, conversations, conferences, policy planning sessions, and so on – there becoming socially actionable. The specific vehicle of neoconservative operation at work in PC is not military force, but particular semantic configurations broadcast through the print and electronic news media.

The neoconservative critique of PC was a media strategy that contested prior meanings of PC. Through this resignification neoconservatives attempted to delegitimize the presence of anti-racist and feminist politics within universities, the social movements that have arguably had the greatest impact on higher education in Canada and the United States. The neoconservative PC offensive represents a response to institutional gains made by a series of social movements over the course of the 1980s. Challenger social movements succeeded in establishing a presence inside powerful social institutions such as the church and the state, including the educational sector, indicating the emergence of a new front of oppositional struggle *within* dominant institutions. The limited success of oppositional politics has predictably provoked ideological resistance.

Existing commentaries on the history of the term PC have noted its use in North American social movements from the late 1960s and within Leninist parties before this time (Berman 1992, 5; Denning 1992, 45n.4; D'Souza 1991a, 44; Epstein 1991, 15; Perry 1992, 15). Berman maintains that ' "politically correct" was originally an approving phrase of the Leninist left to denote someone who steadfastly toes the party line' (Berman 1992, 5), evolving from there into a term of disapproval among leftists for those 'whose line-toeing fervour was too much to bear' (Berman 1992, 5). D'Souza dates 'political correctness' to Marxists who, earlier in the twentieth century, used it devoid of irony 'to describe and enforce conformity to their preferred ideological positions' (D'Souza 1991a, 44). According to D'Souza, it fell out of use until the 1980s. Neither Berman nor D'Souza supplies evidence for his assertion and, while Leninist parties did have a variety of expressions denoting conformity such as 'party line' or 'correct line,' 'political correctness' does not specifically appear to have been used among Marxists prior to the mid-1960s. As Perry documents, 'politically correct' seems to have been a phrase formed under Maoist influence in the mid- to late 1960s (Perry 1992, 14). The early history projected by Berman and D'Souza would therefore be inaccurate, and D'Souza's dating of the social movement usage of PC to the 1980s is simply wrong, as I will show below. This paper documents three sequential phases of PC: a social movement use dating from the late 1960s, a mass media use located in newspapers during the 1980s, and a neoconservative phase that existed orally from the mid-1980s and spread through a mass media news wave from October 1990.

PC in its social movement form acted as an internal critique of social movement culture. The phrase was addressed to other social movement members. As a gesture of self-critique, PC was applied restrictively to the practices of a particular social movement: it pertained to the culture or practices of the women's movement or gay liberation or a Marxist party, but not to a common culture cross-cutting these movements. It defined a shifting line of conflict between the cultural forms of social movements and the cultural capital of the social groups/processes to which particular movements were antagonistic.

In mass-circulation Canadian and American newspapers of the 1980s, PC was also applied critically to the cultural effects of particular social movements. Writer and readers were often positioned as engaging in PC practices, or negotiating their relations with PC, but no commitment to building a social movement was assumed. Like the social movement form of PC, the newspapers manifested a profound ambivalence toward the kinds of cultural change instigated by social movements, positioning readers as negotiating between desire/habit and principle in their choice of Christmas trees, coffee beans, and speech practices.

Unlike the hybridized voice of PC in the mass media of the 1980s, which was derived from and tied to social movement usage, the neoconservative variant of PC situates its speaking position and readership wholly external to social movements; it is about *them*, the dangerous people in universities supposedly stifling democratic rights. PC here operates as a key term in a pattern of contrastive rhetoric distinguishing vice from virtue in civic morality, an attempted expulsion of left challengers from central social institutions.

PC thus has no stable language-external referent cutting across all phases of its usage. But there are some language-internal continuities of sense that can be demonstrated. It has functioned as an interpretive device capable of characterizing any statement as an instance of authoritative speech in the Bakhtinian sense of that word – obedience/conformity lacking persuasive power. In principle capable of being deployed against the right or the left, PC in practice has been used by both the left and the right to criticize the left. As I will show, PC has persistently been characterized as dreadfully conformist and no fun at all; pleasure becomes invested in the non-PC, which, for the neoconservatives, is a defence of unfettered capitalism and dominant cultural forms. The result is an attempt to delibidinize social movement activism and the fight for social justice. The critique of PC has centred for the most part on cultural questions: music, food, textbooks, speech codes, deconstruction, literary canons, sexuality. The challenge that contemporary social movements have made to people's daily practices implicates a complex renegotiation of personal desire and collective everyday practice: small wonder there should be ambivalence and resistance to change, quite apart from questions of social power in everyday life.

'Political Correctness' in Social Movements of the 1970s and 1980s

Ruth Perry, in the best article published to date on the history of the term PC, states that it 'first gained currency in the mid to late sixties in the Black Power movement and the New Left' (Perry 1992, 15). She believes that PC probably derived from the English translation of Mao Tse-Tung's 'On the Correct Handling of Contradictions among the People' (1966).

Mao identified the rooting out of contradictions among the popular masses with the democratic method of persuasion, discussion, and education; through this method the masses would discover 'correct ideas.' Rick Salutin, recalling the influence of the Maoist use of 'correct' on Canadian social movements of the 1960s and early 1970s, has, moreover, noted the ironized reading of 'correct ideas' on the North American left:

> Around the same time, a comic strip called Korrect Line Komix appeared in the alternative press along with the Fabulous Furry Freak Brothers. A chubby little Mao face in the corner of each panel said things like, 'Where do correct ideas come from?' Next panel he'd ask, 'Do they fall from the sky?' Then some guy would get bonked on the head by a falling idea and Mao would chirp, 'Nope!' (Salutin 1991, 20)

Perry notes that no sooner was PC used 'as a genuine standard for socio-political practice – so that we might live as if the revolution had already happened – than it was mocked as ideologically rigid and authoritarian' (Perry 1992, 16). Uttering PC marked the sender as both hostile to dogmatism and aligned with the forces of social change.

In addition to Rick Salutin's retrospective account, I have been able to locate five Canadian feminist texts from the late 1970s and the 1980s that employ the phrase 'politically correct' or 'politically incorrect.' In addition, I have found one American text from the early 1980s that also uses these collocations. The Canadian texts will be presented in chronological order, beginning with Salutin's recollections. The American example follows, together with a more general commentary on the social movement examples as a whole.

Rick Salutin remembers the context in which he first heard the collocation 'politically correct':

> The first time I heard the phrase was in a Chinese restaurant during the late 1960s, after a political meeting or protest march. Those things built an appetite. Someone always has to take charge when you're ordering Chinese food, and someone did. She listed a number of dishes and asked if it sounded okay. 'I don't know,' somebody else said, 'whether that's a politically correct order.' It got a little laugh, as a touch of slightly self-conscious left-wing humour. (Salutin 1991, 20)

Salutin goes on to note that the humour was apropos, given the context of ordering Chinese food and the popularity of Maoism on the left at that time.

Three of the five Canadian texts relate to lesbian feminists organizing in Toronto during 1979 and 1980. The first, a handbill entitled 'A Fine Kettle of Fish,' advertised a meeting in March 1979 to discuss the relation of lesbianism to the women's movement. The handbill, which had a generally playful tone, listed a series of topics for the day, including 'Is the Personal Political?' and 'Politically Correct? Politically Incorrect?' (reprinted in Ross 1990, 85). The second, a letter by Ruth Dworkin in 1979 to the *LOOT Newsletter* (LOOT being the Lesbian Organization of Toronto), asked, 'How many women have become exiles from the women's movement because they were made to feel that their behaviour was "Politically Incorrect?" ' (Dworking in Ross 1991, 125). She went on to state that, since feminists were being attacked from the right, they could not afford to stigmatize each other as 'politically incorrect.' Dworkin's letter argued that criticizing women as 'politically incorrect' inappropriately raised differences in personal behaviour to the same level of significance as substantive political differences. Third, the Toronto feminist newspaper, *Broadside*, carried an article by Val Edwards in September 1980 describing tension in Toronto lesbian organizing efforts over the past year, including attempts to define 'an appropriate lifestyle to express our politics' (Edwards 1980, 4). Despite 'political factionalism,' attempts were made 'to overcome our differences. The words "politically correct" and "politically incorrect" reared their ugly heads, and have since been sent back to the intellectual cesspool from which they emerged' (Edwards 1980, 4).

In the August 1980 issue of the Vancouver feminist publication, *Kinesis*, Marg Verrall echoed Val Edwards' concerns that 'political correctness' within feminism was acting to suppress diversity. Verrall, a performance artist, had come under attack by a personal friend for her contribution to a variety show done for International Women's Day in March 1980: 'Apparently some people feel it is anti-feminist to come on stage in a lacy white dress, or "poor drag," to wear a tuxedo and dance to a man's voice' (Verrall 1980, 18). Verall defended herself, stating in an inspired message that some of her shows

> are so 'politically correct' they leave no room for judgment. But what can I do as a feminist who is stirred by romance and rainbows, and who was born with the spirit of Fred Astaire in my feet? Could you not enjoy the dance? (Verrall 1980, 18)

She argued that feminists have been harshly judgmental of each other and that this has narrowed the membership of the women's movement. As I recall, Verrall's difficulties negotiating a relation with feminist audiences was endemic among feminist artists of the 1970s and early 1980s: the signs of patriarchy were regarded as having fixed, invariant meanings incapable of resignification in artistic practice.

My last instance of a Canadian social movement use of PC that occurred prior to its neoconservative inflection appears in a text written during the spring of 1989 (subsequently published in 1991). Seema Kalia, in the article, 'Addressing Race in the Feminist Classroom,' argues for the importance of an anti-racist perspective in women's studies courses. Kalia cautions teachers that guidelines for anti-racist practice and speech cannot be codified in advance:

> Words of warning about dealing with such a precarious area as race analysis: there are no guidelines, and there is no real structure in terms of 'politically acceptable' and 'politically incorrect' language or behaviour except for the obvious racial slurs. Accept outright that you will use at least one term that offends someone, that opposition to any approach is guaranteed. (Kalia 1991, 277)

The audience here and throughout her article is constructed as feminist and university-based. Readers are presumed to have some prior knowledge of PC, rendered in the above passage as 'politically acceptable' and 'politically incorrect,' the quotation marks indicating authorial distance from the terms, as well as an intertextual relation to discourse outside the Kalia article.

My final example of PC in social movement discourse before its neoconservative use is from the legendary American conference 'Scholar and the Feminist IX: Towards a Politics of Sexuality' at Barnard College in 1982 (often referred to as the Barnyard Conference in feminist circles). The American feminist Muriel Dimen, in an article published in the subsequent conference proceedings, attempted to define PC as a phenomenon characteristic of all social movements:

> Politically correct is an idea that emerges from the well-meaning attempt in social movements to bring the unsatisfactory present into line with the utopian future ... Politically correct behavior, including invisible language and ideas as well as observable action, is that which adheres to a movement's morality and hastens its goals ... The ideology of political correctness emerges in all sorts of movements, applying to behavior, social institutions, and systems of thought and value. (Dimen 1984, 138–9)

Dimen's article assumes a universal human antagonism between individuality and collectivity with any social group capable of enforcing conformity and threatening individuality – a deeply liberal/Enlightenment problematic.

The American feminist Ruth Perry, in her secondary commentary on the history of PC in the United States, has noted the importance of PC and PI (the latter an abbreviated form of 'politically incorrect,' much used in social movement circles although it subsequently gained little currency in the mass media) within what has been called the feminist sex wars/debates of the 1980s (Perry 1992, 16; Vance 1984). These debates involved intense and often bitter discussions ranging over a host of areas from pornography to consensual sado-masochism. Those feminists who argued that there was no single feminist PC standard in sexuality were attacked by other feminists who held them complicit with violence against women. 'Politically incorrect sex' was taken up defiantly in response to attacks, with transgressive sex highly valorized, and 'politically correct' sex devalorized as boring and 'puritan.'

With the exception of the Salutin example, in all the above texts both writer and reader are positioned as feminists. The discourse in which PC appears is thus posited as circulating inside a social movement, here the feminist movement. All uses of 'politically correct' criticize specific aspects of feminist practice, but do not attempt to discredit feminism as a whole. PC consistently connotes rigidity and self-righteousness, the humourless enforcement of an orthodoxy that results in factionalism, though it can be used in a self-mocking fashion, as in the Salutin example about ordering food. The antithesis of PC, political incorrectness, thus links with diversity, art, imagination, wildness, and transgression. The lines of conflict within social movements being signified by PC are consistently cultural: anti-racist speech practices, dress in performance art, pornography, the symbolics of sexual practices, judgments of individual behaviour, lifestyle. The disputes are not about employment equity, health policy, or the party line on the Hitler–Stalin pact.

These kinds of disputes were not confined to feminism. I can remember a series of internal conflicts within Toronto gay liberation circles during the early to mid-1980s that also centred on cultural questions: the use of disco music at demonstrations rather than a mix of ethnically diverse music, with the defenders of disco castigating the opposing position as a PC and anti-populist attack on the spontaneous pleasures of gay culture. A long dispute ran through the pages of *The Body Politic* during 1982–3 regarding race-specific ads, particularly one advertising for a black domestic worker who would also double as the prospective employer's sexual partner. Those objecting to such ads as racist – and these included virtually every non-white organization in the Toronto area – were termed PC by the opposite side.

Many of the feminist PC disputes around dress, speech, and sex were less severe by the end of the 1980s than they had been at the beginning of the decade, as feminism grew from its initial base in separate women's organizations to establish a presence 'inside institutions that have long been male dominated (the church, the military, coeducational universities, the foundation world, the media)' (Katzenstein 1990, 34). The cultural homogeneity characteristic of the earlier period in the feminist movement no longer held over the course of this institutional growth, and likewise the beginnings of a multiracial feminism in the same period were a challenge to the older notion of (white) 'women's culture.'

The kinds of intra-movement cultural struggles that PC indexed have not been investigated within the sociological literature. There is a small literature on youth and subcultural style, literature associated particularly with the Birmingham University Centre for Contemporary Cultural Studies. Dick Hebdige and Angela McRobbie have argued that working-class subcultural styles operate as forms of collective resistance to mainstream culture (McRobbie 1991, 27) and as interventions against ruling ideologies (Hebdige 1979, 138). The tastes in dress, music, ritual, and argot that have been identified as components of style in youth subcultures thus implicate far more than the whims of individual taste: style is a form of resistance to both dominant and parental cultures (Clarke et al. 1976).

The culture of social movements likewise has its own oppositional values and practices acting to distinguish those inside the movement from non-members. This has been noted at the level of the ideological transformation that occurs in individuals after their recruitment to social movements (Snow et al. 1986); but ideology constitutes only one aspect of social movement culture. Melucci (1989) has tangentially referred to social movements as 'cultural laboratories in the production of new meanings and new forms of relationships' (60), and this observation begins to suggest how widely ramified are the cultural forms of social movements. Part of becoming a member of a social movement is learning new dispositions of the body, new forms of daily practice that are signs of a critical distinction from those social forms to which the movement stands in opposition (Bourdieu 1988, 200–1). The kinds of intra-feminist and gay liberation debates around PC were associated, at least in part, with issues of the culture of these movements. Decontextualized, the disputes might appear to involve a great deal of emotion over relatively little of lasting social value. However, social movement activists often read dress or speech or artistic practice as signs of a particular person's belonging to a movement, and/or of the relations between a movement and the social and cultural practices it opposes. Where the relation between signifier and signified was understood by participants as invariant, and particular cultural practices were read as parts standing in for the entirety of social movements or hegemonic culture, the PC stakes could be very high indeed.

PC in Mass Circulation Newspapers

The mass media use of PC is customarily dated to Richard Bernstein's October 1990 report in the *New York Times* (Bernstein 1990) about the 1990 Western Humanities Conference whose theme was ' "Political Correctness" and Cultural Studies' (Berman 1992, 1; Denning 1992, 21; Epstein 1991, 15). However, as I will demonstrate in this section, 'politically correct' and 'political correctness' were employed in the Canadian and American news media throughout the 1980s and with a range of meanings distinct from social movement and neoconservative PC. In addition I will show the kinds of stories in which PC tended to appear and its meaning potential in these contexts.

A word search on the database Infomart of six regionally representative Canadian metropolitan newspapers (*Edmonton Journal, Financial Post, Halifax Daily News, Montreal Gazette, Toronto Star, Vancouver Sun*) and one magazine, *Maclean's*, showed a total of 153 articles in which the terms 'politically correct' or 'political correctness' appeared between 1 January 1987 and 27 October 1990 (the latter date is chosen as an endpoint since Richard Bernstein's article launching the neoconservative PC media wave was published the next day). A DIALOG ONE word search of twelve, regionally representative metropolitan American newspapers[2] (for the period 1 January 1983 to 27 October 1990) showed a total of 492 articles containing one or more uses of 'politically correct' or 'political correctness.'

While neoconservative uses of PC initially focused on education, particularly university education, relatively few news articles from the 1980s had anything to do with formal education. The search of Canadian sources on Infomart disclosed only two articles having to do with education and the DIALOG ONE search nine.

Canadian and American uses of PC tended to concentrate primarily in arts/entertainment coverage, and secondarily in news coverage. Of the 153 articles found in the Canadian PC sample, 93 involved arts/entertainment coverage, while 14 were in news coverage. In the U.S. sources arts/entertainment comprised 202 of the 492 articles and news a further 81. Thus, during the 1980s, Canadian and American newspapers overwhelmingly placed PC in the context of news and entertainment coverage. It is also the case that both American and Canadian sources from this time period occasionally deployed PC for anti-Communist purposes. PC was used to portray socialist/communist countries as anti-individualist, conformist, and dreary. The majority of references, however, pertained to particular social movements or to cultural change associated with social movements that were not specified in the texts, e.g., in concert reviews of Parachute Club, Holly Near, or John Cougar Mellencamp. While PC might have been formally intended to criticize state institutions and right-wing policies during the 1980s it was very rarely used to do so.

Throughout the Canadian and American media PC was associated with smugness, humourlessness, tedium. For example, it has been said of Ed Schreyer, Canada's former governor general, that he 'is not known for his effervescent personality or his thrilling prose, but in Ontario, at least, he is politically correct' (*Maclean's* 1990, A11). We may surmise that PC varies independently of effervescence and thrills. In the *Edmonton Journal* we are informed: ' "Sexuality and desire," muses Riis, a self-described post-feminist ... are aspects of humanity "you cannot make politically correct" ' (*Edmonton Journal* 1989). A book reviewer in *Newsday* is surprised that the novel under review can 'accomplish the seemingly contradictory feat of being at once uproariously funny and politically correct' (Gabree 1987). The consistency with which PC comes to be characterized as anti-libido and the 'politically incorrect' with libido has the effect of equating social movement culture with drudgery and hegemonic culture with unproblematic fun and joy.

By the end of the 1980s, then, PC had been firmly lodged in the Canadian and American print media. Most articles containing an occurrence of PC had to do with arts and entertainment, often poking fun or sometimes simply undermining the influence of social movements on movies, music, books, the visual arts, and other media. PC is frequently, though not exclusively, associated in these media texts with left-wing social movements, generally with particular movements. The cumulative effect, however, of the individual occurrences is to set the stage for a global association of PC with movements of the left. However, the implied reader of the mass media is not a social movement activist; the element of critique present in PC is thus no longer internal to social movements. The voicing of the newspapers appropriates a term from leftist social movements, together with many of the axes of conflict found in those movements, particularly the opposition between habitual vs. desired dispositions of the body and well-known vs. transformed practices of everyday life. The newspapers thus have a hybrid voicing. When the mass media in the 1980s relocated PC from its previous social movement location, the dialogic positioning of PC shifted radically. The moment of self-critique present in its social movement meanings became vulnerable to being appropriated as a purely external critique.

Neoconservative PC

I propose in this section to locate the neoconservative reaccentuation of PC as an aspect of American neoconservative politics on formal education. I then proceed to analyse two texts, Richard Bernstein's 'The Rising Hegemony of the Politically Correct' (Bernstein 1990) and George Bush's convocation address at the University of Michigan (Bush 1991) as case studies in order to show how neoconservatives resignified PC. The analysis will draw on systemic functional grammar, a school of linguistic theory and social semiotics, and concentrate for the most part on the new patterns of lexical cohesion (defined below) introduced to define PC, to give it a new 'value' in Saussurean terms. Systemic functional linguistics interprets grammar as a repository of social process, language as a realization of social organization. It is thus attractive for a sociology of language that has as one component the close analysis of texts.[3]

American neoconservatives had been interested in the politics of formal education long before their deployment of PC during late 1990 as a line of attack against liberals and leftists in universities. During the 1980s neoconservatives regarded universities as the last significant bastion of liberalism. William P. Bennett, while secretary of state in the second Reagan administration, fought against cooperative learning models in public schools. He attacked the use of education as a vehicle for social change, arguing that this gave rise to divisiveness and undermined the creation of a 'common culture' in the United States. Like other neoconservatives, he held that achievement in schooling should be judged by uniform national 'objective measures.' As Bennett saw it, schooling was to teach common moral standards, what he called 'the formation of civic character,' and that character was to be modelled on competitive, neoconservative models of subjectivity. Bennett's earlier 1984 report on education in the humanities, *To Reclaim a Legacy*, commissioned when he was chair of the National Endowment for the Humanities, understood the humanities to be a repository of historical memory. The value of the humanities lay in their keeping alive responses made throughout history to what he deemed to be universal human questions: 'What is justice? ... What is noble? What is base? Why do civilizations flourish? Why do they decline?' (Bennett 1984, 3). Bennett attacked university education for purportedly having abandoned the teaching of a common culture and tradition based on canonical authorities, condemning his opponents as 'the academic thought police' and referring to 'the new McCarthyism of the left' before these phrases had become popularized in neoconservative PC discourse.

From the mid-1980s, neoconservatives became preoccupied with the supposedly new politicizing of the humanities. In article after article their flagship journals such as *The New Criterion* and *Commentary* put forward the position that the humanities had a higher purpose: the creation of a 'common culture' and the maintenance of a certain ideal of 'the educated person.' These accounts construct the humanities as a particular form of cultural capital without which the American nation would fall to rack and ruin.

These educational ideals reflected an increased concern for social and cultural values characteristic of neoconservatism since about 1985. It was at this time that they discovered that capitalism was not completely autonomous, but dependent, so they argued, on cultural forces that could not be wholly addressed by economic policy. At this point neoconservatives in Britain and the United States began to emphasize 'the absolute moral values that underlie the nation and its market economy' (Morris 1991, 28). The discovery of 'culture' as a prerequisite to national dominance and capital accumulation paralleled the explosion of concern with 'organizational culture' in management circles from 1982 onwards (Barley and Kunda 1992, 381–4). Given the cultural agenda of neoconservatives from the mid-1980s, it was small wonder that they should become implacable opponents of some of the most exciting trends in the contemporary humanities – feminism, deconstruction, anti-racism, the new historicism – which recover and examine the social in texts, exploring the role of literary and popular culture in iterating and challenging dominant power relations. The 'common culture' of the neoconservatives is, after all, not shared commonly among the people of Canada and the United

States; it is and has been an élite culture, the status and form of which is the bone of contention between neoconservatives and radical scholars. 'Common culture' is a clever, populist advertising tactic.

Lessons from Richard Bernstein

The article credited with beginning the PC media wave, Richard Bernstein's 'The Rising Hegemony of the Politically Correct' (Bernstein 1990), linked PC to a variety of educational initiatives and social movement politics that had been previously vilified by neoconservatives. These are all assembled under the rubric 'PC.' More technically, PC is constituted as the superordinate term (the general class) with the others as co-hyponyms (the members of the subclass), like the relation between 'cutlery' (superordinate gloss)[4] and 'fork' (hyponym), or between 'fork' and 'spoon' (co-hyponyms).

The Bernstein article is didactic, as can be seen by the number of relational verbal processes in the text – verbs having to do with being or having. The text does not presuppose that readers have previously heard about PC, or that they associate PC with feminism, curricular change, or any other of its co-hyponyms. The text makes new meaning through creating new patterns of cohesion among vocabulary items. A word/lexical item in a text is cohesive with other items if it 'presumes some other element in the text for its interpretation' (Halliday 1985a, 50), and the two items are said to be joined by a 'tie' in some form of meaning relation. The Bernstein text forms ties that constitute affirmative action, gay and lesbian studies, anti-racist organizing, and so forth as co-hyponyms and PC as their superordinate gloss (see Figure 1). Some readers may already have received training during the 1980s in the making of these cohesive ties, but, if not, the information in the Bernstein text is sufficient to learn the pattern of meaning entailments between PC and its hyponyms. The hyponyms correlate with a specific knowledge structure (Thibault 1988, 224), that being the enemies of neoconservatism in the universities. The meaning entailment between PC and its hyponyms enabled neoconservatives to simultaneously attack a wide host of changes taking place in the university today, unifying them under a convenient-to-use collocation. Bernstein here is teaching his readership to mean PC in a novel way, how to signify political struggles within universities by producing PC and its set of hyponomous meaning entailments. Over the next few months the number of university programs and policies entailed by PC mushroomed.

FIGURE 1

Hierarchy of Hyponymy in 'The Rising Hegemony of the Politically Correct' (Bernstein 1990)

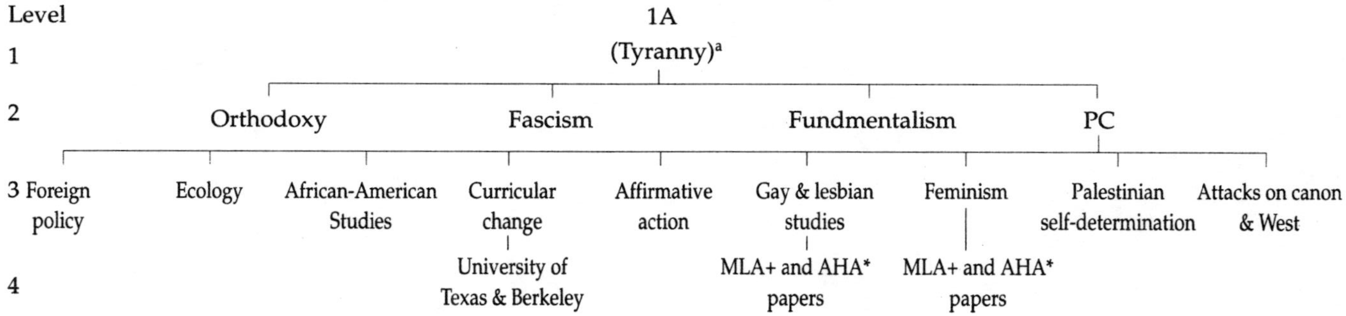

MLA+: Modern Languages Association AHA*: American Historical Association

Level Alternate Reading of Hierarcy of Hyponymy in `The Rising Hegemony of the Politically Correct'

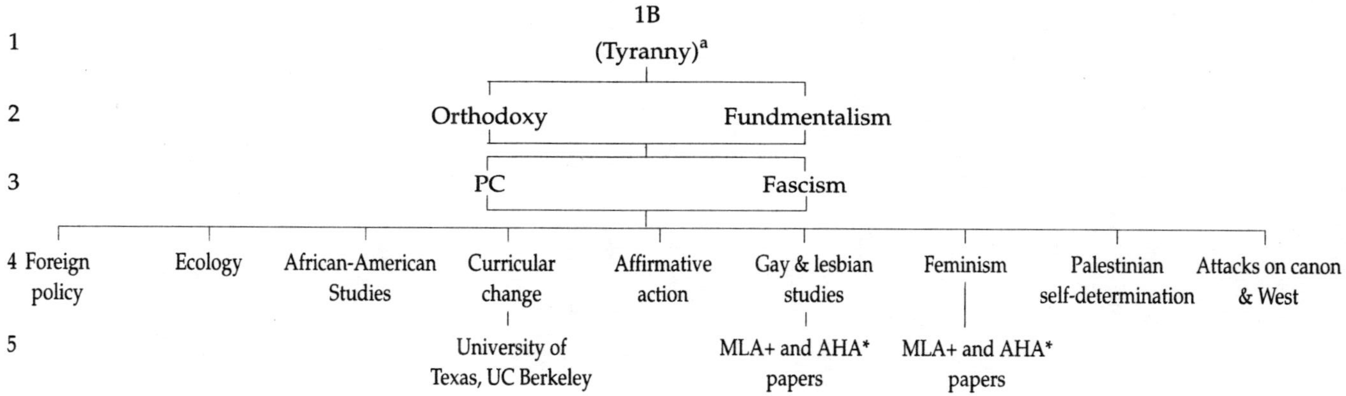

a: Superordinate gloss not present in text.

Readers received further instruction in the use of PC from Bernstein through a series of examples of PC in action: titles of papers presented at the American Historical Association and the MLA, a reference to a Berkeley course on 'contributions that minority groups have made to American Society,' (Bernstein 1990, 4) and curriculum change at the University of Texas (Level 4 in Figure 1A and Level 5 in Figure 1B). These examples create text-specific meanings for PC, but also orient readers to ways of producing cases of PC in their own localities for their own political purposes, thereby making the critique of PC locally actionable.

A further didactic task was taking place in Bernstein's article: the linkage of PC with the semantic field of 'orthodoxy' or what I will call 'tyranny.' Bernstein notes PC's 'suggestion of Stalinist orthodoxy' (1) and repeatedly links it with 'orthodoxy,' which also appears in the subheading to his article, 'America's Fashionable Orthodoxy.' He quotes Roger Kimball's oxymoronic identification of PC with 'liberal fascism' (4). PC is 'a kind of fundamentalism' (4). The text constitutes PC as a co-hyponym of orthodoxy, Stalinism, fascism, and fundamentalism (see Level 2, Figure 1A). The text may also be read as placing PC at the same level of hierarchy as fascism and constituting orthodoxy and fundamentalism as superordinate to PC and fascism (see Levels 2 and 3, Figure 1B). The hierarchy of hyponymy here has areas of ambiguity in the organization of its levels, indicating that all elements in the semantic field of orthodoxy/oppression are not fixed in relation to one another.

Neoconservative media texts subsequent to Bernstein's extended PC's range of co-hyponyms to 'storm troopers,' 'thought police,' and 'crusades.' Locating PC within the semantic field of 'tyranny' creates the possibility for this open-endedness of lexical cohesion. Since, moreover, 'the lexicon of a language is organized into a "hierarchy of hyponymy" so that we have differing degrees of generality' (Hasan in Thibault 1988, 223), hyponymy entailment from PC to feminism, anti-racism, ethnic studies, and so forth is affected by the positioning of PC within the semantic field of tyranny (the superordinate term is not realized in the text, only its hyponyms): these too become constituted as forms of oppression. The semantic field of tyranny is an open set to which new co-hyponyms may be added by a sender of a message, for, as Thibault has noted, 'the hierarchy of hyponymy is neither fixed nor necessarily given' (Thibault 1988, 223). Last, Bernstein repeats the previous social movement and news media association of PC with displeasure, quoting a student: 'Among its features ... are tenacity, sanctimoniousness, huffiness, a stubborn lack of a sense of humor' (Bernstein 1990, 4).

Bernstein's article in the *New York Times* provided a model for the propagation of neoconservative PC. Subsequent neoconservative PC did not simply reproduce Bernstein's model. Rather, his text acted as 'a system according to which new texts can be constructed. Once the constructing begins it becomes again a dynamic process, a "performance" which will inevitably change the model with which it begins' (Threadgold 1989, 108–9). Other neoconservative PC texts adapt Bernstein's hierarchy of hyponymy with its insertion of PC as a new element in the hierarchy of tyranny, coupled with PC's own set of hyponyms.

Bernstein's small contribution to the reorganization of the English lexicon differed from media use of PC during the 1980s.[5] Neoconservative deployment of PC attempts to define a broad axis of conflict within universities against the institutional form of social movements within academia such as women's studies, employment and educational equity policies, and anti-racist curricular change. Unlike newspaper texts of the 1980s, the locus of conflict does not primarily apply to arts/entertainment and to consumer culture under the impact of social movements – the ambivalence of everyday life and the body challenged by new ways of speaking, new desires, new dispositions. And where 1980s media texts often spoke with a voice hybridized with social movement PC, engaging in forms of mild self-mockery, the voice of neoconservative PC has nothing but contempt and ridicule for the presence of social movements inside and outside academe. Although social learning of PC through the mass media during the 1980s may account for some of the success of neoconservative PC, Bernstein's resignification was extensive. Bernstein's article fashioned a new meaning potential for PC: an element in the semantic field of 'tyranny,' superordinate to affirmative action, feminism, educational equity, ethnic studies, and so on, within universities – the grab-bag of neoconservative targets – and desperately dull to boot. These meanings are found wherever neoconservative PC is invoked.

George Bush on Civic Morality

As a second example of neoconservative PC discourse, I will analyse George Bush's commencement speech delivered on 4 May 1991 at the University of Michigan (see Bush Oration, pages 68–70). He spoke to about 63,000 people that day in a speech prepared for him by Anthony Snow, his new head speech writer and ex-editorialist for the *Washington Times*.[6] The speech being ceremonial, Bush used the time-honoured topic for these occasions – virtue and vice – to speak about civic morality. Bush's address took issue with Lyndon Johnson's May 1964 commencement address, also at the University of Michigan. To Johnson's 'Great Society,' Bush counterposed the 'Good Society,' a society that shone with all the national and capitalist virtues of Johnson's ideal, but without the welfare state encumbrances that, Bush claimed, had incited Americans to give up responsibility and learn dependency, and that generally tended to 'weaken people's moral sensitivity' (Bush 1991, 565). As befits a neoconservative, Bush's rhetoric was positioned in a Scottish Enlightenment idyll where the invisible hand of the market solves all social problems, and where less government frees the market to promote the prosperity of all – as though the path of capital over the past two centuries had been blamelessly bloodless. With a seeming complete lack of irony, Bush claimed that 'no system of development ever has nurtured virtue as completely and rigorously as ours.' However, in the passage on freedom of enterprise, speech and spirit, a discussion that forms the bulk of the speech, Bush acknowledged that in this land of maximal good lurked non-virtuous citizens, those who follow the base ways of the politically correct.

BUSH ORATION

George Bush, 'Remarks at the University of Michigan Commencement Ceremony in Ann Arbor,' 4 May 1991. *Weekly Compilation of Presidential Documents: Administration of George Bush* 27(19): 563–5.

Paragraph number

1 President Duderstadt, thank you all very much. Thank you for that warm welcome. I want to salute the president, salute Governor and Mrs. John Engler, Representatives of the Congress – Pursell, Upton, and Vander Jagt – and distinguished Regents, and especially I want to pay my respects to our fellow honoray degree recipients. Barbara and I are very grateful for this high honor. Before this, there wasn't one lawyer in the family, and now we have two.

2 The last time I was in Ann Arbor, we commemorated John Kennedy's unveiling of the Peace Corps. And as your commencement program indicates, Lyndon Johnson introduced the Great Society in a University of Michigan commencement address.

3 Today, I want to talk to you about this historic moment. Your com-

mencement – your journey into the 'real world' – coincides with this nation's commencement into a world freed from cold war conflict and thrust into an era of cooperation and economic competition.

4 The United States plays a defining role in the world. Our economic strength, our military power, and most of all, our national character brought us to this special moment. When our policies unleashed the economic expansion of the 1980s, we exposed forever the failures of socialism and reaffirmed our status as the world's greatest economic power. We sent troops to the Gulf, we showed that we take principles seriously enough to risk dying for them.

...

5 But the power to create also rests on other freedoms, especially the freedom – and I think about that right now [*applause*] – to think and speak one's mind. [*applause*] You see – thank you. The freedom – I had this written into the speech, and I didn't even know if these guys were going to be here.

6 No, but seriously, the freedom to speak one's mind – that may be the most fundamental and deeply revered of all our liberties. Americans to debate, to say what we think – because, you see, it separates good ideas from bad, it defines and cultivates the diversity upon which our national greatness rests, it tears off the blinders of ignorance and prejudice and lets us move on to greater things.*

7 Ironically, on the 200th anniversary of our Bill of Rights, we find free speech under assault throughout the United States, including on some college campuses. The notion of political correctness has ignited controversy across the land. And although the movement arises from the laudable desire to sweep away the debris of racism and sexism and hatred, it replaces old prejudice with new ones. It declares certain topics off-limits, certain expressions off-limits, even certain gestures off-limits.

8 What began as a crusade for civility has soured into a cause of conflict and even censorship. Disputants treat sheer force – getting their foes punished or expelled, for instance – as a substitute for the power of ideas.

9 Throughout history, attempts to micro-manage casual conversation have only incited distrust. They have invited people to look for an insult in every word, gesture, action. And in their own Orwellian way, crusades that demand correct behavior crush diversity in the name of diversity.

10 We all should be alarmed at the rise of intolerance in our land and by the growing tendency to use intimidation rather than reason in settling disputes. Neighbors who disagree no longer settle matters over a cup of coffee. They hire lawyers, and they go to court. And political extremists roam the land, abusing the privilege of free speech, setting citizens against one another on the basis of their class or race.

11 But, you see, such bullying is outrageous. It's not worthy of a great nation grounded in the values of tolerance and respect. So, let us fight back against the boring politics of division and derision. Let's trust our friends and colleagues to respond to reason. As Americans we must use our persuasive powers to conquer bigotry once and for all. And I remind myself a lot of this: We must conquer the temptation to assign bad motives to people who disagree with us.

12 If we hope to make full use of the optimism I discussed earlier, men and women must feel free to speak their hearts and minds. We must build a society in which people can join in common cause without having to surrender their identities.

13 You can lead the way. Share your thoughts and your experiences and your hopes and your frustrations. Defend others' rights to speak. And if harmony be our goal, let's pursue harmony, not inquisition.

* Grammatical problem present in oration.

The Bush oration is an exercise in contrastive rhetoric, defined for sociological purposes by Hargreaves as an

> interactional strategy whereby the boundaries of normal and acceptable practice are defined by institutionally and/or interactionally dominant individuals or groups through the introduction into discussion of alternative practices and social forms in stylized, trivialized and generally pejorative terms which connote their unacceptability. (Hargreaves 1981, 309)

One can discover a pervasive use of antithesis as a contrastive device in the Bush address. Examples from Bush include:

> What began as *a crusade for civility* has turned into *a cause of conflict and even of censorship.*
> Disputants treat *sheer force* ... as a substitute for the *power of ideas.*

... the growing tendency to use *intimidation* rather than *reason* in settling disputes.

The concluding sentence of paragraph 9 sounds a crescendo of double paradox:

And in their own Orwellian way, crusades that demand correct behavior *crush diversity in the name of diversity.*

The use of antithesis and paradox, in the 'freedom of speech' section clusters in paragraphs 7, 8, and 9 where PC is centrally being identified and described; it teaches rather transparently the purportedly shifty character of PC.[7]

The presence of antithesis and paradox in PC discourse allies neoconservatives with one of the common patterns found in the European right-wing press in articles dealing with racism: a pattern of denial and reversal. Attributions are simply reversed, and criticisms of racists as intolerant, aggressive, and tyrannical are turned and used against anti-racists (van Dijk 1991, 193–5; Essed 1991, 271; Murray 1986). Van Dijk has observed that reversal occurs when the right is defending its own self-image, and its 'ideological and political opponents are seen as symbolic competitors in the realm of moral influence' (van Dijk 1992, 108). In Bush's oration and elsewhere in neoconservative PC, attributions, such as intolerance and authoritarianism, made by the left about racism, sexism, and homophobia on campus are reversed and often posed in antithetical or paradoxical form.

Neither PC nor those engaging in PC are constructed as thinking, feeling, or perceiving, such activities being reserved for the Americans in whose name Bush speaks throughout the presentation. This can be shown from a technical analysis of the Bush speech. In Bush's passage on freedom of speech, PC is nominalized. PC functions, together with its co-referents (a meaning relation between separate lexical items that establishes identity of reference in particular texts), as the sayer in verbal processes (saying, reporting), the actor in material processes (doing, happening), and the carrier in relational processes (being, having). PC does not appear as the sensor in mental processes (perception, affection, cognition); in these processes the role of sensor is reserved for 'us,' the American people.

Within Bush's speech, 'we' and 'our' have shifting senses (Guespin 1985). In his opening remarks, Bush refers to 'Barbara (his partner) and I' as 'we' (paragraph 1). In the second paragraph, 'we' appears to be used in the sense of majesty, shifting to the sense of 'Americans/the American nation' at the point when Bush assumes an imperialist voice: 'The United States plays a defining role in the world. Our economic strength, our military power, and, most of all, our national character brought us to this special moment ... When we sent troops to the Gulf, we showed that we take principles seriously enough to risk dying for them' (paragraph 4 Bush 1991, 563). This third sense of 'we' as the American nation, with Bush speaking on its behalf as its delegated authority, is the predominant sense given to 'we' throughout the speech. As President, the delegated representative of the American people, acting in an official capacity at Ann Arbor, Bush had the warranted power to recreate 'we' in speech, elaborating its meaning, disseminating new significations of the American nation.[8] His remarks on freedom of speech inscribe PC and its inherents as 'they,' as people outside the American nation, who must be expunged from it.

Following the progression of personal pronouns and possessive adjectives in paragraphs 5 to 12 enables the resistant reader to see how they are used by Bush as a means to constitute a pattern of contrastive rhetoric, and to identify PC as a threat to the American nation. In paragraph 5 Bush breaks with his prepared text, turning to directly address his audience, positioning himself as 'I' and the audience as 'you.' The applause that greets this direct address, the confusing exophora (situationally specific reference: parts of a text that require reference to the text-external context of situation for interpretation) in the printed text, are explicable as a gesture of acknowledgment and solidarity on Bush's part. Bush goes on to construct PC as an attack on freedom of speech in paragraphs 6 to 8, beginning in the final sentence of paragraph 8 to characterize PC in the third person, and in the two successive paragraphs repeatedly referring to PC advocates as 'they' and 'their.' Paragraph 11 begins an appeal to 'us,' the American people, to fight back and expel the 'them' of the previous paragraphs, shifting to the vision of a unified society in paragraph 12 and a final appeal to 'you' in paragraph 13 to act like Americans should.

The sequence in the development of personal deictics in the passage is co-patterned with the use of modulation, and to a lesser extent, modality. In systemic functional grammar, modality and modulation are understood as aspects of the interpersonal function of language, the aspect of language coding the sender's judgments about the communication. Modality realizes speaker's attitude, evaluation, and opinions, while modulation is a realization of obligation/necessity. Little modalization or modulation of verbal processes occurs in the first six paragraphs of the 'freedom of speech' section (paragraphs 5–10), but there is a great concentration of both in the last three paragraphs – the expulsion and exhortation paragraphs mentioned above. The interpersonal is carried in the section identifying PC (paragraphs 7–11) primarily through the use of attitudinal epithets such as 'outrageous,' '*boring* politics,' '*laudable* desire.' A glance at the final paragraphs will reveal the repeated use of modulation: 'As Americans we *must* use ... We *must* conquer' (paragraph 11); 'men and women *must* feel free ... we *must* build a society' (paragraph 12). Two modal auxiliaries (verbal processes having a compound verb, with one element expressing speaker judgment) are found in the two final paragraphs: 'You *can* lead the way' (paragraph 13), and 'people *can* join in common cause' (paragraph 12).

The pattern of modulation and modalization in Bush's speech is in turn co-patterned with the use of mood structure (explained immediately below), another aspect of the interpersonal, with sentences in paragraphs 6–10 being in the declarative, but those in the final three paragraphs being in the optative imperative – 'let us fight back' (paragraph 11) – and the jussive imperative – 'Defend others' rights to speak' (paragraph 13). Mood realizes the semantics of speech function – language as action and interaction – and also assigns roles to addresser and addressee. In paragraphs 5–10, the statements give information and position the addressee in the role of acknowledging the statement, while in the last three the speaker is positioned as demanding goods and services, and addressee compliance is required.

The Bush speech reproduces and reinforces forms of meaning entailment for PC that neoconservatives had been concertedly propagating through the mass media since Bernstein's article appeared in October 1990. The section of Bush's address dealing with PC would have been difficult for his audience, then and later, to comprehend without this prior period of social learning. Like Bernstein and other neoconservatives before him, Bush fashions a position for PC within the semantic field of tyranny. In order to show how his speech accomplishes this task, we must follow the cohesive chains of which PC forms a part, that is, the set of lexical items in the text to which PC is related through ties of identity, opposition, synonymy, hyponymy, and part–whole relations.[9]

The collocation, 'political correctness,' first appears in Bush's address in paragraph 7 of its 'freedom of speech' section, immediately preceded by the statement 'we find *free speech* under assault throughout the United States' and followed by 'And although *the movement* arises.' Because 'movement' is preceded by 'the,' receivers of the message know that the meaning of 'movement' is recoverable in the immediate textual environment. 'Political correctness' is the most likely candidate for meaning entailment, making PC a kind of movement – that is, 'movement' and PC have a co-extensive tie, with 'movement' superordinate to PC. Now 'movement' is co-referential with 'it': the references are situationally identical. Thus, the text receivers are instructed to read PC as a movement that 'replaces old prejudices with new ones' and 'declares certain topics off-limits, certain expression off-limits, even certain gestures off-limits.' The initially mysterious link between 'free speech' in the topic sentence of paragraph 7 and PC has been clarified by the end of the paragraph: 'free speech' and PC have the relation of antonyms. A speaker of English unacquainted with PC on 5 May 1991 would have been required to make these kinds of cohesive links between 'free speech,' 'political correctness,' and 'the movement' simply to make the passage coherent, in so doing creating new forms of lexical ties among the terms.

In addition to being constructed as the opposite of 'free speech' and as a kind of 'movement,' PC is a chain with 'disputants' (by part–whole relation, 'disputants' being part of a 'movement'), and as a hyponym in a large set of superordinate terms: 'crusade,' 'conflict,' 'censorship,' 'correct behaviour,' 'bigotry,' 'bullying,' 'intimidation,' 'intolerance,' 'inquisition,' and so forth. This lexical chain, of which PC forms a part, and which I called 'tyranny' in the above analysis of the 1990 Bernstein article, stands in a contrastive/antonymic relation to a second lexical chain: 'tolerance,' 'respect,' 'trust,' 'optimism,' 'common cause,' 'harmony,' and so on. These latter are constructed as the virtues of the 'Good Society' to which PC is opposed. Bush's speech differs from Bernstein's October 1990 article in being far less explicit about agency. Where Bernstein made PC superordinate to feminism, ethnic studies, anti-racism, Palestinian self-determination, affirmative action, curricular change, attacks on the canon and the West, international solidarity, Bush was far more abstract. PC in the Bush text was not made superordinate to a set of discrete co-hyponyms, but rather was characterized at the level of the clause as an activity of unspecified participants in verbal processes – for example, 'Although the movement arises from the laudable desire to sweep away racism and sexism and hatred, it replaces old prejudice with new ones. It delcares certain topics off-limits ... They have invited people to look for an insult in every word, gesture, action.' The meaning entailment from the superordinate gloss, PC, is to the implicit hyponym 'speech codes,' evoked but not mentioned in the text.

We can thus see that the political claims made in the deployment of neoconservative 'PC' are enacted through particular skewings of the meaning potential of English, necessitating a level of analysis distinct from economics or psychology, a level of analysis capable of analysing meaning formation within texts. The news media in disseminating neoconservative PC did not simply reproduce pre-existing discourse. In the case of neoconservative PC, North Americans were taught how to resignify a collocation with which some were already familiar either through its presence in the mass media during the 1980s and/or through their own participation in social movements.[10] Social movement PC signified an axis of intra-movement conflict on the terrain of culture. Mass circulation newspapers during the 1980s employed PC to variously signify conflicts within consumer culture, the culture industries, and everyday life occurring under the impact of social change associated with social movements. Neoconservative PC projected an axis of conflict between the forces of democracy and tyranny on the terrain of education, particularly higher education. Neoconservative PC is a form of contrastive rhetoric intended to discredit, ridicule, and trivialize the gains and presence of social movements institutionalized within higher education.

In the analyses of the Bernstein and Bush texts, I have argued that neoconservatives resignified PC by locating it within a hierarchy of hyponymy, which in part mobilized and reorganized pre-existing semantic fields. However, the place of PC in this hierarchy was new to the mass media in the autumn of 1990. Figure 2 sketches a general model of the PC hierarchy of hyponymy. In Level 2 (see page 76) of Figures 2A and 2B appear co-hyponymous elements – 'crusades,' 'inquisition,' 'fascism,' 'Stalinism,' and so forth; this list is not fixed and may be expanded or contracted in any given text. These elements entail a superordinate gloss that was not realized in the Bush or Bernstein texts; I have called this superordinate analytical structure 'tyranny.' If included, it would form an additional level in this hierarchy of hyponymy (Level 1 in Figures 2A and 2B). The base level of the lexical hierarchy consists of a series of co-hyponyms typically realized by 'speech codes,' 'feminism,' 'multiculturalism,' 'affirmative action,' 'curriculum change' (Level 4 in Figure 2A and Level 3 in Figure 2B). Again, these elements are an open set; the list expands and contracts, but many terms pertain to formal education. Typically, local cases are indexed to the base level (Level 5 in Figure 2A and Level 4 in Figure 2B). The location of PC within the hierarchy of hyponymy may be interpreted in at least two ways, as illustrated in Figures 2A and 2B. In Figure 2B, PC is construed as a co-hyponym of 'crusades,' 'inquisition,' and so on (Level 2, Figure 2B) and in Figure 2A as hyponym

FIGURE 2
PC Hierarchy of Hyponymy
2A

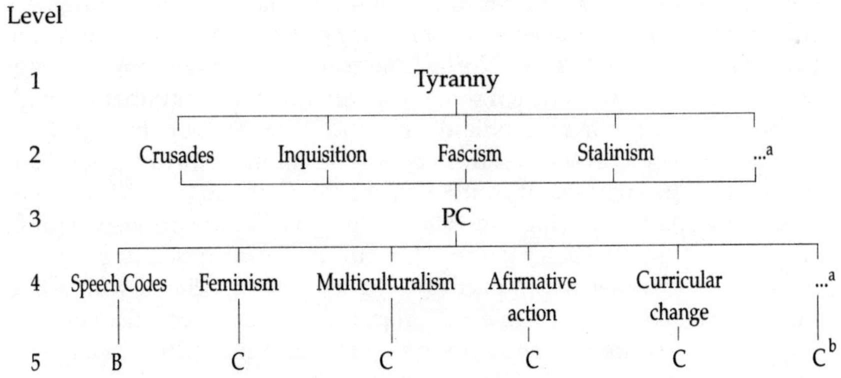

a: Indicates terms of Level may be expanded.
b: Indicates local examples indexed in specific texts.

2B

Alternate Reading of PC Hierarchy of Hyponymy

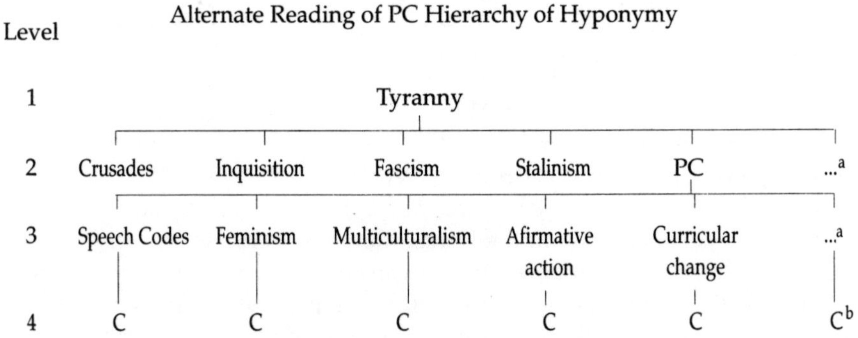

a: Indicates terms of Level may be expanded.
b: Indicates local examples indexed in specific texts.

of the superordinate 'crusades,' 'inquisition.' In the former case, PC is given the meaning of an entirely new type of tyranny; in the latter, PC is construed as a particular case of fascism, Stalinism, crusades, and so forth.

Through this hierarchy of hyponymy, neoconservatives are able to put into circulation their own standpoint on the changes taking place in formal education, a convenient rubric that unifies these heterogeneous phenomena, associates them with tyranny, and pits them against democracy. The contrastive rhetoric of neoconservative PC was further typically characterized by the use of antithesis and paradox, all the better to assist the overall pattern of reversal: neoconservatives claim the mantle of being the truly liberal, tolerant defenders of diversity, while their foes supposedly tolerate intolerance, crush diversity in the name of diversity.

It was through this pattern of discursive innovation that neoconservative PC became a news theme in the fall of 1990. Operating as a theme, it made events newsworthy: stories are chosen for print or broadcast if they are or can be typified as instances of a newsworthy theme (Fishman 1978). Of course, the kinds of social change associated with neoconservative PC predated the PC media wave, which began in late 1990. The success of this media wave should not, therefore, simply be read as reflecting social change within universities. In any case, these forms of social change might have been, and were, criticized on other grounds by conservatives. This form of explanation misses the particular brilliance and virulence of neoconservative PC that was constituted in its specific combination of discourse innovations. Through these discursive features, PC was resignified, became a news theme, and local events thereby became newsworthy, although without the political struggles taking place within universities there would have been no motivation for neoconservatives to mobilize discursively, nor, indeed, any events for news reports to index.

Canadian Deployment of Neoconservative PC

President Bush's speech at the University of Michigan was not well publicized in the Canadian print media. The Canadian neoconservative news wave began in earnest with the 27 May 1991 issue of *Maclean's*. Shortly before this date, neoconservative PC had appeared in the Canadian media (e.g., Kingwell 1991), but its use had yet to become thematic. During the early period of the American neoconservative PC news wave from October 1990 to May 1991, Canadian newspapers continued to use PC in the sense that had circulated during the 1980s: as a pesky form of social change principally impinging on everyday habits and consumer culture.

The *Maclean's* issue introduced a new voicing into Canadian PC discourse. The three texts about PC in that issue of the magazine – the editorial by Kevin Doyle (1991) and articles by Tom Fennell (1991) and Rae Corelli (1991) – reproduce the forms of contrastive rhetoric found in American neoconservative PC. They reaccentuate PC by deploying the patterns of lexical cohesion found in American neoconservative PC, placing PC within a hierarchy of hyponymy that resignifies PC as a form of tyranny contrastive to freedom of speech, democracy, and toleration. This pattern of lexical cohesion attempts to reverse at a semantic level the moral high ground and legitimacy claimed by social movement politics acting both independently of, and within, dominant social institutions. There are few instances of antithesis and paradox in these three texts, but the figures of speech are found elsewhere in Canadian neoconservative PC.

Examining the similarity chain to which PC has ties in the Doyle, Fennell, and Corelli texts, we see the superordinate gloss to PC named as 'repression,' 'movement,' 'puritanism,' 'totalitarianism,' 'censorship,' and 'Nazis.' The texts may also be read as placing 'Nazis' and 'puritanism' as co-hyponyms of PC since Nazis and puritanism may, like PC, signify particular historical instances of movement, repression, or totalitarianism. This field of terms is constructed as antonymic to 'freedom of speech and behaviour' and 'democracy.' PC in turn is superordinate to an enormous range of co-hyponyms: 'codes of conduct,' 'feminism,' 'homosexual rights,' 'native rights,' 'animal rights,' 'deconstruction,' 'affirmative action,' 'non-drinking,' 'nonsmoking,' 'non-meat-eating,' 'high cholesterol foods,' 'environmentalism,' 'garbage disposal,' 'logging,' 'conventional English usage.' This open-ended list is then made antonymic to 'classics,' 'Western civilization,' and 'humour.'

The pattern of lexical cohesion operating in the *Maclean's* texts is therefore the same as that in American neoconservative PC. Interestingly, the editorial for the issue does in fact extensively quote from Bush's speech at Ann Arbor (Doyle 1991, 4).[11] However, the similarity chain in which PC is an element has a further level of elaboration through which neoconservative PC comes to be Canadianized. 'Feminism,' 'animal rights,' and the other co-hyponyms and antonyms that have meaning-entailment ties to PC are indexed to Canadian examples. Through the rich documentation of Canadian instances, neoconservative PC acquires situational relevance for Canada; the Fennell and Corelli texts constitute neoconservative PC as meaningful and potentially actionable *in Canada*. American-specific examples of PC are minimal in the *Maclean's* articles, with Fennell's article concentrating on Canadian universities and Corelli's on the depredations of Canadian 'special-interest groups' (Corelli 1991, 48) for consumer culture and everyday practice. Sad tales abound: the persecuted University of Toronto professor forbidden to smoke in his office, petitions at the University of Alberta and the University of Waterloo against employment equity, protests against 'Into the Heart of Africa,' an exhibit at the Royal Ontario Museum in 1989–90. These examples suggest the range and kinds of targets against which PC might be used in Canada, teaching the discursive means for producing PC in a variety of particular, local practices.

The *Maclean's* texts implicate Canadian universities as major sites of PC, as did subsequent media coverage such as the broadcasts on the CBC Radio show 'Sunday Morning': 'PC in the Universities' (28 July 1991) and 'Witch Hunts and P.C.: Is Political Correctness the New McCarthyism?' (15 December 1991) (see Smith this volume). Canadian newspaper stories in which PC had appeared before 1991 had not used PC to criticize higher education. The article by Tom Fennell, 'The Silencers: A New Wave of Repression Is Sweeping through Universities' (Fennell 1991, 40), followed the trend of American neoconservative PC in making universities a topic of PC. He established a precedent in linking neoconservative PC to the critique of Canadian universities. Nonetheless, neoconservative PC in Canada was not exclusively about universities, as may be surmised by scanning the *Maclean's* issue in question: both Corelli's 'Saying "No" to the Old Ways: Personal Habits Are under Attack' (Corelli 1991), and Kevin Doyle's editorial, 'The Evils of the Nons' (Doyle 1991), deal extensively with challenges to customary body practices and consumer culture.

American neoconservatives initially aimed PC as an attack against universities, but a broader range of topics has consistently been deployed in both Canadian and American neoconservative PC. Thus, for instance, in an interview with Phil Bryden, president of the British Columbia Civil Liberties Association, the questioner from *B.C. Business* reproduces the neoconservative penchant for antithesis and paradox together with the similarity chain prototypical of PC. The questioner uses this pattern when posing questions about university education and other topics:

> There appears to be a new wave of Puritanism sweeping the continent in which the only acceptable posture is what's been dubbed 'politically correct.' Are individuals like Philippe Rushton ... not also entitled to freedom of expression? (Mitchell 1991, 69)

In an effort to promote openness and tolerance towards women and minorities, are the advocates of political correctness merely creating new forms of intolerance? (73)

While neoconservative PC has attacked social and cultural reform within Canadian universities, it would be a mistake to confine its relevance to the educational sector.

The neoconservative PC news wave has now dissipated in English Canada, although PC is still used as a theme in news reports and in headlines. At present PC is multiaccentual, bearing the traces of its various historical uses over the past three decades. Media sources still signify PC in the senses in which it was used before October 1990. Joey Slinger of the *Toronto Star* still wondered in December 1991 about the environmental wisdom of buying Christmas trees and was bemused by his own dilemmas of how to engage in consumer capitalism with a good conscience (Slinger 1991). Columnists in the *Globe and Mail* continued to make snide remarks about radical cultural events in arts reviews and fashion columns (Livingstone 1991; Vincent 1991). Nancy Millar of the *Calgary Herald* fled earnest PC types who wanted her to write on 'PC topics' like bilingualism instead of what she longed to memorialize – the flies in her kitchen. This older voicing co-exists with a neoconservative PC voice that is hostile to PC, portraying it as a form of tyranny (Smith 1991; Conlogue 1991; Hurst 1991; *Globe and Mail* 1992). As in the United States, neoconservative attacks on feminism and other progressive movements preceded the PC news wave in Canada (e.g., Byfield 1991), but it was the neoconservative version of PC that discursively unified these movements into a single phenomenon with the purported attributes of being tyrannical and anti-democratic and thus as something to attack rather than to feel ambivalent about.

Over the course of the neoconservative media wave, PC was dispersed into everyday speech within English Canada. Its meanings in speech are polysemic, sometimes being used within social movements in the senses found since the 1960s as a sign of rigidity, particularly at the level of culture and the interactive order. Another sense is more consistent with media uses of the 1980s – ambivalence and defence of the repetitive pleasures of the habitus in resistance to the cultural and social reforms ultimately connected with social movements. The neoconservative sense of PC as a form of tyranny proliferates freely in oral and printed forms, and is present as well in speech practices. Lastly, PC appears as a simple term of insult meant to undermine a statement or behaviour of an addressee. All these senses are co-present in contemporary Canada.

Conclusion

Neoconservative PC has succeeded in disseminating a new meaning potential for PC, one that unifies a diverse number of democratic struggles under the rubric of PC, and then associates PC with tyranny. Canadian and American neoconservatives mobilized PC to try to establish a coherent axis of conflict within universities against the institutional forms of social movements within academia. We see in neoconservative PC an attempt to resist the politics that has gradually gained a (small) hold in major social institutions over the past generation. Thus, the front of democratic struggles has now shifted to the management levels of governance. Resignifying democratic struggles as PC was an attempt by neoconservatives and their allies to delegitimize these struggles and to claim the mantle of toleration and democracy for themselves: a reconsolidation of moral authority. The reversal of attributions characteristic of PC has been typical of neoconservative media strategies with respect to specific democratic struggles: anti-racists have, by way of example, been termed the 'real racists' in more than one country.

The Russian psychologist Lev Vygotsky argued that language is a device for carrying out co-operative activities (Vygotsky 1978, 19–30). The neoconservative reaccentuation of PC functioned as a device for unifying the opponents of varying democratic struggles into a loosely co-ordinated bloc. Neoconservative PC also facilitates objections not simply to employment equity or women's studies, but to a broad gamut of democratic struggles. Calling a specific speech code PC is both to delegitimize it and also to locate the speech code as a particular practice within a broader objectionable field. An example of such a move would be the motion passed by the Alberta Association of Provincial Court Judges to request that funding be approved only for such educational courses that were 'free of political correctness' (Moysa 1992, A9); the judges had tired of anti-sexist and anti-racist education. The meaning potential of neoconservative PC is sufficiently general to enable the local indexing of virtually any form of democratic struggle, a necessary preliminary to situational action in the form of political attack – a co-operative activity in Vygotsky's sense.

Whatever its site of use, PC has always been a sign of social conflict. Neoconservatives have typified PC as a social/political movement, the best response to which has been Judy Rebick's (past president of the National Action Committee on the Status of Women) retort: 'I've never known a movement without a newspaper, without a publication of any kind, without any spokespeople and with no one claiming to belong to it' (*Vancouver Sun* 1992, A3). By all known social scientific and political definitions of 'movement,' Rebick is, of course, right. However, when those on the left simply deny the existence of a PC movement, we evade defending the combined and cumulative impact of social changes initiated by social movements and democratic struggles. Neoconservative PC may prove to be the first phase of open and systematic resistance to the modest gains that have been made by social groups struggling for a variety of social reforms. These reforms need to be defended in a concerted way, and not separately as ecologists, anti-racists, feminists, and so forth. Like PC, this exercise of concerting meaning and activity across various attempts at social change will require discourse innovation and new organizational practices and forms.

Notes

Many thanks to Gertrud Neuwirth, Mariana Valverde, Becki Ross, Carol-Anne O'Brien, and Stephen Richer for their critical comments; to Heather Jon Maroney for discussions; to Ki Namaste for sources; and to Nancy Peden (MacOdrum Library, Carleton University), Jennifer Quaile, and Merv Taylor for their research support.

1 The neoconservative critique of 'political correctness' has no corresponding term in the Québécois mass media. The comments in this paper hold solely for English Canada.

2 *Boston Globe, Christian Science Monitor, Chicago Tribune, Detroit Free Press, Los Angeles Times, Miami Herald, Newsday, Philadelphia Inquirer, San Francisco Chronicle, Star Tribune, Washington Post, USA Today.*

3 It is beyond the scope of this paper to show why systemic functional grammar is neither a structuralism nor a formalism. On this question, see Thibault (1991) and Hodge and McHoul (1992) for discussion.

4 The relation between PC and affirmative action, anti-racist organizing, and other members of the similarity chain might also be read as meronymy (part–whole relations).

5 It should be noted that there arguably do exist a few examples of neoconservative PC texts about university education that reached print prior to Bernstein's 1990 article in the *New York Times*, e.g., Starr (1989).

6 Snow had been hired to make Bush's speeches tougher and more topical (Dowd 1991, 32).

7 Rhetoric manuals have, since antiquity, warned against the overuse of antithesis, its witty effect quickly degenerating into contrivance and then into

demagogy. Antithesis and, secondarily, paradox are strongly characteristic of neoconservative PC texts; they abound in the work of Dinesh D'Souza (1991a, b, and 1992).

8 On delegated authority and speech, see Bourdieu (1991, 107–16).

9 Co-classification does not arise in the lexical chain of which PC is a member in the Bush speech, although it is a type of cohesive tie giving rise to lexical chains. In co-classification the elements in a tie belong to the same class, but are different members of the class (Halliday and Hasan 1989, 74).

10 Electronic and printed news media disseminate discourse innovations over large and spatially disparate populations with a rapidity unprecedented in human history. Their influence should be investigated as a new source of collective variation in language.

11 The passage quoted runs from 'The notion of "political correctness" ' to 'certain gestures off limits' in paragraph 7 of the Bush address (Doyle 1991, 4).

References

Balz, Dan. 1993. 'Glenn's Swing South Shows Gaps between Promise, Performance.' *The Washington Post* (21 Nov.): A03

Barley, Stephen R., and Gideon Kunda. 1992. 'Design and Devotion: Surges of Rational and Normative Ideologies of Control in Managerial Discourse.' *Administrative Science Quarterly* 37: 363–99

Bazerman, Charles. 1988. *Shaping Written Knowledge.* Madison: University of Wisconsin Press

Bennett, William J. 1984. *To Reclaim a Legacy: A Report on the Humanities in Higher Education.* Washington, DC: National Endowment for the Humanities

Berman, Paul. 1992. 'Introduction: The Debate and Its Origins.' In Paul Berman, ed., *Debating P.C.*, 1–26. New York: Laurel

Bernstein, Richard. 1988. 'Youthspeak.' *San Francisco Chronicle* (18 Dec.): 20/Z5

– 1990. 'The Rising Hegemony of the Politically Correct.' *The New York Times* (28 Oct.) (sec. 4): 1, 4

Bizjack, Tony. 1989. 'New Dictums of the "Politically Correct." ' *San Francisco Chronicle* (17 March): B3

Bloom, Allan. 1987. *The Closing of the American Mind.* New York: Simon and Schuster

Blumenthal, Sidney. 1986. *The Rise of the Counter-Establishment.* New York: Times Books

Bourdieu, Pierre. 1988. *Homo Academicus.* Peter Collier, trans. Stanford: Stanford University Press

– 1991. *Language and Symbolic Power.* Cambridge: Polity

Bush, George. 1991. 'Remarks at the University of Michigan Commencement Ceremony in Ann Arbor.' *Weekly Compilation of Presidential Documents: Administration of George Bush* 27(19): 557–96
Byfield, Virginia. 1991. 'Fembos in Academe.' *Western Report* (7 Jan.): 24–30
Clarke, John, Stuart Hall, Tony Jefferson, and Brian Roberts. 1976. 'Subcultures, Cultures and Class.' In Stuart Hall and Tony Jefferson, eds., *Resistance through Rituals*. London: Hutchinson
Conlogue, Ray. 1991. 'Political Correctness and the Roots of Rage.' *Globe and Mail* (27 June): C5
Corbett, Edward P. 1971. *Classical Rhetoric for the Modern Student*. New York: Oxford University Press
Corelli, Rae. 1991. 'Saying "No" to Old Ways: Personal Habits under Attack.' *Maclean's* (27 May): 48–50
Denning, Michael. 1992. 'The Academic Left and the Rise of Cultural Studies.' *Radical History Review* 54: 21–47
Dimen, Muriel. 1984. 'Politically Correct/Politically Incorrect.' In Carole S. Vance, ed., *Pleasure and Danger*, 138–48. Boston: RKP
Dowd, Maureen. 1991. 'Bush Sees Threat to Flow of Ideas on U.S. Campuses.' *The New York Times* (5 May): 1, 32
Doyle, Kevin. 1991. 'The Evils of the Nons.' *Maclean's* (27 May): 4
D'Souza, Dinesh. 1991a. ' "PC" So Far.' *Commentary* 91(10)(Oct.): 44–6
– 1991b. *Illiberal Education: The Politics of Race and Sex on Campus*. New York: Free Press
D'Souza, Dinesh, and Robert MacNeil. 1992. 'The Big Chill? Interview with Dinesh D'Souza.' In Paul Berman, ed., *Debating P.C.*, 29–39. New York: Laurel
Durkheim, Emile, and Marcell Mauss. [1903] 1963. *Primitive Classification*. Rodney Needham, trans. London: Cohen and West
Edley, Christopher, Jr. 1983. 'Congress Will Have to Change Its Ways.' *The Washington Post* (26 June): O1
The Edmonton Journal. 1989. 'After a Long Break, Author Riis Travels the Tourist Zone' (11 Nov.)
Edwards, Val. 1980. 'The Invisible Community.' *Broadside* 1(10)(Sept.): 4–5, 14
Epstein, Barbara. 1991. ' "Political Correctness" and Collective Powerlessness.' *Socialist Review* 91(3–4): 13–36
Essed, Philomena. 1991. *Understanding Everyday Racism*. Newbury Park, CA: Sage
Fennell, Tom. 1991. 'The Silencers.' *Maclean's* (27 May): 40–3
Finn, Chester E. 1989. 'The Campus: An Island of Repression in a Sea of Freedom.' *Commentary* 88(3)(Sept.): 17–23
Fishman, Mark. 1978. 'Crime Waves as Ideology.' *Social Problems* 25: 531–43

Fleming, Michael, et al. 1987. 'Inside New York.' *Newsday* (27 Nov.): News 6
Fontanier, Pierre. [1830] 1977. *Les Figures du Discours*. Paris: Flammarion
Gabree, John. 1987. 'Paperbacks New and Notable.' *Newsday* (18 Oct.): Ideas 12
Gardin, Bernard, and Jean-Baptiste Marcellesi. 1974. *Introduction à la sociolinguistique*. Paris: Larousse-Université
Globe and Mail. 1992. 'Death Notice Points to Political Correctness.' (23 Dec.)
Goar, Carol. 1988. 'Mila Is Owed More Credit and Respect.' *The Montreal Gazette* (8 Jan.): B3
Goodman, Ellen. 1985. 'America Exporting Birth Control Ban.' *Chicago Tribune* (5 Sept.) Tempo 1
Guespin, Louis. 1985. '*Nous*, la langue et l'interaction.' *Mots* 10 (March): 45–62
Halliday, M.A.K. 1985a. 'Dimensions of Discourse Analysis: Grammar.' In Teun A. van Dijk, ed., *Handbook of Discourse Analysis*. Vol. 2, 29–56. London: Academic Press
– 1985b. *An Introduction to Functional Grammar*. London: Edward Arnold
Halliday, M.A.K., and Ruquaiya Hasan. 1989. *Language, Context and Text*. Oxford: Oxford University Press
Hargreaves, Andy. 1981. 'Contrastive Talk and Extremist Talk: Teachers, Hegemony and the Educationist Context.' In Len Barton and Stephen Walker, eds., *Schools, Teachers and Teaching*, 303–29. Sussex: Falmer
Hasan, Ruquiya. 1984. 'Coherence and Cohesive Harmony.' In J. Flood, ed., *Understanding Reading Comprehension*, 181–219. Newark, DE: IRA
Hebdige, Dick. 1979. *Subculture: The Meaning of Style*. London: Methuen
Heller, Scott. 1990. 'Colleges Becoming Havens of "Political Correctness," Some Scholars Say.' *Chronicle of Higher Education* 37(12) (21 Nov.): A1, A14–15
Hodge, Bob, and Alec McHoul. 1992. 'The Politics of Text and Commentary.' *Textual Practice* 6(2)(Summer): 189–209
Hurst, Lynda. 1991. ' "Politically Correct"? Think before You Speak.' *Toronto Star* (2 June): A1–2
Iannone, Carol. 1988. 'Feminism vs. Literature.' *Commentary* 87(1)(July): 49–53
Kalia, Seema. 1991. 'Addressing Race in the Feminist Classroom.' In Jane S. Gaskell and Arlene Tigar McLaren, eds., *Women and Education* (2nd ed.) 275–82 Calgary: Detselig
Katzenstein, Mary Fainsod. 1990. 'Feminism within American Institutions: Unobtrusive Mobilization in the 1980s.' *Signs* 16(1):
Kelner, Robert K. 1991. 'We Conservatives Wage a Phony War on Political Correctness.' *The Wall Street Journal* (21 Dec.): A11
Kimball, Roger. 1986. 'Debating the Humanities at Yale.' *The New Criterion* 4(6)(June): 23–33
– 1990. *Tenured Radicals*. New York: Harper Perennial

Kingwell, Mark. 1991. 'Enter the Campus Thought Police.' *Globe and Mail* (15 April)
Levinson, Stephen C. 1983. *Pragmatics*. Cambridge: Cambridge University Press
Livingstone, David. 1991. 'Negligent Chic in New Styles.' *Globe and Mail* (28 Feb.): C6
McKenna, Kristine. 1987. 'The Art Galleries: La Cienaga Area.' *Los Angeles Times* (20 March): 14
Maclean's. 1990. 'A Politician in Print' (22 Oct.): A11
McRobbie, Angela. 1991. *Feminism and Youth Culture*. Boston: Unwin Hyman
Melucci, Alberto. 1989. *Nomads of the Present: Social Movements and Individual Needs in Contemporary Society*. Philadelphia: Temple University Press
Menchu, Rigoberta. 1984. *I, Rigoberta Menchu*. London: Verso
Millar, Nancy. 1991. 'My Worries Fly in the Face of Political Correctness.' *Calgary Herald* (26 Jan.): B4
Mitchell, Don. 1991. 'A Civil Libertarian's View on "Political Correctness".' *B.C. Business* (Sept.): 69–74
Morash, Gordon. 1989. 'Bulk, Specialty Shops Provide Healthy Variety.' *The Edmonton Journal* (25 Oct.): C2
Morris, Paul. 1991. 'Freeing the Spirit of Enterprise.' In Russell Keat and Nicholas Abercrombie, eds., *Enterprise Culture*, 21–37. London: Routledge
Moysa, Marilyn. 1992. 'Judges Bristling at Flood of Courses.' *Edmonton Journal* (19 Feb.): A9
Murray, Nancy. 1986. 'Anti-Racists and Other Demons: The Press and Ideology in Thatcher's Britain.' *Race and Class* 27(3): 1–20
Perry, Ruth. 1992. 'Historically Correct.' *Women's Review of Books* (5)(Feb.): 15–16
Ross, Becki. 1990. 'The House That Jill Built: Lesbian Feminist Organizing in Toronto, 1976–1980.' *Feminist Review* 35(Summer): 75–91
– 1991. 'Whatever Happened to "A Is for Amazon?": The High-Wire Performance of Lesbian Subjectivity in the 1990s.' *Resources for Feminist Research* 20(3/4): 122–7
Salutin, Rick. 1991. 'Loose Canons.' *Saturday Night* (Dec.): 20–4, 74
Slinger, Joey. 1991. ''Tis the Season to Be Jolly Politically Correct.' *Toronto Star* (15 Dec.): A1, A20
Smith, Jean Edward. 1991. 'The Dangerous New Puritans.' *Globe and Mail* (21 Oct.): A15
Snow, David A., et al., 1986. 'Frame Alignment Processes, Micromobilization, and Movement Participation.' *American Sociological Review* 51: 464–81
Starr, Frederick S. 1989. 'The Right to Hear and Be Heard.' *The Washington Post* (19 Nov.): Ro1
Thibault, Paul J. 1988. 'Knowing What You're Told by the Agony Aunts: Lan-

guage Function, Gender Difference and the Structure of Knowledge and Belief in the Personal Columns.' In David Birch and L.M. O'Toole, eds., *Functions of Style*, 205–33. London: Pinter
– 1991. *Social Semiotics as Praxis*. Minneapolis: University of Minnesota Press
Threadgold, Terry. 1989. 'Talking about Genre: Ideologies and Incompatible Discourses.' *Cultural Studies* 3(1)(Jan.): 101–27
Tye, Larry. 1987. 'From LA to Chesapeake, Water Cleanup Starts with Citizen Interest.' *Boston Globe* (31 Aug.): Metro 1
Vance, Carole, ed. 1984. *Pleasure and Danger*. Boston: RKP
Vancouver Sun. 1992. 'Politically Correct Trend Attacked as "Phantom." ' (11 Feb.): A3
van Dijk, Teun A. 1991. *Racism and the Press*. London: Routledge
– 1992. 'Discourse and the Denial of Racism.' *Discourse and Society* 3(1): 87–118
Verrall, Marg. 1980. 'Has the Women's Movement Become a Club of Correct-Liners?' *Kinesis* (Aug.): 18–19
Vincent, Isabel. 1991. ' "Political Correctness" Hallmark of Festival.' *Globe and Mail* (2 April): D3
Vygotsky, Lev. 1978. *Mind in Society: The Development of Higher Psychological Processes*. Cambridge: Harvard University Press
The Washington Post. 1989. 'Politically Correct Expression' (23 June): A22
Whitney, D. Charles, and Ellen Wartella. 1992. 'Media Coverage of the "Political Correctness" Debate.' *Journal of Communication* 42(2)(Spring): 83–94
Wieder, Bob. 1990. 'There Is No Way to Live "Politically Correct." ' *San Francisco Chronicle* (21 Sept.): A27
Wilmen, Chris. 1987. 'Holly Near Edges Closer to Maintown Sound.' *Los Angeles Times* (4 Nov.): Calendar 4

Framing the 'Western Tradition' in Canadian PC Debates

VICTOR SHEA

In English studies the concept of Arnoldian culture, a homogeneous tradition of 'the best which has been thought and said in the world' from *Beowulf* to Virginia Woolf, from Homer to T.S. Eliot (any number of metonymic figures can be substituted), has been extensively challenged for many years.[1] Many of us on the left had become confident that under such challenges the ideology of a disinterested and transcendent 'Western tradition,' inherently superior to any other cultural tradition, had been relegated to historical surveys, a thing of the discipline's past, a victim of its own self-evident contradictions, functioning in the present institutional conjuncture only as what Raymond Williams calls 'the residual.'

Matthew Arnold defined 'culture' most extensively in *Culture and Anarchy* (1867). He was responding to a particular social crisis, the second Reform Bill of 1867, which extended the franchise to certain portions of working-class men. 'Culture,' opposed (as the title indicates) to the potential 'anarchy' of this extension, offered a prescription for this crisis not in the political or social terms of his contemporaries, but in the language of Platonic idealism:

> The whole scope of the essay is to recommend culture as the great help out of our present difficulties; culture being a pursuit of our total perfection by means of getting to know, on all the matters which most concern us, the best which has been thought and said in the world; and through this knowledge, turning a stream of fresh and free thought upon our stock notions and habits, which we follow staunchly but mechanically. (Arnold 1965, 233–4)

This 'culture' presupposes an autonomy of the aesthetic, 'fresh and free' from 'our present difficulties.' This autonomy of 'the best' is precisely what has been challenged in recent years by an insistence that art or literature is always defined and determined by historical moments, within historically specific social practices. As Terry Eagleton has remarked, 'there is no such thing as literature which is "really" great, or "really" anything, independently of the ways in which that writing is treated within specific forms of social and institutional life ... Literary criticism selects, processes, corrects and rewrites texts in accordance with certain institutionalized norms of the "literary" – norms which are at any given time arguable, and always historically variable' (1983, 202–3).

Patricia Jasen has traced the extensive influence of Matthew Arnold's notions of 'culture' in the establishment of Canadian university departments of English in the late nineteenth century: 'A look at the first occupants of new chairs of English at Toronto, Saskatchewan, Queen's, and Dalhousie will reveal the attitudes they held in common,' a commonality 'based on an acceptance of Arnold's definition of culture' (Jasen 1988, 558). Following the trajectory of Eagleton (1983, 17–51) and Chris Baldick (1983), she traces Arnoldian humanism through the Newbolt Report of 1921, to the Leavisite and New Critical domination of the discipline in Britain and the United States respectively. In effect, Arnoldian 'culture' and its canonical norms provided a frame of reference that translated nineteenth-century ideologies across national borders and through over 100 years. Jasen concludes by locating the demise of the ideology as a dominant institutional determinant around 'the early 1960s,' citing the reduction of students taking English courses. Her final word, however, finds Arnoldianism still lingering despite 'new developments': 'even now, when new developments in critical theory are challenging and (in the opinion of many scholars) discrediting virtually all traditional assumptions about the nature and function of literature, the Arnoldian association between culture and human values still exerts a subtle influence' (Jasen 1988, 564). According to Jasen, this 'subtle influence' still determines policy and pedagogy in the contemporary Canadian academy: 'it continues to affect the design of university curricula by justifying the prescription of English in certain programmes and faculties, and, behind closed classroom doors, it still influences the way English professors teach their subjects' (564).

Less than three years after Jasen published her study, 'the Arnoldian association between culture and human values' went from being a 'subtle influence' functioning 'behind closed classroom doors' to being a blunt instrument in media wars – invoked particularly in relation to 'our present difficulties.'

Translating Frames of Reference

Within a two-week period in spring 1991, three of the largest Canadian mass media publications imported 'political correctness' (PC) discourse into Canada by carrying articles with ominous warnings about the threat of 'political correctness' in Canadian cultural institutions, particularly our universities. In the first part of a *Maclean's* (27 May 1991) cover story, reporter Tom Fennell made repeated reference to 'traditional cultural values' and 'Western civilization.' In the course of the article, he identified three canonical authors embodying these 'traditional cultural values': 'Shakespeare' (twice), 'the ancient Greek thinker Plato,' and 'the eighteenth-century German philosopher Immanual Kant.' The article concluded with an Arnoldian appeal to keep 'the best of the Western tradition.' In a companion piece to Fennell's article, D'Arcy Jenish wrote on PC in American universities, similarly referring to 'Western civilization' and 'Western culture.' Less than a week later (2 June) the *Toronto Star* published a feature article on PC in which Lynda Hurst also referred to 'Western culture' and 'Shakespeare.' Nine days later (11 June), Ray Conlogue in the *Globe and Mail* discussed 'Shakespeare' in the context of PC, concluding with allusions to 'a love of literature' and 'beautiful literature.'

These repetitions of 'Western tradition' represented the Canadian media's almost wholesale importation of the frames of reference from American PC debates. Allusions to 'Western culture' and to a few canonized writers, particularly Shakespeare, were as oligatory in Canadian and American mass media articles on PC as is the repetition of the same half-dozen anecdotes that caricature current academic debates regarding curricular reform in a wide range of disciplines. This caricature, however, does have determinant strategic effects. Most important, it provides PC discourse with a distinguished historical pedigree on which to base its claims. The circulation of 'Western tradition' within PC also displaces the social determinations of specific historical struggles, both past and present, on to the terrain of timeless universal values, aligning oppositional positions into a binary that represents reformers of curriculum (and of academic hiring practices) as attacking advocates of universal human values embodied in canonical works of literature, philosophy, and the fine arts. The 'Western tradition,' as well as listing self-evidently great writers in the literary canon, establishes the terms of the debates by centring on traditionalist concepts of the Western canon as the norm, and by marginalizing all forms of questioning of or opposition to this canon as variations. Once established, this norm also aligns a number of specific social practices, particularly affirmative action and multiculturalism, as variations of the norm, or marginal oppositions to it, the products of specific interest groups advocating political and ideological interventions.

I shall resist rebutting specific charges launched in PC discourse against the political and academic left, nor shall I rebut the general arguments in the mass media coverage – such rebuttals in the United States and Canada have been numerous and convincing.[2] An important task now before the left is to redirect in a productive way the discussions of the academy in the mass media. In examining the 'media discourse' of British immigration policy, Stuart Hall has indicated some of the difficulties of this task:

> Changing the terms of an argument is exceedingly difficult, since the dominant definition of the problem acquires, by repetition, and by the weight and credibility of those who propose or subscribe it, the warrant of 'common sense.' Arguments which hold to this definition of the problem are accounted as following 'logically.' Arguments which seek to change the terms of reference are read as 'straying from the point.' So part of the struggle is over the way the problem is formulated: the terms of the debate and the 'logic' it entails. (Hall 1982, 81)

I shall argue that the appeal to the canon within these articles is an important component of the series of interlocking PC propositions. My position presupposes John Frow's argument 'against the assumption that cultural norms, whether "high" or "low," have an intrinsic value which is distinct from any institutional and interpretive frame' (Frow 1986, 123); my methodology is informed by remarks on 'framing' made by Jonathan Culler.[3] In what follows, I shall 'frame' PC in three distinct ways, each of which will trace specific effects of PC's translation of aspects of cultural debate from one institutional frame to another. First I shall examine how academic canon debates are translated into the mass media, how they are represented and how they function in the Canadian PC articles mentioned above; second, I shall examine the 'canon' in books by Roger Kimball and Dinesh D'Souza, whose works have framed Canadian (and American) PC; and third, I shall examine 'political correctness' and the canons of fine art in mass media discussions of a specific controversy, the decision of the Art Gallery of Ontario to close to the public from 4 July 1992 to 24 January 1993. The untangling of the propositions within each of these frames will display the indebtedness of PC discourse to the unexamined universal values assumed as inherent in the traditionalist canon, and will also demonstrate their displacement of any notions of the canon's constructedness in specific contestations and historic struggles.

Canon and PC Discourse

In the academy, 'canon' generally signifies the range of 'traditional cultural values' similar to 'Western civilization' in PC discourse. 'Canon' comes from the Greek *kanon*, a 'reed,' 'rod,' or 'rule' used in measurement. Modern usage derives from controversies from the first to fourth centuries A.D. when the books of the Bible and the authority of the church fathers (both as a 'rule' of faith and as a list of books for determining orthodox as against heretical belief) were fixed in a series of institutional decisions defined as the 'canons' of church councils, canons of scripture, and a canonical body of acclaimed authors and their works. The selection processes of certain texts to the exclusion of others in fixing the biblical and classical canons has been well documented, as has the canon formation of modern national literatures (see, for instance, Curtius 1953, 247–73; and Kennedy 1990). In ecclesiastical usage, four ranges of meaning for the term can be distinguished: the scriptural and doctrinal books that the church recognizes as authentic or authorized; liturgical formularies, such as the canon of the mass; the canonization of saints by the institutional church; and rules concerning life and discipline within the institution (canon law). Similar diversity obtains in the canonization of classical texts in the institutions of education in antiquity and the Middle Ages (see Marrou [1956] 1964). Such diversity of usage, concerning both verbal and written documents and institutional practice, implies a process of normalization in situations of conflict; necessarily, this process involves interpretation, classes of interpretive functionaries, and the exercise of institutional power. Contemporary literacy critics often trace the history of current canon debates to processes of biblical and classical canon formation, framing these debates within social and institutional practices (see, for instances, Guillory 1987 and 1990; and Kermode 1983. For a rejection of this framing, see Harris 1991, 110).

Generally speaking, the 'new developments' alluded to by Jasen have challenged the univeralism of the 'Western tradition' or canon from two directions. The first concentrates on opening the canon to include those who have been systemically excluded: women, women of colour, Afro-Americans, gays and lesbians, First Nations peoples, as well as various postcolonial national literatures. The second challenge comes from new theoretical reading practices, grounded in post-Saussurean linguistics, and developed in French structuralism, and, more recently, in deconstruction. These strategies are often given a political edge by Marxist and feminist influences. The proliferation of these 'new developments' has undermined the assumptions of liberal humanism, redrawing the already crumbling boundaries and divisions of the disciplines, and has enabled the disiplines to redefine their practices, methodologies, and shifting canonical sites. Advocates of a modified traditional canon have adopted the methods and categories of those arguing for inclusivity (Fromm 1991 and Lipkin 1984); others advocate a re-evaluation of the aesthetic criteria that the political critics and deconstructionists have, according to them, left out (Adams 1988 and Altieri 1984). Defenders of the traditional canon have denounced both positions (Bate 1983 and Bloom 1987).

To write about 'canon' from within the academy is now a complex undertaking: it is a *topos* with its own generic conventions, its own obligatory gestures to its own canonic sites, most particularly *Canons* (von Hallberg 1984), a collection of seventeen essays by prominent American critics that still in many ways sets the terms of canon debate. The Modern Language Association computer search facility on CD-ROM lists 646 entries under the title and subject headings 'canon' from January 1981 to the end of April 1992, the vast majority published after 1986. There have been at least six recent monographs and collections on the topic written from a variety of viewpoints.[4] From a Canadian perspective, there have been recently at least three major interventions on the issue of canon: *Canadian Canons*, a collection of thirteen essays (Lecker 1991); and a special issue of *English Studies in Canada* (December 1991) on 'The Canon and the Curriculum,' with seven essays; *Critical Inquiry* (Spring 1990) devoted over 40 pages to Robert Lecker and Frank Davey's debate on Canadian canons. My purpose is not to enter into any particular aspects of the debate, but to acount for its representation and function in Canadian PC discourse.

My first concerns are generic. Both the *Maclean's* and *Toronto Star* articles are documentary surveys that attempt to give some in-depth coverage to a current-affairs phenomenon, making gestures to balance, objectivity, and comprehension. Within this balance, the two sides of the debate are represented as defenders and reformers: those defending the Western tradition against radical attacks and those advocating curricular reform against 'Dead White European Males' (Drainie 1990, C1). Conlogue's opinion column in the *Globe and Mail*, on the other hand, is an advocacy essay, championing the retention of traditionalist reading practices grounded in an affective aesthetics, the 'love of literature,' and the traditionalist monuments of the past, 'beautiful literature.' The distinction between objectivity in current-events reportage in the first two articles and advocacy in Conlogue's opinion article is blurred, however, by hieratic references in all three to the literary canon, epitomized metonymically by 'Shakespeare.' These references already marginalize those advocating any modification of traditionalist practices. Journalistic conventions demand a 'middle ground,' a balanced view presenting both sides of the argument: first those whom Fennell calls 'the Silencers' of individual human rights and personal freedoms, those who advocate 'a number of liberal causes – from feminism to homosexual and native rights,' along with deconstructionists and 'black and other non-white students'; and second, the critics of 'the Silencers':

> Those who oppose the forces of political correctness say that they fear the new reformers will stifle democratic processes – and bury a rich cultural tradition in the same of equality ... As the struggle between the two sides intensifies, Canadians will increasingly have to occupy the middle ground – taking the most worthy ideas from the reformers, while keeping the best of the Western tradition. (Fennell 1991, 43)

The 'middle ground' is constructed by an opposition between the custodians of 'the best of the Western tradition' (echoing Arnold and representing a self-defined, self-evident, and self-contained concept) and 'the reformers' (different groups lumped together as a single voice, eliminating all difference, and specified as united in opposing the 'Western tradition' as the creature of the 'dead white male'). Hence this 'middle ground' locks us into a binary opposition that aligns various positions throughout the article: on the one hand, 'the Silencers,' 'the new reformers' of curriculum and critics of academic hiring practices are depicted as suppressing individual rights and attacking universal human values embodied in canonical works of literature and philosophy; on the other, 'those who oppose' these 'forces' are portrayed not only as defenders of 'the best of the Western tradition' and 'democratic processes,' but also as victims of an overzealous puritanism and a too-narrowly-focused political agenda. We can question these alignments and their effects by asking what is the 'Western tradition,' let alone the 'best of' it. In PC, 'Shakespeare' and 'Western culture' function as self-evident constructs needing no historical specification, to be invoked as easily as, and in contrast to, 'Nazi,' 'Communist witch hunt,' and 'Red Guards'; yet, the *Maclean's* article is compelled to identify Plato and Kant as 'the ancient Greek thinker' and 'the 18th-century German philosopher' respectively. Rather than belabour the contradictions within the frame of this article, however, I shall turn to another frame, the American right and its deployment of 'Western tradition' in PC.

Cultural Translation: From Them to Us

In the most direct sense, Canadian mass media took their leads from their American counterparts. In late 1990 and early 1991, major features on PC appeared in the *New York Times* (Bernstein 1990), *Newsweek* (Adler 1990), *Time* (Henry 1991), *The Atlantic* (D'Souza 1991b), and *New York* (John Taylor 1991): the timing, form, and content of the Canadian PC articles demonstrate that their writers, after adding a few Canadian examples for local colour, copied their stories directly from American journalists. The translation of academic canon debates into PC is mediated, however, almost entirely by two books, Roger Kimball's *Tenured Radicals: How Politics Has Corrupted Our Higher Education* (1990) and Dinesh D'Souza's *Illiberal Education: The Politics of Race and Sex on Campus* (1991a). These books, supported by well-funded right-wing organizations in the United States – the John Olin Foundation, the American Enterprise Institute, and the Institute for Educational Affairs – established the terms of reference and the frames of argument used subsequently in PC discourse. Behind their advocacy of the 'Western tradition' lies the position asserted by Reaganite cultural pundits such as William Bennett in *To Reclaim a Legacy: A Report on the Humanities in Higher Education* (1984), Allan Bloom's *The Closing of the American Mind* (1987), and Lynne V. Cheney's *Humanities in America: A Report to the President, the Congress, and the American People* (1988).

Kimball argues that the collapse of the centres of cultural influence in American life is caused by the domination of the left, specifically sixties radicals now occupying positions of academic power. The discussion of canon in the opening chapter of Kimball's *Tenured Radicals* establishes a basis from which to launch his attack on contemporary literary theory, affirmative action, and a host of other sins. D'Souza extends this argument, assuming the hegemony of the left in educational institutions, and reading three aspects of this domination symptomatically: a lowering of intellectual standards as a result of affirmative action in university 'admissions policy' and hirings; attacks on Western canon 'in the classroom'; and restrictions on academic freedom in 'life on campus.' Hence, one-third of *Illiberal Education* discusses canonical issues: two sites of canon controversy, the 'Western culture' debate at Stanford and critical theory at Duke, position him to launch attacks against affirmative action and attempts to control racist, sexist, and homophobic behaviour on American campuses.

Kimball begins by pillorying recent attacks on 'the ideals of objectivity and the disinterested pursuit of knowledge':

> More and more, one sees the traditional literary canon ignored as various interest groups demand that there be more women's literature for feminists, black literature for blacks, gay literature for homosexuals, and so on. The idea of literary quality that transcends the contingencies of race, gender, and the like or that transcends the ephemeral attractions of popular entertainment is excoriated as naive, deliberately deceptive, or worse. (1990, xv)

He accepts unquestioningly the importance of 'the traditional literary canon' in a narrative where a radical agenda will soon destroy the long-accumulated heritage of Western civilization. His first chapter, 'The Assault on the Canon,' underwrites the authority of his entire argument by inscribing his position in contemporary academic politics as a defender of those transcendental standards of 'objectivity' and 'disinterested pursuit of knowledge' represented in 'the traditional literary canon':

> The term *canon* comes to us from the Roman Catholic Church, where it refers to an official rule or decree, a particular section of the Mass, or the list of canonized saints. Today, as applied to the academy, *canon* refers to the unofficial, shifting, yet generally recognized body of great works that have stood the test of time and are acknowledged to be central to a complete liberal arts education. (1990, 1)

Kimball adopts without demur the Arnoldian notions of the 'Western tradition' as self-evident, universal value. Any questioning of its 'substance,' any challenge to its assumptions, is dismissed as politically interested and motivated, and self-evidently ridiculous: 'It is my aim in *Tenured Radicals* to expose these recent developments in the academic studies of humanities for what they are: ideologically motivated assaults on the intellectual and moral substance of our culture' (xviii). Kimball's method, employed repeatedly, takes arguments out of their theoretical context, and extrapolates sentences from the arguments in which they occur, quoting them for their apparent absurdity. His main object of attack is departments of literature, but his exposé encompasses most of the humanities disciplines, including history, philosophy, art history, and architecture. All opposition to the canon is caricatured as Marxist-motivated subversion. Hence deconstructionsts, feminists, Afro-Americans, gays and lesbians tend to slide inexorably toward the category of Marxist intellectual.

While Kimball extrapolates meaningless snippets of complex arguments, D'Souza's argument proceeds anecdotally, using the Duke English department and the Stanford canon debates metonymically, to represent two aspects of the general decay of liberal education in America. His 'idea of a canon' is simpler than Kimball's: 'a set of required great books' (D'Souza 1991a, 61) is the only definition required before moving to polemic against those who would ask what constitutes the 'great.' A reviewer argued that D'Souza's 'book resembles a debater's brief, written by a bright college debater who has before him, on tabbed, colour-coded index cards, all the points he wishes to make in the assigned time ... In order to reveal [a] Manichean world, he shamelessly stacks the deck – all the better to portray the unprincipled and corrupt denizens of this institution. Almost every page contains examples of his ability to overstate and exaggerate' (Olivas 1991, 58–9).[5] This description could serve for the method of representation in the *Maclean's* article on Canadian PC; Conlogue's column, like D'Souza's book, not only 'shamelessly stacks the deck,' it obliterates the other side. A homogeneous tradition of Western culture allows 'this Manichean world' to be constructed, dividing canon supporters and reformers between the categories of good and evil, battling it out in narratives of the decline and fall of the West, the eclipse of the good, and the sickness of values.

In *Orientalism*, Edward Said (1978) has written of 'the culturally sanctioned habit of deploying large generalizations by which reality is divided into various collectives' (227). He identifies some of these collectives: 'languages, races, types, colours, mentalities, each category being not so much a neutral designation as an evaluative interpretation' (227), connecting the representation of essential values in the defence of the Western canon with 'the right to make generalities about race':

> What gave writers like Renan and Arnold the right to generalities about race was the official character of their formed cultural literacy. 'Our' values were (let us say), liberal, humane, correct; they were supported by the tradition of belles-lettres, informed scholarship, rational inquiry; as European (and white men) 'we' shared in them every time our virtues were extolled. (Said 1978, 227–8)

Drawing on Foucault's work on exclusion and confinement, he differentiates the ways in which this 'formed cultural literacy' performs such a division: 'The human partnerships formed by reiterated cultural values excluded as much as they included ... Underlying these categories is the rigidly binomial opposition of "ours" and "theirs," with the former always encroaching upon the latter (even to the point of making "theirs" exclusively a function of "ours")' (227–8). Said's distinction between the hegemonic 'ours' and the excluded 'theirs' constructed as an effect of nineteenth-century culture, literacy, and imperialism, is inscribed in PC discourse as the opposition between disinterested standards ('our' cultural heritage) and ideological interests ('their' attacks on the culture of dead white European males). Such translations of the unexamined universality of disinterested standards with their political affiliations in cultural literacy, corporate board rooms, and élite educational institutions, are assumed to have no ideological base. Attacks on such privileged positions of power and prestige are dismissed as motivated by political interest, from which those with 'standards' are suppposedly free. Just such an argument is made by Alan Bloom in the *Wall Street Journal,* following an editorial and feature article declaiming against the Stanford curricular reforms:

> Stanford students are to be indoctrinated with ephemeral ideologies and taught that there can be no intellectual resistance to one's own time and passions ... This total surrender to which the present and abandonment of the quest with which to judge it are the very definition of the closing of the American mind, and I could hope for no more stunning confirmation of my thesis. (quoted in Lindenberger 1990, 160)

The binary 'ours' and 'theirs,' inscribed in terms of 'standards' and 'ideologies,' is articulated in a number of homologies. Some have a long association with the debates over the canon – such as the quarrel between the ancients and moderns in seventeenth-century France and England, or eighteenth-century debates between passion and reason, or between sense and sensibility – as 'frames' of reference for larger cultural debates. Those in power within the academies have tried to retain the unchanging canon in a fixed rigidity as a monumental structure of intrinsic worth, transcending the vagaries of such historically specific struggles; simultaneously canon is continually changing, a site of conflict, where the opposing parties align around changing banners for their forces: primary works of the imagination versus secondary criticism; creative art versus parasitical theory; the primacy of certain national traditions with a pedigree genealogy (the classics of Greece and Rome through the Renaissance to neoclassicism and contemporary England and America) versus colonized and derivative traditions, or foreign influences; writing divided between genres of 'literature' (that is, poetry, drama, and fiction) versus the non-literary genres such as reportage, political polemic, popular writing, pulp fiction, and so on. The manipulation of such binaries in PC discourse confers value on the first term, on 'our standards,' denigrating the second, 'their ideology.' The translation of canon debate into its caricature in PC discourse with its Manichean opposition of 'our' good and 'their' evil depends on the violation of the most elementary laws of evidence and support for a premise; on the reduction of complex intellectual positions to simple oppositions; on the use of either/or arguments; and on hyperbole and demonization – such reductions as the comparisons made in *Maclean's* between advocates of curricular reform and McCarthyites, Nazi book-burners, and Maoist Red Guards.

The alignment of canon within PC with 'the best' of 'Western tradition' has allowed the importation of an aggressive right-wing American agenda: 'political correctness' in many ways resembles 'Willie Horton,' 'Family Values,' 'Free Trade,' 'Level Playing Fields,' and 'Character Issues': the various discursive ploys that the right has used to translate a specific political agenda into neutral, universalist categories without a history. There are, however, significant differences between Canadian and American PC: while both rely on British figures, particularly Shakespeare, to signify transcendental values, the Americans have their Franklins and Hemingways, which circulate within the economy of their PC debates; nowhere in the Canadian frame is there mention of a Canadian canon. In Canadian PC, there is almost no red-baiting – the opposition to 'universal values' is here mainly represented by feminists and multiculturalists.[6] I do not think these differences cause for celebration; nevertheless, I should like now to turn to a controversy where such an opposition functioned extensively.

Framing 'Art': PC and the AGO

One year after its importation into Canada, PC indeed acquired 'by repetition, and by the weight and credibility of those who propose or subscribe it, the warrant of "common sense"' (Hall 1982, 81). Earlier PC needed extensive definition and explanation; now it is a commonplace in the mass media. To demonstrate its currency in framing and referencing the grounds of appeal for 'common sense' values, I should like to examine a recent controversy surrounding the closing of the Art Gallery of Ontario

(AGO). PC enables a government decision undertaken in the midst of the longest and most serious economic downturn since the 1929 depression to be translated into a wholesale attack on the Western tradition of art. Not surprisingly, inscribed in this reading is a broadside attack on affirmative-action policies, specifically concerning the funding of cultural institutions, as well as attacks on the province's first New Democratic (socialist democrat) government.

The AGO's fiscal problems are complex, including high operating costs and a costly pay-equity adjustment. Furthermore, the AGO is currently midway through the third stage of a long-term building expansion program, a project currently running 70 per cent over budget. The provincial government pays about 90 per cent of the operating costs. For years chronic over-spending by the AGO beyond its base operating budget was made up by supplementary grants from the Ministry of Culture and Communications. In 1990–1 the one-time deficit reduction grant was $4 million, added to an operating base budget of $8.1 million. The previous Liberal government had made gestures toward increasing the operating budget to the total level of expenditures, but this arrangement had not been formalized, and as a result of the recession AGO director Glenn Lowry was informed in February 1992 that the base allocation of $8.5 million was all that they could expect for 1992–3. In the budget tabled in April 1992 for 1992–3, the Ministry, one of fifteen ministries that had reduced allocations, nevertheless allotted another $1 million deficit reduction grant, along with a further $1 million for education and outreach programs undertaken by the gallery. At the same time, the operating grants for other cultural agencies in the province such as CJRT-FM, TVO, and the Royal Ontario Museum were reduced. It is the allocation of this additional $2 million to the basic operating grant in the 1992–3 budget – an 'addition' said the Ministry, a 'reduction' said the AGO – that was the immediate source of the dispute that led the AGO to close its doors to the public in July 1992. In July, the Minister of Culture, Karen Haslam, announced the appointment of a task force – composed of an artist, a former director of an art gallery, and a financial expert – to advise both the Ministry and the AGO on long-term solutions to the Gallery's fiscal woes.[7] My task is not to question details of, or to take a position on, this debate, but rather to examine how PC and canon function within mass media reporting of the dispute.

Toronto Star art critic Christopher Hume responded to the appointment of the task force with a full-page article, 'Politically Correcting the Arts':

The NDP's lame arguments about culturedom not living within its means and being poorly managed are diversionary tactics ... No, the real issue here is political correctness ... Despite everything that the NDP would have us believe, not one jot of evidence exists that people seek out art because its contents are politically correct and government approved. All of us make judgements. We have to and, for the most part, it's not difficult. Most of us choose one thing over another because we prefer it, because we think it better. The idea that quality is a white male conspiracy aimed at keeping minorities in their place is dangerous nonsense. (Hume 1992a, G3)

Important fiscal aspects of the decision are dismissed as an aside before a full-scale attack, under the umbrella of 'political correctness,' is launched. In Hume's reading the government's policy of diversifying representation on the boards of cultural institutions to address the systemic barriers to funding faced by individuals and groups outside traditional bases of power is translated directly into an attack on consensus: 'Most of us ... think it better.' On the editorial page of the same day, Hume's argument is translated into an editorial pronouncement, 'NDP Frames AGO':

To the casual observer, the beleaguered Art Gallery of Ontario has been forced to close for lack of money. But money isn't the problem. NDP ideology – and a culture minister determined to put a politically correct stamp on the arts – is the more sinister force threatening one of Ontario's oldest and most important cultural institutions. (*Toronto Star* 1992, D2)

The wholesale transference of the frame and terms of Hume's opinion piece onto the editorial page demonstrates my argument that 'political correctness' – 'the more sinister force' – and its relations to 'the Western tradition' – the appeals to antiquity and universal consensus in 'one of Ontario's oldest and most important cultural institutions' – enables an individual's position to become the supposedly more objective editorial voice, speaking for the entire newspaper.

Less than a week earlier Robert Fulford had written a similar attack in his opinion column in the *Financial Times*. Fulford does not use 'politically correct' in his attack, but throughout makes various rhetorical gestures compatible with PC discourse. Attacking the minister, he appeals to the canonical status of the institution: 'She's brought to its knees a proud and, by Canadian standards, an ancient institution, founded in 1900.' Fulford gives an interesting democratic twist to the appeal to universal consensus: 'A museum like the AGO is by its nature democratic and anti-elitist: it shows to all of us art that once could be seen mainly by the rich'; but, as if to contradict himself, he refers immediately to the minister's being uncomfortable with 'the circles of financial and cultural power that provide most of the leadership for museums.' In Fulford's formulation the universally agreed status of 'art' provides the means for this contradiction to be constructed: the 'rich' who once owned the art and the 'financial and cultural power' that now provide its 'leadership' in no way determine the value and conceptualization of 'art.' Throughout the argument this 'art,' like the literary canon, is assumed to possess self-inherent value, a value under attack by the special interests within NDP circles: 'She's surrounded by people (her political aides, not her civil servants) who believe, not for what they imagine are good reasons, that museums and symphonies and ballet companies are inherently elitist and need fixing by progressive political persons.' Rather than use the more appropriate (for his argument) term *apparatchik* to designate a socialist party apparatus, Fulford instead uses Matthew Arnold's term for the taste of unenlightened middle-class Victorians: 'Haslam and several other New Democrats (some in the Premier's office) ... automatically view the gallery with Philistine suspicion.' This phrase, used in Fulford's title, attests to the staying power of Arnold's terms in defining canonical politics and class positions in specific struggles.[8] Fulford ends by reducing the whole controversy to *ad hominem* arguments pitting the minister, 'a lifelong outsider' against 'the brilliant and highly articulate director of the AGO, Glenn Lowry, a Ph.D. from Harvard' (Fulford 1992, 23).

The *Globe and Mail* followed the *Toronto Star* and *Financial Times* with a similar piece on the controversy on 1 August, in which Kate Taylor uses Fulford's *ad hominem* opposition to frame her article. 'A Clash of Two Cultures' lays out the AGO dispute as that between two personalities from different social backgrounds, epitomized in two juxtaposed paragraphs:

Glenn Lowry is a 37-year-old American, a specialist in Islamic art with a Ph.D. from Harvard University who speaks six languages. He took over as AGO director nearly two years ago.

Karen Haslam, 45, is a former teacher and school trustee from Stratford, Ont., who has led Girl Guide troops and sat on little theatre boards. She was sworn in as Culture Minister on July 31, 1991. (Kate Taylor 1992, A1)

Large separate photos of Haslam and Lowry face each other; above both is a detail of a painting with the caption: 'From the AGO's permanent collection: Battle of the Gods and Giants, oil on canvas; Luca Giordano

(1634–1705), Italian.' Beside the photo of the painting is the following comment: 'Ms Haslam aligned herself with critics for whom the gallery is an elitist institution, patronized by relatively few people and gobbling up money that might otherwise go to smaller community-based arts groups' (Kate Taylor 1992, A4). This frame, elaborately constructing a context to present financial data with charts, skews the interpretation of that data between a normative centre appropriate to the appreciation of the fine arts and the ephemeral marginalized special-interest groups, between an art specialist and a politician.

After the *Globe and Mail* feature article, mass media attention shifted from the funding crisis and the gallery's response to focus attention on the task force. Although Fulford and Hume attacked the task force as political hacks with foregone conclusions, the tabloid *Toronto Sun* on 16 August supported the establishment of the task force – with one qualification:

> Gallery defenders fear that task force members – no matter how objective – will become pawns in the hands of a government determined to force the AGO to fulfil the NDP's own politically correct agenda. (Bowen 1992)

Throughout the summer Hume continued to rail against the funding decision, using familiar Arnoldian terms and arguments. For instance, on 12 August, in 'AGO's Responsibility Is to Art, Not to Artists,' he argued:

> The AGO owes nothing to the artists of Ontario. Rather, the gallery's responsibility is to *art* ... The AGO's role in the contemporary art scene can't be measured in dollars and cents. As the province's leading fine arts institution, the gallery is in a unique position to showcase the *best* of what's current and legitimize it. The AGO functions as a setter of standards. (Hume 1992b; italics in original)

The next day he reviewed a mural by Toronto artist Joanne Tod, calling it 'an abject failure':

> Unveiled just last month, the work is so poorly conceived and slavishly politically correct that it can't be taken seriously, even as an artwork commissioned by a large corporation to decorate its shiny new headquarters ... It consists of several dozen disembodied heads ... white and black, male and female, young and old, turbaned and bare ... Tod's painting will thrill the multiculturists but for reasons that have nothing to do with art. If there were a way to remove the logos, the New Democrats could use the image on their Christmas cards. (Hume 1992c)

'Politically correct' and references to canonic 'standards' are used not only by disgruntled art critics. 'Politically correct' appears at least twice in the *Toronto Star* almost exactly contemporaneously with the passages quoted above; significantly, it was used by participants (who were being quoted) in cultural confrontations not involving the arts. On 15 August a report was published on the studies undertaken by Philippe Rushton (no stranger in PC discourse) and his colleague at the University of Western Ontario, Dave Ankey. Their work investigates whether women's brains are smaller than men's. Ankey comments: 'Some biologists may be too "politically correct" to report differences in brain size, even if they find them' (Michael Smith 1992, A6). Two days later the *Toronto Star* reported on the annual General Council of the United Church in which homosexuality was a matter of controversy. The leader of a small group of church members opposed to the church's recognition of same-sex unions was led by Bill Morris, a retired United Church minister from Dundas, Ontario: 'He said the United Church, like general society wants to be "politically correct" in its attitudes, but in being so is trying to rewrite the Bible and reinvent the "wheel of morality and ethics" ' (McAlteer 1992, A10).

In each instance PC discourse converts a historically specific position within cultural controversy into one representing universal consensus; the historic specificity of the AGO's current problems, however, can also be located in the history of the institution itself. The Art Museum of Toronto, under its first president, Sir Edmund Walker, was incorporated by the Ontario Legislature in 1900; its name was changed to the Art Gallery of Toronto in 1919 and the Art Gallery of Ontario in 1966. Its first permanent home was The Grange, a Georgian mansion donated by the estate of Goldwin Smith in 1912; subsequent expansion and alterations added to the exhibition space in various ways, chiefly in the period from 1926 to 1935.

Further building expansions were needed to store and exhibit the growing acquisitions. In his 'Preface' to a 1974 *Handbook* to the AGO, William J. Withrow lists 'the acquisition[s] of some of the most important individual works in the collection' decade by decade, a chronology and encomium that attaches the name of a donor to each 'work of art' in a catalogue that, taken collectively, constitutes a considerable selection of the Canadian corporate élite, upon which so much of the support of the Gallery depends for the purchase of new works. Withrow collapses the moneyed interest of the patrons of the Gallery on to the ideology of the masterpiece in the canon of painters: 'These years were rich in gifts and bequests and many treasures were added to the Old Master collection' (Withrow 1974, 2–3). By 1985 there were over 10,000 'paintings, sculptures, prints, and drawings of the permanent collection includ[ing] examples from the Old Master traditions, the Impressionists and early 20th-century movements – paintings by such masters as Rembrandt, Hals ...' (Withrow 1985; s.v. 'Art Gallery of Ontario'). The language describing the acquisition policy is similar to that of the literary canon in that a stable of canonic proper names signifies the establishment in the 'permanent' collection of criteria of transcendent value. The same language recurs in AGO publications. In the 1974 *Handbook*, for instance, Richard Wattenmaker writes of a transition in the acquisitions policy from 'a distinct randomness' based on donor tastes and finances to 'a unified interrelatedness' governed by its relation to 'the ideal selection of works from any period or tradition' – that totality of 'art' and its history that presumably governs every gallery's acquisition policy (Wattenmaker 1974, 16).

Wattenmaker uses gender-specific language to articulate this universalist conception of art and an affective poetics of individualist creativity to discuss its construction:

> To grasp the multiform results of the feelings and values expressed by a panoply of artists across the ages in many countries throughout the world, we must acknowledge that art is a universal currency in the emotional and intellectual expression of mankind. The subtle essences which in works of art are distilled from their natural and man-affected surroundings have the capacity to broaden the perspective and deepen the aesthetic responsiveness of all men regardless of temporal or geographic boundaries. This is one of the essential meanings of universality as the term is applied to art. Artists in times past and today express the ethos of an indescribable variety of aspects of the world; these unseen but evocative transformations of inner experience, no less than the more immediately documentary side of art, derive their sources from some aspect of the artist's experience. (Wattenmaker 1974, 17)

Wattenmaker's aesthetic categories make an appeal on the basis of what is supposedly valued everywhere, always, and by all;[9] to what is supposedly expressed 'across the ages' and 'in times past and today'; to what supposedly has 'universal currency' and 'essential meanings of universality,' 'regardless of temporal or geographic boundaries'; and to what supposedly is common to 'many countries throughout the world,' which accords with what 'we must acknowledge,' as agreed to by 'all men.' Such a concept of the Old Masters can be found in subsequent AGO publications. It is also contradicted, however, by new language in discussions of the gallery's current expansion.

According to the AGO's publication *Stage Three* (1987), a summary of the finalist architectural proposals, 'the Board of Trustees of the Art Gallery of Toronto and the Government of Ontario cooperated to give the Gallery a new mandate' in 1966. The agreement would take the form of a different financial arrangement and enable the 'three-stage expansion program to become an excellent visual arts museum' meeting the 'tremendous need for more exhibition, storage, preparation, and administration space,' to have it continue as 'a first-rate, world-class art institution ... as Canada's leading art museum' (Art Gallery of Ontario 1987, 5, 8). The necessity for expansion is discussed in the language of the 1980s economic boom – the language of the developers, Skydome, the Olympic bid – Toronto's achieving 'world-class' status as a 'cosmopolitan city' with 'spectacular and innovative structures' that enable it to compete with other cities in the 'unprecedented building boom of art museums around the world' and in 'a stable and mature international art market' (7). In the midst of the ensuing economic recession, it was no longer acceptable for any public institution to describe its projects in such language of imperialist ambition. Nevertheless, it is worth noting that this language is compatible with the descriptions of the Permanent Collection of Old and Contemporary Masters, insofar as the economics and politics of expansion are viewed merely as the historical accidents within which the transcendental works exist.

The ideology of a canon of transcendent great art, when inscribed in PC, allows Hume, Fulford, and the others to align their specific political position with what are asserted to be timeless, universal values; other political interests are relegated to the accidents of history, along with art markets, world-class booms, the specific fiscal problems, and world-wide economic recessions. These 'accidents' are either silenced or dismissed when the rubric 'political correctness' is deployed.

Framing the Institution: 'Whose Museum Is This Anyway?'

Students in my classroom this fall have at least twice referred to 'political correctness' as a means of dismissing particular points of discussion: first a feminist position, and second, a reading practice that set out Hollywood narrative formulas in the context of American cultural imperialism. A colleague mentioned it in disagreeing with proposed changes in a course we are teaching, changes that would have increased the number of women writers on the reading list. Like it or not, PC has 'acquire[d], by repetition ... the warrant of "common sense" ' among many in the academy. In order to move forward, it is imperative to return to the trenches of PC to find points of departure: canon debates, which John Guillory argues is 'precisely the site in the practice of criticism responding so actively to perceived social pressures' (1987, 485), will always be a crucial point. I do not mean to imply that were we somehow able to rid ourselves of the canon, PC would fall like a house of cards: canons – lists of books, methods of interpretation, and institutional sanctions to these lists and methods – are a given in any matter of cultural politics. As John Frow argues, 'Although the process of canon formation is thoroughly political, and although the canon is constantly being challenged, defended, and reconstituted, it is nevertheless a historical given with determinate historical effects. The history of the formation of a literary canon is something like a crystallization of the regimes of valuation which have governed this process' (121). To oppose the 'regime of valuation' constituted by PC, we must focus upon canon not as a problem of universal or self-evident value, but of value formation.

Bronwyn Drainie, in a *Globe and Mail* article that appeared the same week as the *Newsweek* PC cover story (December 1990), argues that Canada's multicultural policies and recent developments in feminism are at the root of the 'gloomy ... state of knowledge, education and culture in Canada in 1990.' She discusses 'the legacy of DWEMs (Dead White European Males),' citing a multiplicity of different 'voices,' and arguing that 'at this stage in their cultural development, such groups ['women,' 'other ethnic groups,' 'the non-white races,' 'gays,' 'the disabled,' 'youth,' and 'the poor and disadvantaged'] are not interested in some academic definition of excellence or quality.' She discusses 'the study of great monuments of Western art,' 'the principles of individual scholarship and historical accuracy,' and 'independent standards of intellectual achievement.' To these she opposes multiculturalism, treated with contemptuous irony, and rhetorical questions to which the imperial answers are only too clearly implied:

> Here in Canada we have our own aggressive policy of multiculturalism, which lends official weight to cultural fragmentation and educational relativism. Why should children from a Sikh or West Indian background be required to learn British or European history any more than any of the other world's histories? And since we can't possibly teach them all, better to transmute history into social studies and current events, which 'validate' all children by letting them voice their own opinions instead of intimidating them with the unfamiliar, which might make them feel inferior. (Drainie 1990, C1)

The divide-and-conquer tactics, by means of a universal standard ('British or European history') being assumed at the expense of various accidentals, are consistent with PC, but what makes her argument even more familiar is that one of her illustrations is a canonic gesture in Canadian PC (referred to in Fennell and Hurst), the 'Into the Heart of Africa' exhibit at the Royal Ontario Museum:

A show full of content and thought-provoking ironies for educated white Torontonians was being 'read' in a completely different way by some black visitors (by no means all), who saw in it only shame, humiliation and racism. One had to be very literate and sophisticated to appreciate the show as the curator intended, which raised the broader question: whose museum is this anyway? How can an institution like the ROM become more responsive to a population that comes from a hundred different countries, with a functional literacy rate of 38 per cent? How can it do it without abandoning the principles of individual scholarship and historical accuracy on which it was founded? These questions have been raised this year, but none of them answered. (Drainie 1990, C1)

These questions, for the most part, are fine; the problem is that PC discourse frames the answers in an unacceptable manner. With a different interpretative frame, however, a different set of answers could be posited: ones that draw different conclusions about the ownership of public institutions and the rights of all citizens to have their interests represented.

November 1992

Postscript: Creating 'Noise' (April 1994)

In February 1993 Karen Haslam was demoted from Minister of Culture and Communications to Minister without Portfolio. She resigned from the cabinet that summer, when she voted against her government on a new social contract, which, she maintained (along with every public-sector union), violated the principles of collective bargaining. Karen Haslam is now MPP for Perth, Ontario.

Glenn Lowry is still the director of the AGO.[10] On 16 April 1994, his feature article, 'Legacies of the Past Provide a Key to the Future,' appeared in the *Toronto Star*.

Art museums throughout North America have come under a great deal of pressure recently to justify their existence in real and theoretical terms. Rapidly changing demographics, constrained finances, new technologies, and politics, among other issues, have led to the accusation that museums are elitist, are out of touch with the diversity of contemporary society, and are possibly obsolete ... Museums ... are both repositories of past achievements and venues of current debate. As such, they are one of the primary means of ordering and understanding experiences that have shaped and will continue to shape our consciousness ... A museum's importance depends upon its ability to be a site of learning and encounter, where individuals can explore great works of art in an environment that allows them to come into direct contact with these objects. In doing so museums create, whether intentionally or not, historical and aesthetic narratives that tell the 'story' of their collections, interests and evolution. And it is this process, more than anything else, that creates tension between the institution and the general public ...

In a culturally pluralistic society it is ... a highly contentious exercise. For there will always be those who disagree with a museum's decisions and with its authority to make these decisions. How can a white male curator, for instance, assess the importance of a work by a woman of color? Or a curator of European background judge the work of an Asian artist? At a time when there is no consensus over what constitutes our national identity, not to mention our patrimony, the narratives constructed by museums inevitably will be at odds with large numbers of people.

This does not mean, however, that museums cannot or should not engage in the work that they do. On the contrary, it is incumbent upon them to share their knowledge about works of art in their collections and to ensure that they are lively centres of debate. To do this well, they need to recognize that in a heterogeneous society such as ours, the key to intelligent decisions must be a commitment to making those decisions based on knowledge and experience combined with a willingness to embrace the diversity of contemporary culture. Knowledge, experience and tolerance are not subject to gender or ethno-racial affiliation, though they are qualities that tend to get lost in the noise created by the current arguments over entitlement and identity. (Lowry 1994, L10)

There is no direct mention of 'politically correct,' nor does Lowry make any shrill denunciations or outrageous analogies between those who would question his authority and nazis. Absent as well is all language of the 1980s economic boom: what I have referred to above (quoting an AGO publication) as the language of the developers, Skydome, the Olympic bid – Toronto's achieving 'world-class' status as a 'cosmopolitan city' with 'spectacular and innovative structures' that enable it to compete with other cities in the 'unprecedented building boom of art museums around the world' and in 'a stable and mature international art market' (Art Gallery of Ontario 1987, 7). Instead, Lowry defends the existence of the museums in relation to what Arnold would have called 'our present difficulties' in a tone, it would seem, filled with what Arnold called 'sweetness and light.' Perhaps PC has already become a thing of the past.

How then, we might ask, is Lowry's argument different from PC? I would argue, aside from a more sophisticated articulation of the aesthetic and a more subtle style of argumentation, that PC's frame of reference, and its alignments, are still in place. The vantage point, a position of power under threat defending itself against what Arnold called 'anarchy,' remains the same. What has shifted is the focus of the argument: from an attack on those making the 'noise' to the expertness of the keepers of the gates, those who, like a department of immigration, judge who is worthy for status as a citizen of the nation of 'great ... art.' Much of the difference in tone can be accounted for in this shift of emphasis; what is astounding about Lowry's call for 'tolerance,' however, is that from the way his argument is constructed, the emphasis on the need for toleration falls disproportionately on the side of those out of the positions of power. Underlying Lowry's call for 'tolerance' are the same oppositions that structure PC: between 'great works of art' and 'current arguments'; between those with 'knowledge' and 'experience' and those making all the 'noise ... over entitlement and identity'; between a 'museum's ... authority' and 'those who disagree'; between 'a white male curator' or 'a curator of European background' and 'a woman of colour' or 'an Asian artist.' Lowry's argument resolves these oppositions by relating 'great works of art' to 'contemporary society' in a strategy resembling that of T.S. Eliot's in 'Tradition and the Individual Talent' (1919):

> The existing monuments form an ideal order among themselves, which is modified by the introduction of the new (the really new) work of art among them. The existing order is complete before the new work arrives; for order to persist after the supervention of novelty, the *whole* existing order must be, if ever so slightly, altered; and so relations, proportions, values of each work of art toward the whole are readjusted; and this is conformity between the old and new. (Eliot 1975, 38–9)

Whereas Eliot in this essay avoids 'present difficulties,' the conditions in post-war Europe, Lowry explicitly connects the 'old' art and 'new' conditions, a 'culturally pluralistic society' – presumably one that includes 'an Asian artist' who may argue that her art is worthy of display at the AGO. Those making the 'intelligent decisions,' however, may not agree.

I should like at this point to recall the title of an article by Christopher

Hume quoted above: 'AGO's Responsibility Is to Art, Not to Artists' (Hume 1992b). 'Art' as canonical appeal does not deal with the realities of 'an Asian artist' in a 'culturally pluralistic society' dominated by 'a white male curator.' It has been estimated that by the year 2000 the South Asian communities of Metropolitan Toronto will make up 20 per cent of the total population. I would wager that these communities, along with other 'ethno-racial affilations,' as well as women, gays and lesbians, and other marginalized groups, will continue to demand their 'entitlement,' as citizens and taxpayers, to representation in 'our' public institutions. Because of these demands, and because in all likelihood those in positions of privilege will continue to dismiss them, the frames of reference of PC will be with us for a long time; therefore, it will be necessary to continue to make 'noise.'

Notes

1 I would like to thank Sharmini Peries and William Whitla for a careful reading of this paper and for their many helpful suggestions; I would also like to thank Gregor Campbell for bibliographic help. Adrianna Tetley of the office of the Ontario Minister of Culture and Communications was very generous with her time; the Public Relations Department of the Art Gallery of Ontario was also helpful.

2 For rebuttals to Canadian PC, see Keefer (1991a, 1991b, and 1992a); McCormack (1991); Perkin (1992); and Doug Smith (1991). Michael Keefer has produced an annotated bibliography on PC that has proven invaluable to my research (Keefer 1992b).

3 Culler explains the rationale for the title of his recent collection of essays as follows: 'The expression *framing the sign* has several advantages over *context*: it reminds us that framing is something we do; it hints of the frame-up ("falsifying evidence beforehand in order to make someone appear guilty"), a major use of context; and it eludes the incipient positivism of "context" by alluding to the semiotic function of framing in art, where the frame is determining, setting off the object or event as art, and yet the frame itself may be nothing tangible, pure articulation. Although analysis can seldom live up to the complexities of framing and falls back into discussions of context, with its heuristically simplifying presumptions, let us at least keep before us the notion of framing – as a frame for these discussions' (Culler 1988, ix). These remarks serve to remind us of the limited strategic value of denunciations of PC within a generalized 'context' of American right-wing ideologies.

4 The books include Fromm (1991), a reactionary attack on theoretical modes of reading; Lindenberger (1990), a traditionalist approach to genre incorporating new paradigms of reading; Kaplan and Rose (1990), a study written from an American liberal feminist perspective; Lauter (1991), an overview of the canon debate in the United States in the last decade, arguing for new protocols of canon formation; and Easthope (1991), an interrogation of canonicity accomplished by juxtaposing popular cultural texts with those of the traditional canon, written from a British cultural materialist perspective.

5 Olivas' review is a companion to one by Nathan Glazer, who argues in support of D'Souza:

> I call the book 'journalistic' in no pejorative sense – it is a balanced, well-researched, meticulously documented account of disputes around race in a number of major American universities, with brief accounts of and references to similar conflicts in scores of other colleges and universities ... D'Souza reviews ... the conflict over revising a required course in Western civilization at Stanford, which, after much faculty discussion, conducted under pressure from a militant student movement, became transmuted into a course in culture, institutions, and values that was to include the study of non-Western writings and ideas of class, race, and gender ... The soil on which all these disputes feed is black academic deficiency. Twenty years of effort have done little to change the situation. I doubt an infusion of black content into the curriculum will do anything to affect the problem. (Glazer 1991, 56, 58)

6 A feature article in the *Toronto Star* by Nicholas Bradbury demonstrates that PC provides a frame for red-baiting as well. Published five days before Hume (1992a) (see below), the article denounces 'the PCs' who reduce the 'beauty of truth' of art to

> one level of understanding – the racial, the sexual, in short, strangely enough, the political ... The leveling of all values to the one sphere of politics is far from new. Indeed, it represents one of the main social movements of the century – totalitarianism. The regimes of the Communist bloc and of fascism, particulary Nazism, all subscribed to this idea ... Reducing culture, and indeed everything, to politics is the very core of totalitarian methods of thought control and propaganda ... Those who appeal to beauty or truth are dismissed as apologists for, or devious agents of, capitalist bourgeois ideology (in the U.S.S.R.) or Jewish bourgeois ideology (in Nazi Germany), or white patriarchy (in North America). (Bradbury 1992, A17)

Except for assertions about their reductionism and the analogy to totalitarianism, Bradbury does not examine his opponents' arguments in any specific way; instead, his argument relies on an appeal to the autonomy of the aesthetic, 'the "artness" of art': 'art and literature is essentially about freedom from ideology, at least in intention ... If "truths" do not exist, even ideally, but only in politics, where does that leave us?' (Bradbury 1992, A17).

7 My account of the fiscal situation is drawn from press releases from both the AGO and the Ministry of Culture and Communications, as well as from Stevenson (1992) and Kate Taylor (1992).

8 The Philistines are in the Old Testament the warlike opponents of the Israelites. Arnold uses the term along with 'Barbarians' for the aristocracy and 'Populace' for the working classes 'to denote roughly the three great classes into which ... society is divided' (Arnold 1965, 143). Conservative American columnist George Will uses the same term in drawing the same opposition that functions in PC: 'Many of the most enlightened defenders of our cultural patrimony are now out in the "practical" world, including government, and many philistines are in the academies shaping tomorrow's elites, and hence tomorrow's governance' (Will 1991, 72).

9 A phrase drawn from the *Commonitorium* (434 A.D.) of Vincent of Lerins:

> Also in the Catholic Church itself we take great care that we hold that which has been believed everywhere, always, by all. For that is truly and properly 'Catholic,' as the very force and meaning of the Word show, which comprehends everything almost universally. And we shall observe this rule if we follow universality, antiquity, consent. (Vincent [434] 1914, 26)

The appeal of the 'Vincentian canon' to the criteria *quod ubique, quod semper, quod ab omnibus creditum est* – 'that which has been believed everywhere, always, by all' – inscribes a notion of correctness or authorized interpretation of the canon of scripture, not in terms of institutionally approved methods, but rather in terms of an appeal to sameness located in transcendental categories. In the first sentence Vincent makes an appeal to the grounds of belief in terms of extension of religious practice through space and time; in the third sentence this notion is generalized into transcendental terms: universality (*universitas*), antiquity (*antiquitas*), and consensus (*consensio*), terms that continue to be inscribed in the academic debates on the literary or Western canon.

10 In December 1994, Glenn Lowry announced that he was leaving the AGO to take up the post of director of the Museum of Modern Art in New York.

References

ACCUTE Newsletter. 1992. 'Supplement of the "Political Correctness" Controversy.' (March)

Adams, Hazard. 1988. 'Canons: Literary Criteria/Power Criteria.' *Critical Inquiry* 14 (Summer): 748–64
Adler, Jerry. 1990. 'Taking Offence: Is This the New Enlightenment on Campus or the New McCarthyism?' *Newsweek* (24 Dec.): 48–54
Altieri, Charles. 1984. 'An Idea and Ideal of a Literary Canon.' In Robert von Hallberg, ed., *Canons*, 41–65. Chicago: University of Chicago Press
Arnold, Matthew. 1965. *Culture and Anarchy. The Complete Prose Works of Matthew Arnold.* Vol. 5. Ed. R.H. Super. Ann Arbor: University of Michigan Press
Art Gallery of Ontario. 1987. *Stage Three: Architectural Proposals by Competition Finalists.* Toronto: Art Gallery of Ontario
Baldick, Chris. 1983. *The Social Mission of English Criticism, 1848–1932.* Oxford: Oxford University Press
Bate, Walter Jackson. 1983. 'The Crisis in English Studies.' *Scholarly Publishing* 14: 195–212
Bennett, William J. 1984. *To Reclaim a Legacy: A Report on the Humanities in Higher Education.* Washington, DC: National Endowment for the Humanities
Bernstein, Richard. 1990. 'The Rising Hegemony of the Politically Correct.' *New York Times* (28 Oct.), sec. 4: 1, 4
Bloom, Alan. 1987. *The Closing of the American Mind.* New York: Simon and Schuster
Bowen, Lisa Balfour. 1992. 'The Task at Hand.' *Toronto Sun* (16 Aug.)
Bradbury, Nicholas. 1992. 'The New Flat World of the Politically Misguided.' *Toronto Star* (13 July): A17
Cheney, Lynne V. 1988. *Humanities in America: A Report to the President, the Congress, and the American People.* Washington, DC: National Endowment for the Humanities
Conlogue, Ray. 1991. 'How Long Might It Take to Repair Damage Wrought by the PC Movement?' *Globe and Mail* (11 June): C1
Culler, Jonathan. 1988. *Framing the Sign: Criticism and Its Institutions.* Oxford: Basil Blackwell
Curtius, Ernst Robert. 1953. *European Literature and the Latin Middle Ages.* New York: Harper and Row
Davey, Frank. 1990. 'Canadian Canons.' *Critical Inquiry* 16 (Spring): 672–81
Drainie, Bronwyn. 1990. 'Food for Thought or Anorexia of the Mind.' *Globe and Mail* (29 Dec.): C1
D'Souza, Dinesh. 1991a. *Illiberal Education: The Politics of Race and Sex on Campus.* New York: The Free Press
– 1991b. 'Illiberal Education.' *The Atlantic* (March): 51–79
Eagleton, Terry. 1983. *Literary Theory: An Introduction.* Minneapolis: University of Minnesota Press

Easthope, Antony. 1991. *Literary into Cultural Studies.* London: Routledge
Eliot, T.S. 1975. 'Tradition and the Individual Talent.' *Selected Prose of T.S. Eliot.* Ed. Frank Kermode. London: Faber
English Studies in Canada. 1991. 'The Canon and the Curriculum' (Dec.)
Fennell, Tom. 1991. 'The Silencers: A New Wave of Repression Is Sweeping through the Universities.' *Maclean's* (27 May): 40–3
Fromm, Paul. 1991. *Academic Capitalism.* Athens: University of Georgia Press
Frow, John. 1986. *Marxism and Literary History.* Oxford: Basil Blackwell
Fulford, Robert. 1992. 'The Philistines Strike Back: How the NDP Crippled a Proud Art Gallery.' *The Financial Times* (13 July): 23
Glazer, Nathan. 1991. Review of D'Souza's *Illiberal Education. Change* (Sept.–Oct.): 56–8
Guillory, John. 1987. 'Canonical and Non-Canonical: A Critique of the Current Debate.' *ELH* 54: 483–527
– 1990. 'Canon.' In Frank Lentricchia and Thomas McLaughlin, eds., *Critical Terms for Literary Study*, 233–49. Chicago: University of Chicago Press
Hall, Stuart. 1982. 'The Rediscovery of "Ideology": Return of the Repressed in Media Studies.' In Michael Gurevitch et al., eds., *Culture, Society and the Media*, 56–90. London: Routledge
Harris, Wendell V. 1991. 'Canonicity.' *PMLA* 106 (Jan.): 110–21
Henry, William. 1991. 'Upside Down in the Groves of Academe.' *Time* (1 April): 62–4
Hume, Christopher. 1992a. 'Politically Correcting the Arts.' *Toronto Star* (18 July). G3
– 1992b. 'AGO's Responsibility Is to Art, Not to Artists.' *Toronto Star* (12 Aug.): B2
– 1992c, 'Talented Tod Fails with Wrong-Headed Mural.' *Toronto Star* (13 Aug.): E11
Hurst, Lynda. 1991. ' "Politically Correct"? Think Before You Speak: New Watchwords "Politically Correct" Cause Controversy.' *Toronto Star* (2 June): A1, A12
Jasen, Patricia. 1988. 'Arnoldian Humanism, English Studies, and the Canadian University.' *Queen's Quarterly* 95(3) (Autumn): 550–66
Jenish, D'Arcy. 1991. 'A War of Words: Academics Clash over "Correctness." ' *Maclean's* (27 May): 44–5
Kaplan, Carey, and Ellen Cronan Rose. 1990. *The Canon and the Common Reader.* Knoxville: University of Tennessee Press
Keefer, Michael. 1991a. 'Political Correctness.' *Canadian Federation for the Humanities Bulletin* (Summer): 7–8
– 1991b. 'Tensions Exist but *Maclean's* Article Not Acceptable Account of Developments.' *University Affairs/Affaires Universitaires* (Aug.–Sept.): 19

– 1992a. 'Ellis on Deconstruction: A Second Opinion.' *English Studies in Canada* 28 (March): 83–103
– 1992b. ' "Political Correctness": An Annotated List of Readings.' *ACCUTE Newsletter*. Supplement on the 'Political Correctness' Controversy (March)
Kennedy, George A. 1990. 'Classics and Canon.' *The South Atlantic Quarterly* 89 (Winter): 217–25
Kermode, Frank. 1983. 'Institutional Control of Interpretation.' *The Art of Telling*, 168–85. Cambridge, MA: Harvard University Press
Kimball, Roger. 1990. *Tenured Radicals: How Politics Has Corrupted Our Higher Education*. New York: Harper & Row
Lauter, Paul. 1991. *Canons and Contexts*. New York: Oxford University Press
Lecker, Robert. 1990. 'The Canonization of Canadian Literature: An Inquiry into Value.' *Critical Inquiry* 16 (Spring): 656–71
– , ed. 1991. *Canadian Canons: Essays in Literary Value*. Toronto: University of Toronto Press
Lindenberger, Herbert. 1990. *The History in Literature: On Value, Genre, Institutions*. New York: Columbia University Press
Lipkin, Lawrence. 1984. 'Aristotle's Sister: A Poetics of Abandonment.' In Robert von Hallberg, ed., *Canons*, 85–107. Chicago: University of Chicago Press
Lowry, Glenn. 1994. 'Legacies of the Past Provide a Key to the Future.' *Toronto Star* (16 April): L10
McAlteer, Michael. 1992. 'United Church Grapples Again with Gay Issue.' *Toronto Star* (17 Aug.): A10
McCormack, Thelma. 1991. ' "Politically Correct." ' *Canadian Forum* (Sept.): 8–10
Marrou, Henri I. [1956] 1964. *A History of Education in Antiquity*. New York: New American Library
Olivas, Michael A. 1991. Review of D'Souza's *Illiberal Education*. *Change* (Sept.–Oct.): 56–60
Perkin, J. Russell. 1992. 'Literary Studies and Society: Some Reflections on the Political Correctness Debate.' *Queen's Quarterly* 99 (Summer): 314–27
Said, Edward. 1978. *Orientalism*. New York: Pantheon Books
Smith, Doug. 1991. 'The "New McCarthyism." ' *Canadian Dimension* (Sept.): 8–13
Smith, Michael. 1992. 'Female Brain Smaller, Rushton Report Says.' *Toronto Star* (15 Aug.): A6
Stevenson, Mark. 1992. 'Ontario's Art Gallery Needs a Lesson in Business.' *Financial Times* (13 July): 1, 4, 5
Taylor, John. 1991. 'Are You Politically Correct?' *New York* (21 Jan.): 32–40
Taylor, Kate. 1992. 'A Clash of Two Cultures: How the AGO Lost Out.' *Globe and Mail* (1 Aug.): A1, A4

Toronto Star. 1992. 'NDP Frames AGO.' Editorial (18 July): D2

Vincent of Lerins. [434] 1914. *The Commonitory of St. Vincent of Lerins*. Trans. T. Herbert Bindley. London: SPCK

von Hallberg, Robert, ed. 1984. *Canons*. Chicago: University of Chicago Press

Wattenmaker, Richard J. 1974. 'Introduction.' *Handbook: Art Gallery of Ontario*. Toronto: Art Gallery of Ontario

Will, George F. 1991. 'Literary Politics.' *Newsweek* (22 April): 72

Withrow, William J. 1974. 'Preface.' *Handbook: Art Gallery of Ontario*. Toronto: Art Gallery of Ontario

– 1985. 'Art Gallery of Ontario.' *The Canadian Encyclopedia*. Edmonton, AB: Hurtig

Academic Freedom *Is* the Inclusive University[1]

JANICE DRAKICH, MARILYN TAYLOR, AND JENNIFER BANKIER

Introduction

The present is, in America, a period of academic transition, and great changes are immediately impending. (Adams 1907, quoted in Carnochan 1993, 58)

Curricular battles and academic transitions have a long history in the academy (see Carnochan 1993; Vickers 1993). The current challenges to the traditions of higher education from women and members of other traditionally marginalized groups constitute another chapter in academe's history. Whereas earlier debates focused on matters such as 'the idea of the university,' liberal education, and disciplinary wars, the current emphasis is on ensuring that the differing values, perspectives, and insights of women and other marginalized groups are fully represented in the academy. Interdisciplinary studies, multicultural studies, inclusive curriculum projects, women, minorities, and other changes to the landscape of academe have important implications for the institutional, pedagogical, intellectual, and interpersonal cultures of the academy. These changes confront the androcentric and ethnocentric conceptualizations of the university and push the boundaries of traditional academic convention to encompass diversity of thought and diversity of community. As the conception of the university has evolved, so too has the understanding of academic freedom.

The formulation of the concept of academic freedom can be traced to Germany in the nineteenth century (Fuchs 1967; Jones 1967). The original formulation of academic freedom emphasized teaching freedom for faculty and learning freedom for students. The American Association of University Professors (AAUP) in its initial statement on academic freedom in 1915 recognized these two complementary principles but failed to address learning freedom for students. The AAUP 'General Declaration of Principles' states:

> The term 'academic freedom' has traditionally had two applications – to the freedom of the teacher and to that of the student, *Lehrfreiheit* and *Lernfreiheit*. It need scarcely be pointed out that the freedom which is the subject of this report is that of the teacher. Academic freedom in this sense comprises three elements: freedom of inquiry and research; freedom of teaching within the university or college; and freedom of extramural utterance and action. (Joughin 1967, 157–8)

In the AAUP '1940 Statement of Principles on Academic Freedom and Tenure,' academic freedom is defined as having a teaching aspect and a learning aspect:

> Academic freedom in its teaching aspect is fundamental for the protection of the rights of the teacher in teaching and of the student to freedom in learning. It carries with it duties correlative with rights. (Joughin 1967, 34)

The Canadian Association of University Teachers (CAUT) has had policy statements on academic freedom since 1967. The current 'Policy Statement on Academic Freedom' states:

> The common good of society depends upon the search for knowledge and its free expression. Academic freedom in universities is essential to both these purposes in the teaching function of the university as well as in its scholarship and research. Academic staff shall not be hindered or impeded in any way by the university or the faculty association from exercising their legal rights as citizens, nor shall they suffer any penalties because of the exercise of such legal rights. The parties agree that they will not infringe or abridge the academic freedom of any member of the academic community. Academic members of the community are entitled, regardless of prescribed doctrine, to freedom to carry out research and in publishing the result thereof, freedom of teaching and of discussion, freedom to criticize the university and the faculty association, and freedom from interpersonal censorship. Academic freedom does not require neutrality on the part of the individual. Rather, academic freedom makes commitment possible. Academic freedom carries with it the duty to use that freedom in a manner consistent with the scholarly obligation to base research and teaching on an honest search for knowledge. (CAUT 1977)

Despite its long history and entrenchment in collective agreements, the concept of academic freedom continues to be ambiguous. University faculty in Canada do not share a single view of academic freedom yet they believe that it is something to be preserved. Although faculty have wholeheartedly accepted the basic premise of academic freedom – that they have the unfettered right to research, teach, and publish – the boundaries of academic freedom are vague. Recent media discussions[2] of academic freedom have revealed some aspects of the ambiguity of the concept and the disagreement surrounding its boundaries. Many have argued that academic freedom extends to extramural utterance and action, while others have argued that academic freedom does not apply beyond the scholar's area of competence. Academic freedom has been identified with unrestricted free speech. Some have even argued, perhaps unknowingly, that free speech extends to the dissemination of unethical research (Sopinka 1994). The conflation of the concepts of academic freedom and free speech that occurs in academia ignores the fact that academic freedom should be anchored by responsibility and a recognition of corresponding rights and freedoms to foster a culture of academic freedom that supports free inquiry in teaching, research, and learning. At the core of the truly inclusive university is a culture of academic freedom that will welcome changing pedagogies, fields, and university populations and promote equality. It is important to note that the concept of academic freedom was designed to accommodate oppositional views. According to Menand (1993, 12), if the university is unable to accommodate conflicting political and ideological views, the problem is structural and philosophical, not ideological. He goes on to argue that 'since the concept of academic freedom is fundamental to the structure and philosophy of the modern university, the concept of academic freedom is at the centre of the whole affair.'

The current characterization of the relationship between academic freedom and the inclusive university as an oppositional one, in the 'political correctness' debate,[3] gives rise to the impression that academic freedom cannot compatibly coexist with the commitment to fostering diversity in the university. By contrast, in this paper, we wish to elaborate the position that the practice of academic freedom *is* the inclusive university. We view academic freedom as a dynamic concept that is practised by the university community rather than as a static policy entrenched in collective agreements for the protection of faculty.

We acknowledge that the principle of academic freedom is central to the highest purposes of the university and, ultimately, a democratic society. Academic freedom is commonly understood to mean that faculty and the academy itself are protected against retribution by the state and economic/political élites, outside and within the university, when they advance knowledge that is at odds with the extant policies and priorities of the state or the university itself. This policy ensures that faculty have the freedom to carry out research and discussion; faculty have the freedom to criticize the university; and faculty are protected from institutional censorship. Thelma McCormack (1991) has forcefully made the point, for example, that women's studies owes its very existence to the principle of academic freedom. She observes, however, that an expanded interpretation is needed if academic freedom is to respond adequately to the new reality of a diverse academy. According to the principles of academic freedom, the pursuit of new or unorthodox or challenging ideas is a legitimate activity for faculty. Indeed, it is the central mission of the university. Yet, professors and students who represent diversity in the university today and are advancing new and unsettling perspectives and projects are more often opposed than welcomed. The opposition to the pursuit of the academic imperative of intellectual inquiry, examination, and re-envisioning reveals that there is a considerable gap between the *precept* and the actual *practice* of academic freedom in the academy. Expanding the precept of academic freedom to the practice of academic freedom requires a shared culture of academic freedom that will encourage a variety of intellectual ideas growing out of differences and welcoming both individuals and groups who represent these differences.

In this paper, we explore barriers as well as avenues to the *practice* of academic freedom. We begin by discussing two major limitations in the current interpretation of academic freedom: (1) its emphasis on individual actions to the exclusion of attention to their context or social, institutional relationships; and (2) its emphasis entirely on intellect to the exclusion of other human dimensions – identities, emotions, and feelings. We then examine the intersection of the social-relational context and affect. We assert that an important avenue to the practice of academic freedom is the recognition of academic freedom as a reciprocal right and obligation of all members of the academic community – faculty, staff, librarians, and students. We argue that the precept of academic freedom reflects the social-relational context of the university and recognizes the differences in values, experiences, needs, and power present in the university community. Finally, we present the existence of supporting frameworks in CAUT policy and the Charter of Rights and Freedoms for the implementation of the practice of academic freedom.

The Social-Relational Context of Individual Actions

Academic freedom is currently discussed from an atomistic, a-contextual perspective. As now defined, academic freedom refers to a specific 'piece' of behaviour of a specific 'individual' that ignores the intersubjectivity of all persons in the setting. We think that such an approach conceals the vulnerability of women and other historically excluded groups who are still marginal in the academy, and does not take account of the historic advantages enjoyed by white, heterosexual, able-bodied males. Specifically, it does not acknowledge power imbalances in relations based on gender, race, sexuality, class, and other dimensions of difference. And it ignores the dimension of accountability attached to social relations in the academy. Given the demography of universities, narrowing the focus of academic freedom exclusively to the rights of the individual professor tends to perpetuate the exclusion of traditionally disadvantaged groups through curriculum, pedagogy, and social behaviour.

To women and members of excluded groups, it is obvious that many assumptions and practices of the academy still reflect a time when the university was a virtually homogeneous white male environment. White, male, androcentric assumptions underlie the practice of exclusion. For example, at a recent conference working session on the topic of academic freedom and the inclusive university, a white male professor, who was defending his view of academic freedom, stated emphatically that it was his job to upset his students in the classroom. A black woman administrator, who administers an access program, replied angrily that he had no right to do so. The professor's pedagogical style, in his view, is not directed toward harming students but rather to preparing them to think analytically and critically by challenging their ideas. This is a process that can, at first, be disruptive to old ways of seeing things. However, the black female administrator was also expressing an essential and valid point about the destructive potential of a professor expressing ideas in a way that discounts and disempowers already-marginalized students in the classroom. The white male professor and the black woman administrator live in two different worlds of experience and did not, in that session, manage to bridge those worlds to achieve any kind of mutual understanding (see Smith 1989 for a discussion of this problem). The professor appeared completely unaware of the vast difference in entitlement between the two of them: his existence, as a student and a professor, is one as a white Anglo-Saxon male in an institution that has been populated for most of its history exclusively by white males. By contrast, the black administrator knew that black students are often not 'at home' in the university; university practices and rituals that are premised on white, middle-class, male experiences do not reflect black students' experiences. That the white male professor was oblivious to the problem of differing experiences is not surprising. The existence of a university culture that sustains and enables individuals in institutional settings, like the invisible root system of a tree, tends to be overlooked by the beneficiaries of the status quo. Moreover, the social context of white male privilege in the academy supports the individual's resistance to acknowledging and confronting the changing demography of university communities.

The current statistical reality of the university describes a university that dramatically differs from the one that existed prior to the 1960s. In particular, women's enrolment has increased steadily.[4] In 1990, 56 per cent of undergraduate degrees and 45 per cent of graduate degrees were awarded to women (Statistics Canada 1992). The proportion of women administrators and faculty has also increased, but not at the same rate as the change in the student population. However, some things stay the same. Women faculty remain concentrated in the lower professorial ranks, and women administrators are often members of the 'triple A club – assistant, associate, and acting.'[5] The proportions of other underrepresented groups have increased also, although the extent of the increase is not as clearly documented. The case of gays and, to a lesser extent, lesbians is somewhat unique. They have been represented in the university throughout its history but are only recently beginning to be able to acknowledge openly their sexual identity. The diversity of the university population should significantly alter the social-relational context within which the business of the university is conducted as the participants in the university no longer reflect the monolithic demographic of the white male academy.

This diversity represents a heterogeneity of identities and experiences that deviate from the identities and experiences of the white, middle-class, male norm of the university culture and curriculum. Identities from the margins of academe make visible the need for a re-envisioning of the structures, values, and assumptions of academic conduct and inquiry. The work of Dorothy Smith (1989) and bell hooks (1988, 1993), among others, in describing the social-relational context of female and racial identities in the academy underscore the need for change. And the experiences of members of these diverse groups demand it.

Smith's (1989, 49) argument about the disjuncture between women's lived experiences within the social forms of consciousness in relation to 'the world directly felt, sensed, responded to' is directly applicable to our concerns for the conceptualization of academic freedom. Since the experiences of members of marginalized groups in the academy are determined by social relations and situated in the power relations in the academy, the practice of academic freedom must also address the social-relational context to be inclusive. Moreover, this disjuncture directs our attention to an area that is seldom, if ever, considered in the academic enterprise – 'the world directly felt, sensed, and responded to.' In the next section, we take up the significance of affect to the practice of academic freedom.

The Significance of Affect as well as Intellect

The language of academic freedom assumes that 'the person' is only a 'mind' and the problem is one of a 'clash of ideas.' We agree that the right of all persons to express their own ideas should be protected and that this right is fundamental in a free and democratic society. We would be justified in leaving it at that if reality were exclusively made up of ideas and if people were disconnected intellects. This is not the case, however. An exclusive focus on words and ideas can obscure the fact that we are talking about whole people. For many people, ideas and words may well be referents for highly significant experiences that have powerful meanings, evoke strong emotions, and are not *simply* ideas and words. The meanings and emotions attached to ideas and words render people extremely vulnerable in what, for others, might be a benign intellectual exercise.

Women and minorities, who are not welcomed into the disembodied world of the academy, bring, among other things, consciousness of their emotionality and their vulnerability. For example, the lived experience of women in the academy is one in which we learn that to be successful, we must disassociate our rational selves from the rest of ourselves. The bifurcation of persons, particularly those in marginalized groups, in the academy is supported by the hegemony of objectivity over subjectivity. Thus, learning in the classroom and conducting research are activities in which women and minorities are profoundly vulnerable. In order for women and minorities to open themselves to discovery, they face uncertainty and confusion in balancing their subjective experiences in a world that values objectivity. The learning process provokes fear, anxiety, and loss of self-assurance for everyone, but this is compounded for minorities and women.

The required objectivity surrounding words and ideas embedded in the masculinist culture of the university has obscured the presence of the personal and associated subjective emotions and feelings. 'The canons of science as a constitutional practice require the suppression of the personal' (Smith 1989, 60) and through this suppression perpetuate the obfuscation of the existence of whole persons in the university. The eschewing of the personal and subjective is further evidenced in the masculinist models of discourse and pedagogy.

The masculinist model of discourse is premised on a competitive, confrontational style that seeks to establish/entrench power imbalances without regard for the 'other' in the discourse. This model is most clearly illustrated in its concomitant pedagogy, which demeans students without regard for the impact on students' sense of themselves in the classroom. We are all familiar with the phrase, 'If you can't take it, no matter how tough, you don't belong here.' Refusal to acknowledge the predictable emotionality and vulnerability in response to the expression of inhospitable views and behaviour in the academy – in the classroom, or toward colleagues – is crude incivility. People have deep feelings about their convictions and identities. The reality of personal and subjective experiences must be recognized and formally acknowledged in the academy.

Recognition of others' profound feelings does not suggest that ideas and discourse be restricted. Rather, it is a call for sensitivity or, at minimum, civility. To ignore this call evades the ethical responsibilities of persons who assume positions of institutional authority. The prevailing perspective on academic freedom does not take into account the intersections of institutional power relations (e.g., teacher–student) and dimensions of emotion. We take up these points in more detail in the following section.

The Intersection of the Social-Relational Context and Affect

Does the consideration of the consequential vulnerabilities of students, especially women and members of other underrepresented groups, mean that professors must never upset students? Do the inherent advantages for male professors mean that they should never challenge female colleagues? Of course not. Academic freedom encourages open discussion and intellectual inquiry. Indeed, the quality of our pursuit of knowledge and understanding rests on the existence of a community of scholars, interaction, and exchange among differing perspectives. The exhortation here is that the professor has an obligation to communicate respect, sensitivity, understanding, and tolerance toward her or his students, along with the intellectual content. These qualities, in the context of civility, are essential features of community. The favourable or unfavourable response of a credible authority such as a teacher or senior colleague becomes extremely salient during the exchange of ideas (Taylor 1986). When combined with other power imbalances, the significance of the impact of authority redoubles.

Professors of non-canonical subjects face the challenge of maintaining these qualities in every class. Few people are open to new ideas that contravene their traditional perspectives. However, scholars who support the practice of academic freedom balance the corresponding responsibilities of testing and proposing revisions to the prevailing wisdom with sensitivity to students' feelings. This wilful practice is, for many women and minority professors, a consequence of their experiences with andro-, euro-, and heterocentric traditional education. Their experiences of being excluded as students and professors in the academy have sensitized them to their students' vulnerabilities and contributed to their inclusive pedagogies for enabling students.

Logic and experience indicate that when material, based on sound and honest scholarship, conveys what can be seen as a negative message about women or a particular racial group, for example, a professor should be expected to present the material in a way that does not disempower or demean any members of that group in the class.[6] This material can be presented with an explicit acknowledgment of its potential for disruption and a sound rationale for its inclusion in the course to justify its disturbing consequences.

Difficulties in the application of the principle of academic freedom are most likely to arise when individuals focus exclusively on the professor's unrestricted right of expression while at the same time ignoring the intersubjectivity and power relations that exist in the classroom. Such a complete freedom ignores the reality that when an individual is in a power position, her or his behaviour may have a negative impact on those under her or his power. The need to attend to the effects of as well as the origins of behaviour is widely recognized with respect to physical behaviour: Most people would agree that one person's freedom to swing a fist ends when it collides with another person's nose. To address this problem, Smolla (1990, 222) has suggested that a more appropriate approach to academic freedom would be to accept that a professor is 'an *intellectual* free agent, but not a *behavioral* free agent.' This distinction is helpful, but an issue still remains.

Should all 'verbal behaviour,' such as words in a classroom, automatically be protected by the concept of academic freedom? We would argue that the answer is no. Words cease to be an expression of academic freedom when they have an effect that interferes with the academic freedom of other people, repressing, constraining, or prohibiting scholarship or inquiry. For example, a member of a tenure and promotion committee would clearly violate a colleague's academic freedom if she or he used words to argue that a colleague should be denied tenure because her or his research reflects a feminist, or an aboriginal, or a black, or a gay, or a lesbian perspective. A professor also interferes with students' academic freedom when she or he verbally abuses, belittles, or ignores students who wish to present alternative perspectives to course materials.

There is a significant difference between ideas themselves and the presentation of ideas in a particular manner and context. It is possible to present ideas in a clear and effective fashion that nevertheless reflects respect for the values and perspectives of other people involved in the discussion. This form of respect is particularly important if the listeners are a captive audience, as students are. Adoption of a style of presentation that abuses or marginalizes others is a behavioural choice, and not a matter of intellectual right.

Academic Freedom Based on Reciprocity Rather Than Autonomy

We would like to advance the proposal that academic freedom be interpreted as a reciprocal right that exists within academic relationships (teacher–student, colleague–colleague, etc.). In this perspective, both parties to any given academic relationship have rights to academic freedom, and the exercise of one person's rights must not infringe on the rights of the other. Currently, the practice is constructed on behalf of a single individual faculty member attempting to preserve her or his autonomy against more powerful interests (the administration) generally perceived as acting with malevolent or misguided purposes. Even if this is an accurate characterization of a particular dispute, we wonder how useful an image it is. It may be more helpful, we think, to define an interactive concept of academic freedom: Members of the university community – faculty, students, and staff – are encouraged to express their views and pursue their priorities, and in the exercise of these freedoms the rights of all parties are protected. In this view, the rights of all the persons involved become the focus, not the 'bad' or 'heroic' (depending on your 'side') behaviour of one person. Women and other members of historically excluded groups would be viewed primarily as persons with academic rights, not primarily as victims of harassment, sexism, and/or racism. Under such a model we would enjoy a right of academic freedom based upon our respect of the academic freedom of others through our acknowledgment of the legitimacy of their values and other differences. A system in which professors practice what we preach would be more credible to our students, other members of the academic community, and to the wider society.

The acknowledgment of rights to academic freedom for all faculty including women and members of other minority groups in the academy is, perhaps, a less difficult conceptual adjustment than academic freedom for others, students in particular. However, from the standpoint of promoting equity, this would seem to be an important addition. Women and members of other underrepresented groups are not only more numerous in the lower ranks of the professoriate (and, thus, more vulnerable to punishment for intellectual heresy by more senior male colleagues), but women are more numerous as students than they are as university teachers. Since students are the future professoriate, the learning climate for minorities in the academy has long-range as well as current significance for the future of our universities. Further, it seems reasonable to expect that this would foster an understanding and an appreciation of the importance of preserving academic freedom for our students who will be tomorrow's professors. Students' rights related to academic freedom are not a novel notion. The 'International Statement on Academic Freedom and Tenure' speaks of the university's 'responsibility to society to defend and maintain ... freedom in research as fundamental to the advancement of truth, and freedom in teaching as fundamental for the protection of the rights of the student in learning and the teacher in teaching.' CAUT is one of the nine signatories of this document. CAUT's own definition of academic freedom, however, concerns only the rights of academic staff.

It is often through students' interests and needs for learning that androcentric, Eurocentric, and heterocentric biases in our curricula are challenged. The extension of rights, described above, empowers all members of the academic community, rather than imposes restrictions upon individual behaviour, as one side in the 'political correctness' debate characterizes the issue.

The restriction of initiatives to recognize diversity and practise inclusiveness is a violation of academic freedom as conceptualized here. The movement toward inclusion in our language, our courses, and our scholarship has been one that conforms to academic freedom rather than erodes it. Academic freedom is alleged to provide a forum and protection for the new, the provocative, the disturbing, and the unorthodox. Yet, the practice of academic freedom has been the practice of exclusion and restriction (see Kaplan and Schrecker 1983). 'When we talk about the freedom of the academic to dictate the terms of his or her work, in other words, we are also and unavoidably talking about the freedom to exclude, or to limit the exposure of, work that is not deemed to meet academic standards' (Menand 1993, 14). Professors have been denied tenure, denied promotion, and denied jobs, and their research has been judged unacceptable because it represents a non-traditional perspective. Most junior faculty recognize the danger in engaging in non-canonical work. The protection of academic freedom in the practice of exclusion has also denied students access to their histories, their experiences, and to knowledge – the knowledge of non-Western, non-white, and non-male scholarship.

The phrase 'academic freedom *is* the inclusive university' transforms the conventional interpretation of academic freedom from a protection and a right to exercise exclusion to a practice of integration and inclusion.

Academic Freedom Is the Inclusive University

CAUT's 'Policy Statement on Professional Rights, Responsibilities and Relationships' (revised January 1991) contains several clauses that are pertinent here. These clauses have existed in CAUT's guidelines concerning professional ethics and professional relationships almost as long as CAUT's 'Policy Statement on Academic Freedom.' Their import for our conceptualization of academic freedom as a practice is manifest. The policy embodies the foundation for the idea that 'academic freedom is the inclusive university.' For example, appropriate gender and racial/ethnic representation in curricula are really part of our responsibility to 'be conscientious in the preparation and organization of [our] subject matter, and ... [to] review this periodically in light of developments in [our] field' (Article 2.2). Sensitivity toward and respect for our students, and the acknowledgment of their vulnerabilities in our classes is integral to our responsibility to 'encourage the free exchange of ideas between [ourselves] and [our] students' (Article 2.3). A second section in the policy statement dealing with responsibilities to colleagues states that 'academic staff members should act to ensure a working milieu which is open, non-discriminatory and free from personal, racial or sexual harassment' (Article 4.1).

Support for the implementation of the ideas we have presented can be found in the Canadian Charter of Rights and Freedoms. Catherine

MacKinnon (1993, 78) discusses the practice of power relations as it can be embedded in the defence of freedom of expression: 'Speech theory does not disclose or even consider how to deal with power vanquishing powerlessness; it tends to transmute this into truth vanquishing falsehood, meaning what power wins becomes considered true.' MacKinnon notes that Canada has public legal conditions under the Charter of Rights and Freedoms that have produced opposite results. She cites the Supreme Court decisions against Keegstra and Butler, with interventions by the Women's Legal Education and Action Fund, as examples of limits on freedom of expression on equality grounds: 'The positive spin of the Canadian interpretation holds the law to promoting equality, projecting the law into a more equal future, rather than remaining rigidly neutral in ways that either reinforce existing social inequality or prohibit changing it, as the American constitutional perspective has increasingly done in recent years' (1993, 38).

The Charter of Rights and Freedoms explicitly acknowledges and recognizes a necessary relationship between individual freedoms and equality provisions in a democratic society. The full significance of this relationship can be seen by contrasting the structure and consequences of the U.S. Constitution, where freedom of speech is enshrined in the First Amendment and equality rights in the Fourteenth Amendment. The separation of these two provisions and the negative, rather than positive, application of both (i.e., prohibitions rather than support for social change) have led to powerful circumstance of inequality.[7] The Canadian Charter of Rights and Freedoms, by contrast, defines 'equality in a meaningful way – one more substantive than formal, directed toward changing social relations rather than monitoring their equal positioning before the law' (MacKinnon 1993, 98). The courts in Canada will balance freedom of speech against other rights and values such as equity. Obscenity legislation has been upheld. The Butler case recently established that violence and degradation of women make material obscene. Promotion of equality and restrictions on some kinds of hate speech can be upheld if properly drafted. In other words, social evils such as racial defamation and degradation of women have been balanced against freedom of speech under the Charter of Rights and Freedoms.

Ironically, we have, in Canadian universities, applications of academic freedom, on the one hand, and professional rights, responsibilities, and relationships on the other hand that reflect the U.S. tradition more than Canadian jurisprudence. Policies in these two domains are held out of relation to one another, with the former eclipsing the latter. Thus, the application of academic freedom and professional rights, responsibilities, and relationships is out of step with Canadian jurisprudence.

Conclusion

In this paper we have explored some of the limits of the current perspective and practice of academic freedom. We have tried to reframe what has been characterized as a collision between academic freedom and the commitment to fostering diversity in universities, to a perspective in which a more fully practised academic freedom is at the heart of a more inclusive university, a place where differences in views and values are respected and protected. We have made the point that the concept of academic freedom is improved by including the subjectivity of women and minorities and acknowledging that the personal and experiential are of equal importance to intellectual words and ideas. The argument for including civility recognizes that ideas are not separate, public, and objective but real, emotional, and personal. This is a starting point. We hope that it contributes to evolving a new perspective on university life that fosters not only greater fairness but, through mutual respect, more peace. We hope that it shifts the emphasis from oppositions to resolution.

Notes

1 The Status of Women Committee of the Canadian Association of University Teachers (CAUT) has initiated a critical examination of policies and procedures related to academic freedom in association with the promotion of inclusivity for women and members of other traditionally underrepresented groups in Canadian universities. The other standing committees of CAUT – the Academic Freedom and Tenure Committee and the Librarians' Committee – are participating in this examination. Each committee presented a paper on academic freedom in a session jointly sponsored by the Canadian Sociology and Anthropology Association and the CAUT at the 1993 Learned Association Meetings (Schrank 1993 [AF&T]; Schenk 1993 [Librarians]; Taylor, Bankier, and Drakich 1993 [SWC]). This paper elaborates the ideas presented by Marilyn Taylor at that session.

The authors want to thank Dr Mary Lou Dietz (University of Windsor) for her thoughtful and valuable contributions to this paper. We also want to extend our appreciation to the members of the CAUT SWC – in particular, Dr Dayna Daniels (University of Lethbridge) and Dr Karen Grant (University of

Manitoba) – and to Dr Lynne Phillips (University of Windsor) for their careful reading of various drafts of the paper.

2 A sample of the considerable discussion of academic freedom in daily newspapers, faculty association newletters, *University Affairs*, and *CAUT Bulletin* can be found in, for example, Baker (1994); Brooks (1994); Cook (1994); Fulford (1994); Graesser (1993); Graham (1994); Grogono (1994); Kimura (1993); Letteri (1994); Lougheed (1994); Marlin (1994); Melchers (1994); Milne (1994); Montgomery (1994); Simmons (1994); Sopinka (1994); Storm (1994); Wright (1994).

3 The rhetoric of 'political correctness' is not helpful in this discussion because it obscures the issues of tolerance, equality, and civility. If taken literally, the phrase is meaningless, since committed individuals of all political predispositions believe that their own values are politically correct. However, the phrase is not universally applied to strong participants on all sides of the political debate. Instead, it is applied only to people who are advocating change to the status quo, and is never applied to people who strongly uphold the maintenance of things as they are. The strategy of this usage is to prevent change and avoid addressing the merits of the demands for tolerance and equality.

4 *The Report of the Royal Commission on the Status of Women in Canada* (1977, 170) provides a table summarizing the proportion of undergraduate and graduate degrees awarded to women in Canada from 1930–1 to 1966–7. In 1955–6, 22.9 per cent of undergraduate degrees and 18.5 per cent of graduate degrees were awarded to women.

5 Professor Jill Vickers included this phrase in her acceptance address, for the Sarah Shorten Award, to the Council of the Canadian Association of University Teachers. The Sarah Shorten Award recognizes outstanding contributions to the advancement of women in Canadian universities.

6 We want to emphasize that we are not disputing the professor's expertise in subject matter. Rather, we are asking that the freedom to delivery scholarship not be confused with the form or manner of presentation of material.

7 MacKinnon (1993, 72–3) states:

> Both bodies of law ... show virtually total insensitivity to the damage done to social equality by expressive means and a substantial lack of recognition that some people get a lot more speech than others. In the absence of these recognitions, the power of those who have speech has become more and more exclusive, coercive, and violent as it has become more and more legally protected. Understanding that there is a relationship between these two issues – the less speech you have, the more the speech of those who have it keeps you unequal; the more the speech of the dominant is protected, the more dominant they will become and

the less the subordinated will be heard from – is virtually nonexistent. Issues of equal speech are not framed as problems of balance between two cherished goals, or as problems of meaningful access to either right in the absence of the other, but as whether the right to free speech is infringed acceptably or unacceptably. Equality-promoting provisions on hate crimes, campus harassment, and pornography, for example, tend to be attacked and defended solely in terms of the damage they do, or do not do, to speech. At the same time, issues such as racial segregation, with its accompanying illiteracy and silence, are framed solely in equality terms, rather than also as official barriers to speech and therefore as violations of the First Amendment.

References

Baker, John. 1994. *CAUT Bulletin* (April): 17

Brooks, R.J. 1994. *CAUT Bulletin* (April): 17

Canadian Association of University Teachers. 1977. 'Policy Statement on Academic Freedom,' 3–1. Ottawa: CAUT Information Service

– 1991. 'Policy Statement on Professional Rights, Responsibilities and Relationships,' 25–1. Ottawa: CAUT Information Service

Carnochan, W.B. 1993. *The Battleground of the Curriculum: Liberal Education and American Experience.* Stanford, CA: Stanford University Press

Cook, Deborah. 1994. 'Freedom of Speech Getting Lost in Shuffle.' *Windsor Star* (8 March): A7

Fuchs, Ralph. 1967. 'Academic Freedom – Its Basic Philosophy, Function, and History. In Louis Joughin, ed., *Academic Freedom and Tenure: A Handbook of the American Association of University Professors*, 242–63. Madison: University of Wisconsin Press

Fulford, Robert. 1994. 'Defending the Right to Be Offensive.' *Globe and Mail* (2 Feb.): C1

Graesser, Marc. 1993. *Memorial Faculty Association Newsletter* (Dec.)

Graham, Bill. 1994. 'Don't Sell Academic Freedom Short.' *Globe and Mail* (14 Feb.): A13

Grogono, Peter. 1994. 'Academic Freedom Called Doublespeak.' *CAUT Bulletin* (April): 2

hooks, bell. 1988. *Talking Back: Thinking Feminist, Thinking Black.* Toronto: Between the Lines

– 1992. *Black Looks: Race and Representation.* Toronto: Between the Lines

Jones, Howard. 1967. 'The American Concept of Academic Freedom.' In Louis Joughin, ed., *Academic Freedom and Tenure: A Handbook of the American Association of University Professors*, 224–41. Madison: University of Wisconsin Press

Joughin, Louis, ed. 1967. *Academic Freedom and Tenure: A Handbook of the American Association of University Professors*. Madison: University of Wisconsin Press

Kaplan, Craig, and Ellen Schrecker. 1983. *Regulating the Intellectuals: Perspectives on Academic Freedom in the 1980s*. New York: Praeger

Kimura, Doreen. 1993. 'Universities and the Thought Police.' *Globe and Mail* (28 June): A19

Letteri, Mark. 1994. 'Open Minds, Open Debate.' *Windsor Star* (6 April): A7

Lougheed, Tim. 1994. 'How Far Is Too Far?' *University Affairs* (April): 6–7

McCormack, Thelma. 1991. 'Politically Correct.' *The Canadian Forum* (Sept.): 8–10

MacKinnon, Catharine A. 1993. *Only Words*. Cambridge, MA: Harvard University Press

Marlin, Randal. 1994. *CAUT Bulletin* (April): 17

Melchers, Ron. 1994. 'Self-Serving Media Manipulated University Discrimination Story.' *Ottawa Citizen* (1 March): A9

Menand, Louis. 1993. 'The Future of Academic Freedom.' *Academe* (May/June): 11–17

Milne, Pamela. 1994. 'Zero Tolerance Must Remain the Key.' *Windsor Star* (22 March): A6

Montgomery, Jason. 1994. *CAUT Bulletin* (April): 17

R. v. Butler. [1992] 1 S.C.R. 452

R. v. Keegstra. [1990] 3 S.C.R. 697

Royal Commission on the Status of Women. 1977. *The Report of the Royal Commission on the Status of Women in Canada*. Ottawa: Supply and Services Canada

Schenk, Margot. 1993. 'Academic Freedom and the Role of Librarians and Libraries.' Paper presented at the Learned Societies Meeting, Carleton University, Ottawa, 5 June

Schrank, Bernice. 1993. 'Academic Freedom and the Inclusive University.' Paper presented at the Learned Societies Meeting, Carleton University, Ottawa, 5 June

Simmons, Christina. 1994. 'You Don't Have to Teach Discrimination.' *Windsor Star* (25 March): A7

Smith, Dorothy. 1989. *The Everyday World as Problematic: A Feminist Sociology*. Toronto: University of Toronto Press.

Smolla, Rodney A. 1990. 'Academic Freedom, Hate Speech, and the Idea of a University.' *Law and Contemporary Problems* 53(3): 195–225

Sopinka, Hon. John. 1994. 'Freedom of Speech Under Attack.' *University Affairs* (April): 13

Statistics Canada. 1992. *Education in Canada: A Statistical Review for 1990–91*. Catalogue 81-229. Ottawa: Supply and Services Canada

Storm, Thomas. 1994. 'Political Correctness Claim Angers Reader.' *CAUT Bulletin* (April): 2

Taylor, Marilyn. 1986. 'Learning for Self-Direction in the Classroom: The Pattern of a Transition Process.' *Studies in Higher Education* 1(1): 5–72

Taylor, Marilyn, Jennifer Bankier, and Janice Drakich. 1993. 'Academic Freedom and the Inclusive University: Integrating Civil Libertarian and Egalitarian Values and Practices.' Paper presented at the Learned Societies Meeting, Carleton University, Ottawa, 5 June

Vickers, Jill. 1991. 'Where Is the Discipline in Interdisciplinary?' Paper presented for the Rob McDougall Symposium on Interdisciplinarity

Wright, John. 1994. 'Freedom to Discuss the Unthinkable.' *Windsor Star* (31 March): A7

'Fit and Qualified': The Equity Debate at the University of Alberta

JO-ANN WALLACE

[The Supreme Court of Canada] found in examining the sections of the BNA Act dealing with the selection and appointment of Senators that the word 'persons' was always used in conjunction with either 'qualified' or 'fit and qualified.' On the basis of this, they decided that the question which had to be answered was 'whether "female persons" are qualified to be summoned to the Senate.'

Marchildon 1981, 106

In 1928 the Canadian Supreme Court, ruling on a petition from five Alberta women, found that under the 1867 BNA Act women were not 'fit and qualified persons' and therefore not eligible for appointment to the Senate. This finding was reversed in July 1929 by the British Judicial Committee of the Privy Council, which concluded that 'the word "persons" does include women' (quoted in Marchildon 1981, 110). In 1989 the Department of English at the University of Alberta appointed five women in that year's round of hiring and found itself at the centre of a painful campus-wide debate on 'merit' and employment equity.[1] Given that 1989 was also the much-celebrated sixtieth anniversary of the Persons Act, ironic parallels between the two incidents were not lost on observers; then vice-president (academic) Peter Meekison, for example, noted in a letter to the five new appointees that they could 'justifiably be proud of the fact that you are the 1980's version of the "famous five" who are legendary in Alberta history.' The comparison met with ambivalence from the five professors, some of whom felt that, albeit unintentionally, it belittled the historic achievement of the 'famous five.' Moreover, unlike the earlier women, the five new appointees – who quickly became known in shorthand parlance as 'the five' – felt silenced by the subordination of their individual identities and very different academic projects to a group identity. They were not agents in the controversy occasioned by their hiring and they did not participate publicly in the debate.

The 1989–90 academic year at the University of Alberta was characterized by a series of highly contentious events.[2] In July 1989 five women assistant professors were appointed to the Department of English. On 17 November 1989 two women undergraduate students lodged a formal complaint against *The Bridge*, the Engineering Students' Society (ESS) newspaper, for an 'obscene and sexist' November issue (Kerr 1989, 1). The complaint alleged that in permitting publication of that issue, the ESS 'had failed to comply with two of the conditions required for continued registration as a student group as set out in Section 30.14.4(e)(h) of the Code of Student Behavior'; that is, it failed to 'comply with the stated philosophy of the University' and it did not 'protect the property and good name of the University' (Miller 1989, 1). On 27 November 1989 the *Edmonton Journal* published an interview with a woman engineering student who revealed that, in the first year of her engineering program, *The Bridge* had run 'a false story about her sexual behavior and habits, totally humiliating her' (Boehm 1989, A1). On 6 December 1989 Marc Lepine killed fourteen women engineering students at the École Polytechnique in Montreal. On 10 January 1990, when she appeared on stage in the engineering students' annual skit night, the woman student who had been embarrassed in *The Bridge* and who had criticized the Faculty of Engineering for its unresponsiveness to women's issues was greeted by chants of 'Shoot the bitch!' (see Bhardwaj 1990 and Jackson 1990). She later left the program, the university, and the province (see Cernetig 1990 and Schuler 1990). Two weeks later, and in response to these events, the president of the university struck a Commission for Equality and Respect on Campus; its three tasks were 'to identify factors in the University community which contribute to inequality and disrespect among people,' 'to create an awareness of these factors,' and 'to suggest actions which maintain an environment reflecting the values of equality and respect among all members of the community' ('Commission ...' 1990, 1). The Commission held hearings from early March to mid-April 1990. The Women's Issues Committee of the Association of Academic Staff: University of Alberta (AAS:UA) prepared a brief on behalf of the Association for submission to the president's Commission on 10 April. After requesting a number of changes, the Executive and Representative Councils of the AAS:UA approved the brief, which included six recommendations: an awareness campaign, an equity plan, expanding the pool of job applicants, an equity officer and selection committees, removal of systemic barriers, and support for feminist research. On 9 April a handful of members – citing a seldom-used clause in the Association's by-laws (article 3.4.2) – petitioned the president of the AAS:UA to demand a special general meeting of the Association 'to determine if the brief ... shall become the policy of the Association.' This manoeuvre prevented the submission of the brief in time for the Commission's deadline.

Of this painful series of events, however, it was the hiring of five women by the Department of English that caused the greatest and most sustained controversy among academic staff at the university. This controversy was played out largely within the letters-to-the-editor pages of *Folio*, the university's weekly staff newspaper, between 2 November 1989 and 11 January 1990 and then in various memoranda and factional newsletters. The debate effectively polarized the community and led to – or at least coincided with – the formation of the small, but highly vocal, 'Merit Only' group (which reorganized as the 'Association of Concerned Academics'). This group later focused its efforts on resisting the creation and implementation of employment-equity policies in the university as a whole, but especially in the Faculty of Arts. The fact that the University of Alberta was, in the 1991–2 academic year, under review by the Federal Contractors Program led to an intensification of their efforts.

A cynical reading might suggest that the professoriate did *not* engage in the same degree of public debate regarding the other events of 1989–90 because most of these events touched only the lives of students. An even more cynical reading would point out that these events were perceived as significant primarily by women students. I want to advance a different argument here. When analysed within the context of the 'political correctness' debate, as it originated in the United States and was imported to Canada, it is not surprising that English department hirings should appear so consequential and attract such passionate attention. Prominent right-wing U.S. American critics like Dinesh D'Souza and Roger Kimball have pointed to curricular reform in the humanities in general, and literary studies in particular, as 'ideologically motivated assaults on the intellectual and moral substance of our culture' (Kimball 1991, xviii). Although anti-equity organizers at the University of Alberta did not explicitly use the now-familiar shorthand expression 'PC' – an expression that only entered public debate in the fall of 1990 – their arguments and much of their terminology were drawn from a neoconservative assault on 'culural leftism' that had intensified in the United States following the 1984 release of (then chairman of the National Endowment for the Humanities) William Bennett's pamphlet, *To Reclaim a Legacy*, and the 1987 publication of Allan Bloom's bestseller, *The Closing of the American Mind*. The degree to which anti-equity organizers at the University of Alberta were indebted to a neoconservative discourse that was already well established in the U.S. American academy was evident, for example, in their invocation of what they persistently described as 'merely fashionable' ideologies and their insistence that 'merit' – a quality which they regarded as self-evident, disinterested, and non-'ideological' – is necessarily sacrified by a commitment to employment and educational equity. The controversy that was occasioned by the hiring of 'the five' and the formation of the 'Merit Only' group must be seen not only within the context of events at the University of Alberta, but within the context of the emerging 'political correctness' debate as it developed and played itself out in North America. The remainder of this chapter will analyse the central role of literary studies in the U.S. American political correctness debate, some ways in which that debate has been differently inflected in Canada, and the very specific history of the controversy surrounding the hiring of 'the five' at the University of Alberta. I will conclude by suggesting that the persistent focus of anti-equity organizers on issues of hiring, 'merit,' and, especially, gender – represented, in this case, largely through a language of statistical probability – worked at the University of Alberta to polarize discussion of equity issues and to obscure still more foundational questions regarding the ways in which cultural knowledge is legitimized and (re)produced.

'Political Correctness' and the Function of Literary Studies

The academic year in which 'the five' were hired was the academic year in which a backlash against curricular restructuring and affirmative-action hiring peaked. Over the following two years, scholars across North America, accustomed to nothing more than amused disregard from the media, would be astonished to find themselves and their work featured in the cover stories of such mass-circulation magazines as *Time*, *The Atlantic*, and *Maclean's*. Significantly, much of the U.S. American commentary focused on curricular and hiring policies in the humanities, and especially in departments of literature – areas more typically regarded as 'soft' academic options, far removed from the 'real' world of politics, business, and social policy. In this section I will explore the representation, by conservative intellectuals and journalists, of what has been described as the 'crisis in the humanities' or the new politicization of literary studies. My examples are intended to illustrate neoconservative critiques of canon revision, affirmative-action hiring, and poststructural methodologies.

Of the spate of articles that appeared during the fall and winter of 1990, one of the most reasoned and widely quoted was Berkeley philosopher John Searle's 'The Storm over the University,' a review article originally published in the 6 December 1990 *New York Review of Books*. In that article, Searle describes what has come to be known as the debate over 'the canon' (the generally accepted core of 'great books') – and particularly the highly publicized Stanford University replacement of its required course in Western civilization with a more culturally diverse course called 'Culture, Ideas, Values' (CIV) – as paradigmatic of the increasingly public debate over political correctness. He fairly accurately summarizes the arguments of what he calls 'the cultural left' against simply *supplementing* the canon with texts by women, non-Europeans, and so forth, and notes their call for abolishment of the very idea of 'the canon.' However, like D'Souza and Kimball, Searle expresses dismay at what he sees as a new politicization of the humanities, and especially of literary studies. His dismay seems at times disingenuous, as when he claims he has 'not heard any complaints from physics departments that the ideas of Newton, Einstein ... etc., were deficient because of the scientists' origins or gender' (97),[3] without at the same time noting the real paucity of, for example, women students and professors in that discipline and without speculating about the reasons for that paucity. At other times, his dismay seems real. He notes that 'many members of the cultural left think that the primary function of teaching the humanities is political; they do not really believe that the humanities are valuable in their own except as a means of achieving "social transformation" ' (97). He targets literary studies even more specifically:

> For reasons I do not fully understand, many professors of literature no longer care about literature in the ways that seemed satisfactory to earlier generations. It seems pointless to many of them to teach literature as it was understood by such very different critics as Edmund Wilson, John Crowe Ransom, or I.A. Richards; so they teach it as a means of achieving left-wing political goals or as an occasion for exercises in deconstruction, etc. The absence of an accepted educational mission in many literary studies has created a vacuum waiting to be filled. Perhaps the original mistake was in supposing that there is a well-defined academic discipline of 'literary criticism.' (105–6)

Yet Searle's gesture toward 'earlier generations' of professors of literature is incomplete (indeed, it is limited to those professors whose methods enjoyed especial prominence during the years of Searle's own undergraduate education in the 1950s) and displays an ignorance – albeit an unsurprising one – of the origins and history of English studies. This ignorance is unsurprising not only because Searle is a philosopher and not a literary historian, but because so many professors of literature are themselves unaware of the history of their discipline. As Chris Baldick notes, 'it would seem that the study of English Literature is accepted by most of its practitioners as a "natural" activity without an identifiable historical genesis' (3). However, and as literary historians like Baldick, D.J. Palmer, Gauri Viswanathan, and Brian Doyle have pointed out, from its inception in the Mechanics Institutes of mid-nineteenth-century England to its adoption by the universities in the later-nineteenth and early-twentieth centuries, English studies was *never* intended to function as a disinterested, scientific discipline. On the contrary, it has always had a *productive* function; that is, it was intended to produce appropriate tastes, values, and behaviours. With roots in the movement for mass literacy, English studies was fostered first by the Evangelicals (concerned that every man should be able to read the Bible and attend to his salvation) and by such social reformers as F.D. Maurice, Charles Kingsley, and the Utilitarians (concerned that class and gender unrest brought about by industrial change not culminate in revolutionary violence), and finally by the imperial government (concerned to 'civilize' both its colonial subjects abroad and their English administrators). English studies was not in the first instance addressed to middle- and upper-class men who, well into the twentieth century, still received a primarily classical education, but rather to working men, women, and colonial subjects.[4] It has always had, contrary to Searle's claims, two very well-defined 'educational missions'; that is, English studies has always been caught in a tug-of-war between those interested in furthering (to use Searle's phrase) 'social transformation' and those committed to preserving 'the best that has been thought and said.'[5]

It is only by ignoring the complicated history of English studies in its various national and colonial locations that neoconservative critics can regard the unsettling of the canon, together with the development of poststructural methodologies, as evidence of a *new* 'politicization' of the discipline. This is especially obvious when one considers the more recent history of English studies, particularly the degree to which – since the first quarter of this century – 'English' has been installed as the core element of a homogeneous national (or provincial, or state) curriculum aimed at producing 'properly balanced citizens' (Doyle 1982, 27). The entrenchment of 'English' at the centre of primary and secondary schooling must be seen within the context of such overtly social and political programs as the development of national cultural identity through common systems of education (or the development of 'a common culture rooted in the highest ideals and aspirations of the Western tradition' [Kimball 1991, 59]); the promotion and dissemination of a 'standard' English (Guillory 1990, 240–2); and, through training in reflection, linguistic competence, and recognized cultural values, the development of an administrative élite. In other words, and as historians and theorists of English studies have pointed out, the project of preserving and passing on 'the best that has been thought and said,' is itself hugely political; as Gayatri Spivak argues, 'the matter of the literary canon is in fact a political matter: securing authority' (Spivak 1990, 785). Since, in Spivak's words, 'English is the medium and the message through which, in education, Americans [or Canadians] are most intimately made' (784), the centrality of literary studies in the debate over political correctness is unsurprising.

It is also unsurprising that new critical methodologies that undermine the status of classed or hierarchized culture – by, for example, demanding that the English studies canon be opened up to 'other' cultural interests or abandoned altogether – are targeted as egregious examples of the dangerous excesses of 'the cultural left.' Here I will focus on some of the issues raised by Dinesh D'Souza (a former policy adviser in the Reagan government) in his 1991 book, *Illiberal Education: The Politics of Race and Sex on Campus*. Of particular interest is his discussion of the effects of new hiring policies in the English department at Duke University in Durham, North Carolina.[6] D'Souza notes that in the mid- to later 1980s senior administrators at Duke University made 'two controversial decisions' regarding hiring policy: the first was 'to recruit a new group of scholars to make Duke a frontier for a "new scholarship" in the humanities,' while the second was to require 'every department and program to hire at least one new black by 1993 or face administrative penalties' (157–8). According to D'Souza, 'these two ambitious hiring programs seem unrelated, but in fact there is an underlying unity: both offer a powerful challenge to the notion of standards of merit, on the level of both faculty eligibility and course content' (158). In other words, just as the 'new scholarship' in the humanities refuses to recognize a hierarchy of great books based on inherent literary value and universal truth claims, so affirmative-action hiring policies in the university refuse to acknowledge a hierarchy of ability or achievement.

Is the danger, then, that books of little literary value will be studied in Duke University classrooms staffed by inferior professors, that is, by professors who do not meet the normal standards of academic merit (original research, publication in refereed journals, etc.)? Not exactly. As D'Souza admits, Duke's new humanities (and especially English department) scholars are widely published and enormously influential academic 'superstars,' some of whom – like the African-American literary critic Henry Louis Gates, Jr – are less interested in abolishing 'the canon' than in establishing alternative canons of important but heretofore overlooked literary texts by women and African-Americans. Moreover, D'Souza acknowledges that what he describes as the 'dearth of blacks with doctorates' (167–8) does not mean that departments at Duke University will be hiring unqualified professors but rather that they will be unable to meet their affirmative-action quota. Supporters of the affirmative-action hiring policy nonetheless justify it on the grounds that it raises social awareness regarding institutional racism and puts pressure on the university to meliorate the situation by, for example, instituting graduate scholarships earmarked for particular minority groups.

If most English professors at Duke University more than meet the usual criteria of academic merit, and if many of them still teach 'great' writers like William Shakespeare and Jane Austen, in what way are standards undermined by the new hiring policies? D'Souza suggests that standards are undermined in two ways: non-canonical, even mass-market, texts may be discussed in the classroom (feminist professor Janice Radway, for example, 'applies literary and anthropological techniques ... to study the reasons why women read romance novels' [162]); and, more important, the very notion of merit or value is thrown into doubt by the new scholarship in literary studies. D'Souza's summary of new approaches to literary criticism and theory is less informed than that of other participants in the debate over political correctness and higher education; nonetheless, his conclusions about the *effects* of these approaches are shared by many neoconservatives. He isolates seven 'critical schools' which he describes as 'based on the denial of textual meaning': formalism, hermeneutics, psychoanalytic theory, semiotics, structuralism, Marxism, 'deconstructionism' (177). Of these approaches, only the last could accurately be described as 'new,' that is, post-1968; the others date from the first half of this century, although their roots are in late-nineteenth and very-early-twentieth-century thinkers (de Saussure, Marx, Freud, Jacobson).

Certainly deconstruction has been the most controversial of the new literary theories, particularly since the Paul de Man 'scandal' emerged late in 1987.[7] In many ways, the de Man scandal shaped the terms of the political correctness debate of 1990 by bringing new literary theories to the awareness of a broader reading public. The *New York Times* was particularly active in reporting and following up on this issue. A 17 July 1988 article called 'Decoding Deconstruction' is typical in terms of its tone and premises. It begins: 'Since it is an article of deconstructionist faith that a text has no fixed, single meaning, it probably shouldn't be surprising that books and articles written by deconstructionists are all but impossible for most other people to comprehend' (Johnson 1988, E6). The idea that a text has no fixed, single meaning – that meaning is socially as well as formally constructed, and that it is informed by historical and material contingencies – is seized upon by D'Souza and other neoconservative participants in the political correctness debate as particularly pernicious. D'Souza alludes to 'the prospect of interpretive nihilism' (175) and the dangers of 'radical skepticism' (191), and suggests that those whom he repeatedly describes as the '*au courant*' critics have abandoned their students to philosophical and moral *anomie* – 'listlessness, boredom, and a dulling of the critical faculties' (190).

I will leave aside what would have to be a lengthy critique of D'Souza's understanding of the terms and implications of new literary theories like deconstruction to focus instead on what he describes as the possible social consequences of the new scholarship. D'Souza concedes that

> strange and abstruse literary and philosophical movements have gained the allegiance of large segments of the intelligentsia in the past, and in this respect the current deconstructionist fad is not very different from Cambridge Neo-Platonism or late medieval Averroism; indeed *au courant* esotericism bears a clear resemblance to rigorous scholastic disputations about the number of angels who can dance on the head of a pin. (182)

If, as D'Souza suggests, the new scholarship in the humanities has created a 'meaningless' and 'professionalized jargon' (181), impenetrable to all but devotees, if current debates in the humanities are inherently inconsequential and even slightly ridiculous, why do he and other neoconservative critics feel so passionately about the changes that are taking place in English departments in North America? The answer – as one would expect, given the history of English studies – is that changes in the humanities represent only the thin end of the wedge. 'The implications,' according to D'Souza, 'go beyond the field of literature' (179). By privileging the second term of binary codes that have organized Western philosophy and culture since Plato (e.g., man/woman, speaking/writing, high/low culture), methodologies like deconstruction undermine the status of classed culture. By calling universal truth claims into question – that is, by suggesting that 'meaning' is socially constructed and that 'truth' is inflected by relations of power – the new scholarship in the humanities 'releases relativist and nihilist forces that culminate in coercive ideologies' (190). By aligning itself with what D'Souza calls the 'victim's revolution,' by which he means 'a revolution on behalf of minority victims' whose 'mission is ... to advance the interests of the previously disenfranchised' (13), the new scholarship in the humanities undermines 'the basic systems of American society ... such as democracy, the free market, due process, and so on' (185–6).

These are weighty charges. How have U.S. American literary scholars responded? Some have suggested that the real effect of humanities courses on undergraduate students is minimal in comparison with that of the media culture: 'Madonna has done more to affect the way young people think about sexuality than all the academic gender theorists put together. Perhaps D'Souza should write a book about her' (Menand 1991: 49). University of California (Berkeley) English professor Stephen Greenblatt has pointed out that the vitriol of the political correctness debate has two sources: 'the sheer nastiness of Washington politics' (in reference to neoconservative Lynne Cheney's chairing of the National Endowment for the Humanities), and a broad national anxiety that feminism and multiculturalism represent 'a clear and present danger to our culture' (Greenblatt 1992, 39, 40). He argues that members of the profession must attend to this anxiety by 'explaining to the public what we think we are doing' (40). Duke University English professor Cathy N. Davidson points to parallels between 'attacks on the "leftism" of the academy circa 1951 and 1991' and argues that higher education is being scapegoated 'because it is much cheaper to condemn colleges and universities than to restructure primary and secondary school ... When virtually every state faces huge deficits, blaming the universities can also conveniently justify a reallocation of funds away from universities' (Davidson 1992, 19). In other words, American literary scholars have responded by situating the debate within the larger structures – political, historical, economic – of U.S. American culture.

What happened when the political correctness debate was imported to Canada? Were the humanities targeted to the same degree as in the United States? Yes and no. It is by now well known that the political correctness debate was popularized in Canada largely through *Maclean's* magazine's 27 May 1991 cover story, 'The Silencers,' which announced that 'A New

Wave of Repression Is Sweeping through the Universities.' However, as Guelph University English professor Michael Keefer has pointed out, 'the evidence that [was] offered of a "wave of repression" seems strangely thin' and 'amounts, in fact, to four distinct incidents': the harassment of anthropologist Jeanne Cannizzo, the curator of the Royal Ontario Museum 1989–90 exhibit, 'Into the Heart of Africa,' and a lecturer at the University of Toronto; calls for the dismissal of University of Western Ontario psychologist Philippe Rushton for his research on the links between race and intelligence; feminist criticism of Shakespeare's racism and sexism at a March 1991 Vancouver conference; and feminist protest of the reproduction of Alex Colville's painting, *Western Star*, in Acadia University's calendar (Keefer 1991, 7). While American commentators focused primarily on what they saw as the excesses of race politics and 'leftist' culture in the university, reflected in changes to the humanities canon, Canadian media coverage was much more diffuse.

Nonetheless, some patterns emerge. First, and as Thelma McCormack, director of York University's Graduate Program in Women's Studies, implies in an article in the September 1991 *Canadian Forum*, feminist scholarship and women's studies programs were singled out for particular attention in Canadian media coverage. *Maclean's*, for example, noted that 'much of the pressure for change on campus is coming from women' and that 'feminist studies now are among the fastest-growing areas of research and study on curricula' (Fennell 1991, 42). This is not to say that feminist research and women's studies programs are passed over without comment by U.S. American neoconservatives,[8] or that Canadian feminists have been more successful at bringing their projects to public attention, or that questions of race are not foundational to the political climate of Canadian universities. However, it is important to note that in the Canadian media and universities the question of race has been a question of institutional racism, raised by members of racially disadvantaged groups (as in the case of Jeanne Cannizzo and the Royal Ontario Museum exhibit), or by liberals and 'cultural leftists' concerned about racist research (as in the case of Philippe Rushton), but *not*, as in the United States, by neoconservatives alarmed that 'race' has become a foundational category in terms of hiring policies and curricular reform. Second, although the ways in which local – that is, Canadian – conditions inflect the political correctness debate are alluded to in articles like *Maclean's* 'The Silencers' (which briefly notes the significance of federal and provincial employment equity legislation), there has been little analysis of the specificities of the debate in Canadian higher education. This is especially problematic given the importance of, for example, the Federal Contractors Program whose compliance reviews of various Canadian universities have been directly responsible for the creation of university equity policies and employment-equity work plans. Finally, although the humanities have been targeted to a lesser degree in Canadian media coverage, many of the assumptions, strategies, and rhetorical terms of U.S. American neo-conservative commentators were imported wholesale into the political correctness debate on Canadian campuses. When, as Keefer points out, so few incidents were circulated and recirculated as proof of a political correctness 'movement' in Canada, one must ask why the controversy excited such fierce attention here. In whose interests were the terms (if not the conditions) of this debate imported into Canadian universities and how did they circulate? The remainder of this chapter will trace one local skirmish in the war of words that was the political correctness debate.

'Political Correctness' and the Equity Debate at the University of Alberta

It is important to locate the controversy prompted by the 1989 hiring of 'the five' by the Department of English at the University of Alberta within the context not only of the political correctness debate in the United States and Canada, but within the context of an already simmering equity debate at the University and particularly within the Faculty of Arts. That is, the appointment of five women assistant professors was used by anti-equity organizers as a means of focusing attention on what amounted to an anti-equity (or, as its proponents preferred to call it, 'merit only') campaign.

Although it did not achieve full momentum until fall 1989 (see Taylor and Byfield 1989), this campaign was mobilized in response to a June 1987 revision to the 'Employment Policies' section (section 48) of the University of Alberta's *General Faculties Council [GFC] Policy Manual.* Among other changes, the revision modified the wording of one of the university's 'Basic Principles' from a commitment to 'equal opportunity in employment' to 'equity in employment'; it also committed the university to 'the amelioration of conditions of disadvantaged individuals or groups within the system.' The first principle remained a commitment to appointment 'on the basis of merit.' Anti-equity proponents argued that a commitment to equity and to eliminating systemic discrimination contradicted the university's commitment to merit. Consequently, one of the forms the equity debate at the University of Alberta assumed was essentially hermeneutic and focused on the correct interpretation of GFC policy. However, it is important to note that the changes to the *GFC Policy Manual* reflected the language and spirit of the 1986 federal Employment Equity Act, whose purpose is 'to correct the conditions of disadvantage in employment experienced by women, aboriginal peoples, persons with disabilities, and persons who are, because of their race or colour, in a visible minority in Canada by giving effect to the principle that *employment equity means more than treating persons in the same way but also requires special measures and the accommodation of differences*' (my emphasis). Significantly, anti-equity proponents did not allude to the fact of federal legislation but instead implied that the university had acted capriciously and in response to (to use D'Souza's phrase) 'au courant' or merely fashionable ideological pressures. Thus, in a letter in the university's staff newspaper, Hugh Wilson of the department of History asked 'upon whose authority has this assertion of commitment to a new principle been made?' and suggested that 'an adviser on equity is necessary to keep the President abreast of developments on the liberated front [because] like the Dow Jones average, what is equitable changes from day to day' (Wilson 1988). D.F. Mulcahy of the Faculty of Dentistry similarly suggested that equity policies were a 'deviation from a democratically structured employment process' and that equity proponents had 'fallen victim to that highly prevalent, divisive condition which could be described as minoritygroupitis' (Mulcahy 1989).

Anti-equity proponents ignored not only the existence of federal employment equity legislation but also its targeting of what it terms four 'designated groups.' That is, although much of the U.S. American political correctness debate focused on race and 'cultural leftism' in its discussion of affirmative-action hiring, the anti-equity campaign at the University of Alberta – reflecting trends in Canada – focused almost exclusively on gender, in spite of the fact that federal legislation (and subsequent employment- and educational-equity policy in the Faculty of Arts) identifies four disadvantaged groups: women, visible minorities, native peoples, and people with disabilities. The anti-equity campaign's focus on gender also accounts for the fact that, although pro- and anti-equity proponents had been engaged in public discussion since the fall of 1988, the campaign gained momentum only with the English Department's appointment of five women in a single hiring year. Again, it must be emphasized that it is not so much women's increased presence within the professoriate that accounts for this attention from anti-equity proponents,[9] but the even greater absence of the other three groups (particularly in the humanities) and the subsequent paucity – in Canada – of sustained analyses of systemic discrimination from their point of view.

The anti-equity campaign took a number of forms that included: a prolonged and heated exchange of letters to the editor in *Folio*, the university staff newspaper, between November 1989 and January 1990; the submission of briefs to the President's Commission for Equality and Respect on Campus in March and April 1990; the circulation of a petition in March and April 1991 to 'uphold University hiring regulations'; and the distribution of factional newsletters between February and May 1992. Anti-equity organizers mounted their campaign on the basis of four strategies: an appeal to statistical probability; an appeal to university employment policies as legislated in the *GFC Policy Manual*; an appeal to individual rights together with a criticism of 'group rights'; and a targeting of what they termed 'fashionable ideologies.' Although, as I have discussed above, the equity debate at the University of Alberta can be traced at least as far back as the reaction that followed 1987 changes to GFC policy, it entered a new and more vitriolic phase following a 19 October 1989 *Folio* article about a panel, sponsored by the Academic Women's Association (AWA), on the university's hiring and recruitment policies. Former English Department chair Linda Woodbridge spoke on that panel, and her comments were summarized as follows:

> Relating her recruitment experiences to AWA members, Dr. Woodbridge said it is possible to increase the numbers of women on staff. For example, of the five English Department tenurable positions open last year, five were filled by women, she outlined, adding that the male department members were extremely supportive of efforts to increase the numbers of female department staff members. ('AWA wants ...' 1989, 3)

The 2 November issue of *Folio* contained a letter signed by five anti-equity proponents who responded to Woodbridge's reported comments as follows:

> Even more disturbing to us was the report of what Dr. Linda Woodbridge, former Chair of the Department of English, told the AWA meeting: that her department increased its representation of women by filling each of five openings last year with female candidates. This statement appears to be an admission of a deliberate violation of the GFC hiring policy. We urge President Davenport to follow up his statement of principle by instructing departments that such violations will not be tolerated. (Christensen et al. 1989, 3)

A wave of letters from Department of English members protesting this representation both of the department's hiring practices and its new colleagues appeared in *Folio* over the following weeks. Then-current chair, Maurice Legris (1989), detailed the department's rigorous screening and selection procedures and emphasized that 'merit, only merit' was the criterion for selection of 'the five.' Woodbridge pointed out that 'the efforts made by the department were *recruiting* efforts ... which increased the number of female applicants from about a third of the total in 1988 to about half in 1989. The efforts did *not* include giving preference to female candidates' (Woodbridge 1989a, 4). In their defence, the five signatories to the 2 November *Folio* letter (members of the self-described 'merit only' group) responded that 'as long as there is any hint of preferential treatment at this University, this unfair suspicion will hang over all women on campus. But it is those who promote preferential treatment, not those of us who oppose it, who must bear the blame for the pain it inevitably produces' (Rochet et al. 1989, 7). It is here, with the assumption of 'preferential' or 'affirmative-action' hiring, that the degree to which the terms of the U.S. American political correctness debate has inflected similar *but not identical* debates on Canadian campuses becomes apparent. Canadian employment-equity legislation, on which the University of Alberta's GFC hiring policy must be based, argues that 'employment equity means more than treating persons in the same way but also requires special measures and the accommodation of differences.' While the aggressive recruitment of members of underrepresented groups is an excellent example of 'special measures,' it nonetheless does not address deeper systemic inequities that influence the constitution of the pool of available applicants. The focus of anti-equity proponents on what they described as the potential for 'a policy of quota employment' (Wilson 1988) effectively blocked discussion of specific ways in which 'special measures and the accommodation of differences' might increase the applicant pool.

In their emphasis on gender and hiring, anti-equity proponents turned to arguments based on statistical probability to suggest the unlikelihood that hiring on the basis of merit would culminate in the appointment of five women. The analogies and metaphors that they produced to illustrate their contentions are revealing. Statistical probability was introduced into the equity debate by economist Tom Powrie in his 30 November 1989 *Folio* letter, which pointed out that 'the odds of getting all girls in a family of five are 1:32.' Powrie continued, 'I suppose the odds of getting all women in the best applicants for five positions in the Department of English are about the same – improbable but not incredible.' Powrie's unfortunate analogy, which borrows from conditions of *re*production to examine the production and hiring of professors in an intellectual workplace, suggests that working conditions unfold naturally and that social intervention is inappropriate. Even less fortunate, however, was the 'pink marbles and blue marbles' metaphor introduced into the equity debate when, in February 1992, the 'merit only' group reorganized as the Association of Concerned Academics[10] and issued their first newsletter. In it economist Terry Elrod offered statistical evidence that preferential hiring was already practised at the University of Alberta; hiring data revealed, he noted, that between 1988 and 1990 'women accounted for 19% of the applicants but received 31% of the jobs.' He suggested 'a statistical test for gender-neutrality [in hiring] based on the following metaphor':

> Imagine a huge bin containing 2483 marbles identical except for color – 2019 (or 81%) of them blue and 464 (or 19%) of them pink (representing the male and female applicants, respectively). And imagine blind-folded faculty members reaching in and removing 170 marbles at random (representing the appointees). One would expect to get 32 pink marbles (19% of 170) on average, but the number will usually depart from 32 by chance. A test for gender neutrality must take into account the possibility that as many as 53 pink marbles were chosen out of 170 just by chance. My calculations (using the hypergeometric distribution) show that the probability of selecting 53 or more pink marbles from the bin is less than 1 in 30,000. A probability of less than 1 in 40 is conventionally regarded as *prima facie* evidence of discrimination. (Elrod 1992, 2–3)

Elrod's 'pink marbles and blue marbles' argument attracted comment. University of Alberta president Paul Davenport, for example, noted that 'your analysis runs into trouble with the metaphor of marbles in a bin which differ only in color.' Drawing on eighteen years of experience on university search and hiring committees for appointments in Economics, he argued that 'it was not uncommon to receive applications ... from people who were ... clearly unqualified'; moreover, 'these clearly unqualified candidates are not, in my experience, randomly distributed among the blue and pink marbles: they are overwhelmingly male.' An anonymously circulated, satirical, pro-equity newsletter (*The Asteroid: Newsletter of the Very Concerned {and Busy} Academics at U of A)*, citing the effects of another reduction of provincial financing to Alberta universities, noted that Elrod's 'conclusion [was] that there would have been far too many women hired, had the positions not been frozen and then axed completely' ('Far Too Many ...' 1992, 1).

Although the anti-equity campaign's claims that preferential hiring was already taking place in the Department of English and elsewhere at the University of Alberta were refuted, the campaign nonetheless had long-term effects. Its emphasis on hiring (like its single-minded emphasis on gender), and its concomitant appeal to statistical probability, deflected attention from an examination of deeper systemic inequities at the level of both employment *and* educational equity. As Doris Badir, then special assistant to the president on equity matters, pointed out in October 1988, 'If there is difficulty in finding persons sufficiently meritorious for our standards within the current "pool of eligibles of disadvantaged persons" then it is the University's responsibility to develop persons from those groups to an appropriate level of merit.' Broad and constructive discussion of ways in which the university could provide leadership in the area of educational development did not take place, largely because the terms of the public debate were determined by a small but highly vocal group of anti-equity organizers.

Conclusion

It is ironic that the anti-equity campaign at the University of Alberta – which, for a period of months, was waged over the reputations and careers of five junior women professors – was also frequently waged *in the name of* women. This is especially ironic given that the five women who were at the centre of this controversy felt effectively silenced by the terms of the debate. As they argued in their submission to the President's Commission for Equality and Respect on Campus, 'any responses to the "charge" of preferential treatment in our hirings is doomed to a failure which will be, despite the support and advice of enlightened people in the academic community, borne primarily by the five of us' (Chisholm et al. 1990). The anti-equity claim that 'as long as there is any hint of preferential treatment at this University, this unfair suspicion will hang over all women on campus' was, in spite of its ostensible gallantry, a clear attempt to regulate the terms of public discussion on equity issues.

In terms reminiscent of (though by no means identical to) the 1928 'Persons Case,' anti-equity proponents at the University of Alberta attempted to lay moral claim to a self-evident and unproblematic concept of 'merit.' Arguing from what could be described as a position of radical liberalism, they maintained that justice could only be served by judging candidates as completely discrete or solitary individuals outside of social formations or historical contexts. Thus economist Tom Powrie argued, in terms that slight members of one of the four target groups, that 'we should treat people as individuals, not as representatives of tribes' (Powrie 1991). Richard d'Alquen of the Department of Germanic Languages maintained that 'those who ... defend selective discrimination often claim that, while certain people will suffer, they want to correct a historical injustice. There are serious problems in judging the conditions of yesteryear with the morality of the present, but, beyond that, this argument merely compounds the illogicality by adding a historical dimension' (d'Alquen 1991). Certainly the 'illogicality' of the 'historical dimension' is not lost on women and other target group members. The assumption that members of the four target groups will naturally and inevitably assume their earned positions in the university, as long as the university steers clear of 'social engineering' (Powrie 1991), pales beside the realization that in the decade from 1977 to 1987 – a period that, if we assume ten years between beginning a bachelor's degree and completing a doctorate, comprises an entire academic generation – the percentage of tenured or tenurable women at the University of Alberta increased from only 12 to only 16 per cent. And women, because their numbers cross all four target groups and because some come from privileged backgrounds, are arguably less disadvantaged within the university than, for example, native peoples whose representation in the professoriate across Canada remains less than 1 per cent.

In hindsight, it seems clear that equity proponents at the University of Alberta erred in not publicly interrogating the 'merit vs. equity' dichotomy utilized by anti-equity organizers. Concerned to protect highly qualified junior colleagues from slander, equity proponents instead repeatedly pointed out that merit was the only criterion used *in this round of hiring*. A more productive approach in the long term – though at the time it appeared riskier – would have been to engage in greater public debate regarding the very concept of 'merit.' Certainly, the grounds for this debate had been cleared by philosopher Roger Shiner in a December 1989 panel discussion on employment equity and academic hiring. Shiner's talk, which was published in the 14 December 1989 issue of *Folio*, distinguished between procedural and substantive inequities in hiring to note that disagreements between anti- and pro-equity organizers were profoundly philosophical differences 'about the nature of justice in the distribution of such goods as jobs' (Shiner 1989, 8). Pointing to the ways in which a discourse of individual rights inflected debates on hiring at the University of Alberta – 'such that not merely does each individual candidate have the right to procedural equity, he or she also has the right to the criterion of merit being the only applicable substantive criterion' (8) – Shiner raised the following questions:

But what is this notion of 'what a university is for'? Does it not amount to a normative theory about the proper social role of the social institution that is a modern university? It is not a matter of person-independent scientific fact that a university is a certain kind of thing. Clearly, some notion of expertise in a field is central to the business of university education. But it is a step from that uncontroversial assumption to the idea that merit can be the only relevant criterion for academic hiring, and the step needs arguing for; it is not a self-evident truth. (8)

In a 1991 article on the effects of anti-feminist backlash in North American universities, former English Department chair Linda Woodbridge reflected on anti-equity organizers' responses to the hiring of 'the five,' and particularly on the ways in which they deployed 'merit' as if it is a neutral criterion:

Throughout this whole sordid business, three words kept sounding: 'merit,' 'excellence,' and 'ideology.' We want to hire only on the basis of merit and excellence, not of ideology: when men are hired it's merit and excellence; when women are hired it's ideology. The terms were identical to those of the attack on Women's Studies: the traditional way of hiring professors or canonizing writers was solely on the basis of merit; the feminist way of hiring professors or admitting writers to the canon is solely on the basis of ideology. Merit good, ideology bad. Me Tarzan, you Jane. (Woodbridge 1991, 288)

Unfortunately, however, *sustained* public debate regarding the ways in which merit is socially constructed – varying by time and place, affected by market demand (are the universities hiring?) and by supply (are we, e.g., producing more postcolonial literary critics than medieval literary critics?) – did not take place at the University of Alberta. The consequences of this lack are already obvious. On 19 February 1993 the university, in compliance with the Federal Contractors Program, released *Opening Doors: A Plan for Employment Equity at the University of Alberta*. The preamble to this document reaffirms the university's 'commitment to hiring on merit,' again without defining what 'merit' might mean. Does 'merit' mean that appointees should all have a doctorate? If so, many instructors in the Faculty of Law or in the Department of Drama should not have been hired. Does 'merit' mean that appointees must have a minimum number of publications at the time of appointment? If so, many instructors hired in the late 1960s and early 1970s should not have been hired. Clearly, the concept of 'merit' only makes sense within specific historical, material, and social contexts; it is not a self-evident and neutral standard.

The university, an institution that is in many ways uniquely qualified to produce its own workforce, has failed to produce a representative number of intellectual workers from the four target groups of federal legislation. This suggests three possibilities: that members of the four target groups are not 'fit and qualified' for intellectual work across the disciplines; that it is not the task of the university to ameliorate social injustice; or that the university is not equally hospitable to the knowledge claims, intellectual desires, or material needs of target group members. Unsurprisingly, the first possibility has not been taken up in the equity debate. The second possibility was argued by Tom Powrie in a 1991 *Folio* letter: 'Shouldn't we stick to teaching and research? They are difficult, and important, and they are what we do best. Social policy is the responsibility of the elected government.' Once again the effect of the U.S. American political correctness controversy on equity debate within Canadian universities is apparent. In Canada, the universities have not been leaders in the area of social reform; they have been dragged in the wake of federal legislation and have, in many cases, lagged behind private industry in terms of preparing and implementing equity work plans. The third possibility – that the university is not equally hospitable to the knowledge claims, intellectual desires, or material needs of members of the four target groups – has received insufficient attention in a debate that has been skewed to emphasize gender and hiring, and it is here that progressive intellectuals should be intervening in equity discussions.

Where do we go from here? I want to suggest that we 'go public.' The way in which the U.S. American political correctness debate was imported holus-bolus by the Canadian media, together with the ways in which anti-equity campaigners have been able to define and control the terms of equity debate, suggest that progressive academics (and particularly in the humanities) have not done a good enough job in bringing our skills to bear on these issues. We have allowed ourselves to be locked into defensive positions, responding to accusations rather than helping to shape the terms and consequences of debate. It is clear that the university in Canada is in many ways a profoundly conservative institution and that the humanities, far from undermining (as D'Souza suggests) democratic systems, have been almost totally ineffective in bringing 'new scholarship' to bear on social issues. As English and literary studies professors, our own disciplinary history in the university teaches us that we have a public responsibility to bring these debates into broader forums than the pages of our own professional journals. We cannot afford to wait for the debates to be brought to us.

Notes

I am grateful to my research assistant, Danuta Woronowicz, for her hard work in various university archives, to Professors Bridget Elliott and Susan Hamilton for making their files available to me, and to Garry Watson, Stephen Slemon, Janice Williamson, Steve Richer, Lorna Weir, and 'the five' for their comments on an earlier draft of this paper. I am also grateful to 'the five' for their permission to reopen this painful early chapter of their highly meritorious careers.

1 The five petitioners were Emily Murphy (1868–1933), Nellie McClung (1874–1951), Louise McKinney (1868–1933), Irene Parlby (1878–1965), and Henrietta Edwards (1849–1933). The five appointees – who all agreed to be named in this chapter – are Dianne Chisholm, a specialist in modernist and contemporary avant-garde poetry; Susan Hamilton, a specialist in Victorian prose; Robin McGrath, a specialist in native and especially Inuit writing; Daphne Read, a specialist in contemporary women's writing; and Glennis Stephenson, a specialist in Victorian poetry. In 1993 Robin McGrath resigned from the University of Alberta and Glennis Stephenson accepted a three-year position at the University of Stirling.

2 The University of Alberta was not unique in this regard; see Orland French's 'Sex Wars Still Rage on Campus' (*Globe and Mail*, 1989, D1, D2) and Susan Donaldson and Will Kymlicka's 'No Thaw in Chilly Campus Climate' (*Globe and Mail*, 1989, A8), which document a series of events triggered by anti-feminist backlash at universities across Canada. For a slightly different perspective on the events of 1989 to 1991 at the University of Alberta, see former chair Linda Woodbridge's 'Poetics from the Barrel of a Gun?' (Woodbridge 1991).

3 D'Souza would not agree with Searle's disclaimer that the 'hard sciences' have been exempted from the effects of the 'political correctness' movement. According to D'Souza, 'For the first time, undergraduate and graduate professors in physics, chemistry, and biology are accused by minority activists of practising "white male science" and operating "institutionally racist" departments. While many continue to resist pressures for preferential minority hiring and the inclusion of minority and especially female "perspectives" in the hard sciences, they seem bewildered about, and mute in responding to, accusations of systematic and methodological racism and sexism; consequently, with administrative and activist pressure, the victim's revolution is

beginning its siege of the final bastion of "pure scholarship" ' (D'Souza 1991, 18–19).

4 As Baldick argues, 'three particular factors ... ensured literary study, in particular of English literature, a permanent place in higher education. These are first, the specific needs of the British empire expressed in the regulations for admission to the India Civil Service; second, the various movements for adult education including Mechanics Institutes, Working Men's Colleges, and extension lecturing; third, within this general movement, the specific provisions made for women's education' (Baldick 1983, 61).

5 This is Matthew Arnold's famous term, originally used to further a different argument than the one I am making here. Moreover, in characterizing the history of English studies as the enactment of a crudely binary ideological tug-of-war, I am, of course, simplifying. For a more sustained analysis of the development of English studies – and particularly the place of theory – in Canada, see Heather Murray's 'Resistance and Reception: Backgrounds to Theory in English Canada,' which usefully points out that 'a history of duelling paradigms ... cannot account for materials and points of view that are excluded from the series of debates' (Murray 1990, 52). See also Murray (1991) for a guide to resources on the history of English studies in Canada. In a December 1991 article in *Harper's* magazine, Louis Menand, who teaches English at Queen's College and the Graduate Center of the City University of New York, argues that contemporary English studies programs in the United States have been typically expected to fulfil *three* educational functions – 'scholarly, vocational, and liberalizing' – which he also describes as 'pure speculation, practical application, and general enlightenment' (51). He points out, however, that three developments in contemporary U.S. American society – an increase in the proportion of university students who are not male or white, the spread of contemporary and especially poststructuralist critical theory in the humanities, and the increasing demand for professional degrees – 'have undermined this consensus' (51–2).

6 Much of the Duke University chapter of *Illiberal Education* – 'The Last Shall Be First: Subverting Academic Standards at Duke' – was excerpted in the March 1991 *Atlantic Monthly* shortly before the book was published; consequently, this is the chapter and series of arguments that have circulated most widely.

7 In December 1987 the *New York Times* revealed that the late Paul de Man, a leader of U.S. American deconstruction at Yale University, had published anti-Semitic articles for a Belgian pro-Nazi newspaper in 1941–2. The ensuing controversy focused on the politics of deconstruction and marked an early stage of the political correctness debate.

8 As Susan Faludi notes in *Backlash: The Undeclared War against American*

Women, Allan Bloom's 1987 best-seller, *The Closing of the American Mind* – a flagship text of the neoconservative targeting of political correctness – 'dedicates page after page to an assault on the women's movement' (Faludi 1991, 290).

9 As Linda Woodbridge noted in a 7 December 1989 letter to *Folio,* the percentage of tenured/tenurable female professors at the University of Alberta between 1977 (when the University's *Senate Task Force Report on the Status of Women* published its findings) and 1987 (when the task force published its *Progress Review*) rose from only 12 to only 16 per cent.

10 The new name is reminiscent of the U.S. American 'National Association of Scholars,' which D'Souza describes as 'a small group of faculty crusaders ... launching a bold but somewhat quixotic effort to arrest the pace of the [victim's] revolution' (D'Souza 1991, 18).

References

Allemang, John. 1991. 'The New Puritanism.' *Globe and Mail.* (2 Feb.): D1, D4

'AWA Wants University to Be More Aggressive in Hiring Women.' 1989. *Folio* (19 Oct.): 3

Badir, Doris. 1988. ' "Equity in Employment" Intended to Remove Roadblocks, Take Initiatives.' *Folio,* (6 Oct.): 3

Baldick, Chris. 1983. *The Social Mission of English Criticism 1848–1932.* Oxford: Clarendon Press

Berman, Paul, ed. 1992. *Debating P.C.: The Controversy over Political Correctness on College Campuses.* New York: Laurel

Bhardwaj, Ajay. 1990. 'Skit Night Laughter Simply Isn't Funny.' *The Gateway* (18 Jan.): 4

Boehm, Bob. 1989. 'Woman Student a Target for Crude Engineers' and 'Newspaper's False Claims Humiliated Female Student.' *Edmonton Journal* (27 Nov.): A1, B3

Cernetig, Miro. 1990. 'University's Ivory-Tower Image Darkened by Sexual Harassment.' *Globe and Mail* (25 April): A1, A8

Chisholm, Dianne, Susan Hamilton, Robin McGrath, Daphne Read, and Glennis Stephenson. 1990. 'Brief to the President's Commission for Equality and Respect on Campus.'

Christensen, F.M., G.K. Hunter, G. Faulkner, B. Rochet, and A. Putnam Rochet. 1989. 'Hiring on Merit Only in University's Best Interest.' *Folio* (2 Nov.): 3

'Commission to Examine Sexism on Campus; Engineering Students Come Up with Reforms.' *Folio* (1 Feb.): 1, 3

Correli, Rae. 1991. 'Saying "No" to the Old Ways.' *Maclean's* (27 May): 48–50
d'Alquen, Richard. 1991. 'Of "the Nefarious Concept of Group".' *Folio* (20 Sept.): 2
Davenport, Paul. 1992. 'Comment' [response to Elrod]. *Academic Concerns: A Newsletter from the Association of Concerned Academics* 1(3) (May): 4
Davidson, Cathy N. 1992. ' "PH" Stands for Political Hypocrisy.' *CAUT Bulletin ACPU* (April): 18-19. Originally published in the Sept./Oct. 1991 issue of *Academe*
Donaldson, Susan, and Will Kymlicka, 1989. 'No Thaw in Chilly Campus Climate.' *Globe and Mail* (17 Nov.): A8
Doyle, Brian. 1982. 'The Hidden History of English Studies.' In Peter Widdowson, ed., *Re-Reading English.* London and New York: Methuen
– 1989. *English & Englishness.* London and New York: Routledge
D'Souza, Dinesh. 1991. 'Illiberal Education.' *The Atlantic* 267(3) (March): 51–8, 62–5, 67, 70–4, 76, 78–9
– 1991, 1992. *Illiberal Education: The Politics of Race and Sex on Campus.* New York: Vintage Books
Elrod, Terry. 1992. 'Data on U of A Faculty Hiring Indicate Women Applicants Are Favored 2 to 1 (6 to 1 in Arts).' *Academic Concerns: A Newsletter from the Association of Concerned Academics* 1(1) (9 Feb.): 1–4
Faludi, Susan. 1991. *Backlash: The Undeclared War against American Women.* New York: Anchor Books/Doubleday
'Far Too Many Women in Frozen Positions.' 1992. *The Asteroid: Newsletter of the Very Concerned {and Busy} Academics at U of A* 1(2) (21 March): 1
Fennell, Tom. 1991. 'The Silencers.' *Maclean's.* (27 May): 40–3
French, Orland. 1989. 'Sex Wars Still Rage on Campus.' *Globe and Mail* (11 Nov.): D1, D2
Greenblatt, Stephen. 1992. 'The MLA on Trial.' *Profession 92*: 39–41
Guillory, John. 1990. 'Canon.' In Frank Lentricchia and Thomas McLaughlin, eds., *Critical Terms for Literary Study.* Chicago: University of Chicago Press
Jackson, Rosa. 1990. 'greymatter.' *The Gateway,* (18 Jan.): 9
Johnson, George. 1988. 'Decoding Deconstruction: A Whole New Style of Thinking.' *New York Times* (17 July): E6
Keefer, Michael. 1991. 'Political Correctness.' *Bulletin: The Canadian Federation for the Humanities* 14(2) (Summer): 7–8
Kerr, Doug. 1989. 'Troubled *Bridge* in Hot Water.' *The Gateway* (21 Nov.): 1, 3
Kimball, Roger. 1991. *Tenured Radicals: How Politics Has Corrupted Our Higher Education.* New York: Harper Perennial
Legris, Maurice. 1989. 'Merit Right Down the Line.' *Folio* (16 Nov.): 4
McCormack, Thelma. 1991. 'Politically Correct.' *Canadian Forum* (Sept.): 8–10

Marchildon, Rudy G. 1981. 'The "Persons" Controversy: The Legal Aspects of the Fight for Women Senators.' *Atlantis* 6: 99–113

Menand, Louis. 1991. 'What Are Universities For?' *Harper's* 283 (Dec.): 47–56

Miller, Peter. 1989. 'Findings of a Hearing by the Dean of Students into a Complaint against the Engineering Students' Society and Its Publication *The Bridge*.' December

Mulcahy, D.F. 1989. ' "Minoritygroupitis" Strikes.' *Folio* (2 March): 5

Murray, Heather. 1990. 'Resistance and Reception: Backgrounds to Theory in English-Canada.' *Signature* 4 (Winter): 49–67

– 1991. 'English Studies in Canada to 1945: A Bibliographic Essay.' *English Studies in Canada* 17 (Dec.): 437–68

Opening Doors: A Plan for Employment Equity at the University of Alberta. 1993. 19 Feb.

Palmer, D.J. *The Rise of English Studies*. Toronto: Oxford University Press

Powrie, Tom. 1989. 'Hold to Academic Criteria in Recruiting and Shun Concerns for Statistical Proportions.' *Folio* (30 Nov.): 4

– 1991. 'Teaching and Research, Yes. A Digression into Social Engineering, No.' *Folio* (20 Sept.): 2

Rochet, B., A.P. Rochet, G.K. Hunter, F. Christensen, and G. Faulkner. 1989. 'Department of English Hirings: Faculty Help Clear the Air.' *Folio* (23 Nov.): 7

Schuler, Corinna. 1990. 'Engineering Student Says She Was Forced to Leave City: Classmates, Unwanted Media Coverage Too Much for Woman Who Spoke Out against Sexism.' *Edmonton Journal* (21 Feb.)

Searle, John. 1992. 'The Storm over the University.' In Paul Berman, ed., *Debating P.C.: The Controversy over Political Correctness on College Campuses*, 85–123. New York: Laurel. Originally published in *The New York Review of Books*, 6 Dec. 1990

Shiner, Roger. 1989. 'A Philosophical Look at Employment Practices.' *Folio* (14 Dec.): 7–9

Spivak, Gayatri Chakravorty. 1990. 'The Making of Americans, the Teaching of English, and the Future of Culture Studies.' *New Literary History* 21: 781–98

Taylor, Peter Shawn, and Virginia Byfield. 1989. 'The Women Topped the List.' *Alberta Report* 4 (Dec.): 26–7

Viswanathan, Gauri. 1989. *Masks of Conquest: Literary Study and British Rule in India*. New York: Columbia University Press

Wilson, Hugh. 1988. 'Equality of Opportunity, or "Equity"?' *Folio* (6 Oct.): 3

Woodbridge, Linda. 1989a. 'English Department's Hiring Practices Based on Merit Only.' *Folio* (9 Nov.): 4

– 1989b. 'Former Chair of English Heartened by Colleagues' "high-principled commitment'." *Folio* (7 Dec.): 7

– 1991. 'Afterword: Poetics from the Barrel of a Gun?' In Ivo Kemps, ed., *Shakespeare Left and Right*, 285–98. New York and London: Routledge

PART TWO

Creating Inclusive Pedagogy in Practice

Diversity, Power, and Voice: The Antinomies of Progressive Education

DAIVA K. STASIULIS

Introduction

Since the 1960s, the increased diversity of students entering universities has challenged postsecondary institutions to make curricula, teaching, and staffing more broadly representative of society at large. The move to render more inclusive the curricula of both social sciences and humanities programs, especially of the experiences of oppressed groups, is informed by critical and feminist pedagogy (Giroux 1988, 1992; Luke and Gore 1992; McLaren 1988) and the recent 'haunting' of literary theory and social sciences by postmodernism (Rosenau 1992, 3). University administrators have also been gently prodded, embarrassed, or provoked by student demands, state directives, or incidents of campus-based sexist violence and/or racism to provide a climate of support for such initiatives through the development of institutional policies on sexual harassment, race relations, and employment equity.[1]

At the most general level, progressive (critical and feminist) pedagogy seeks to undermine the 'objectivity' and 'universality' of traditional curriculum or 'the canon,' where these terms have become smoke-screens for the perspectives of privileged, white, European, male authors (Rothenberg 1992, 265; West 1992, 327).[2] In addition to 'democratizing' and increasing the 'inclusiveness' of the curriculum, progressive pedagogy aspires to several other objectives. These include struggling against oppression and 'empowering' students, especially those who have traditionally been excluded or marginalized within schooling[3] (Giroux 1992, 35, 106; Orner 1992, 75), 'examining the comprehensive and interconnected nature of racism, sexism, and class privilege' (Rothenberg 1992, 263), and indeed acknowledging and constructing 'difference that extends beyond the sociological trinity of class, race, gender' (Luke and Gore 1992, 7).

The efforts to produce ever more inclusive forms of knowledge, teaching, and classroom practices, while lauded by many, have also been attacked and ridiculed by critics in the 'political correctness' (PC) debates. For those speaking in defence of what in the American context has been called 'multiculturalism' (an inclusive curriculum that speaks to all forms of diversity – including racial, ethnic, gender, religious, and class differences), there is considerable irony in the self-portrayal by right-wing PC critics as 'defenders of freedom of speech.' Such critics generally represent the constituency of white, male, privileged authors whose writings and teachings have traditionally ignored or silenced the majority in the name of 'universal truths.' However, it is notable that at least within the American context, there have also emerged left critiques of the current educational politics of inclusion. Thus, Barbara Ehrenreich has added a cautionary note to the PC debates in arguing that 'there is a tendency [in multiculturalism] to confuse verbal purification with social change,' and in pointing out how the pluralism inherent in multiculturalism, while 'a big step up from [monocultural education] too often ... leads to the notion of politics as a list' (1992, 335, 337).[4] Edward Said has also decried strategies of building an inclusive curricula by 'simply and obdurately ... reaffirm[ing] the paramount importance of formerly suppressed or silenced forms of knowledge' (1992, 183) or through the 'fetishization and relentless celebration of "difference" and "otherness" ' (1989, 213). In elaborating on the 'woeful insufficiency' of such strategies, he argues that 'the whole effort to deconsecrate Eurocentrism cannot be interpreted ... as an effort to supplant Eurocentrism with, for instance, Afrocentric or Islamocentric approaches. On its own, ethnic particularity does not provide for intellectual process – quite the contrary' (1992, 183).

As the above critiques of 'multiculturalism' suggest, a number of challenges have arisen in the process of fashioning classroom environments, curricula, and practices to reflect a commitment to inclusion, difference, student empowerment, and the awareness of interlocking forms of oppression. This paper examines two such challenges. The first of these stems from the privileging within 'liberatory educational strategies' of 'student voice' and 'experience.' Within progressive pedagogy, the Cartesian dictum 'I think and therefore I am' is inverted by a politics of identity that declares 'I am and therefore I know.'[5]

A significant challenge faced by the educator in responding to the calls for student voice and empowerment, and 'authority of experience' pertains to the multiple, partial, and contradictory forms of experience embodied within each speaking subject as well as among a group of students. It also pertains to a distinction that is sometimes effaced in discussions of radical pedagogy (e.g., Ellsworth 1992) between experiential knowledge and knowledge derived from scholarly research. In considering these issues, I wish to also bring into focus the character of teachers' work in mediating and balancing the tightrope walk between opening spaces for silenced or delegitimated voices, handling 'inappropriate' (racist, sexist, homophobic, and so on) voices, and conveying scholarly knowledge, as well developing among students the art of critical inquiry.

The second challenge I explore is that of simultaneously addressing in one's teaching multiple social relations, forms of oppression, and subjectivities – based on race, gender, class, sexual orientation, and so on. Here the problem can be seen as one of balancing contrary tendencies. These are the epistemological and political demands for complexity, on the one hand, and on the other, the real limits encountered in fashioning a coherent and accessible analysis that simultaneously considers two or more sets of social relations (based on race, gender, class, and other social divisions).

While some of the recent calls for inclusiveness within progressive pedagogy stem from efforts to contest the marginality of other groups within white, Western, masculinist, and heterosexist thought, the failure to address the limits as well as the possibilities of such inclusiveness within teaching and classroom practices leads to unforeseen consequences. These include the emergence of new forms of essentialism reliant on dichotomous categories of thought, tendencies toward turgid and inaccessible language, and premature closure in analyses when dealing with complex issues. Issues of power and oppression are also often obfuscated in postmodernist frameworks of 'difference' wherein there exists a tendency to 'eclipse the political and ethical in favour of issues that center on epistemological and aesthetic concerns' (Giroux 1992, 64).

The two challenges that form the framework for my discussion are clearly related. The structural reality of multiple forms of oppression is mirrored in the existential reality of contradictory and partial subjects. In exploring these two challenges, I will be drawing from debates in critical, feminist, and anti-racist pedagogy and more broadly in social science, as well as from a dozen years of teaching sociology to undergraduate and graduate students in a mid-size, non-élite Canadian university. In so doing, I will also be signalling what I perceive to be significant issues connected to the context of classroom practices that shape the choices made by educators in dealing with such questions as student voice, empowerment, and diversity. The brevity of this paper inhibits my taking up these issues in any comprehensive fashion. My point here is to raise some questions of material, institutional, and cultural constraints that, notwithstanding a few exceptions (Orner 1992; Gore 1992), are given only glancing attention in the progressive pedagogy debates. These include macrostructural issues such as the relationship of universities to the labour market and the effects of this relationship in shaping student educational aspirations. Another urgent issue faced by university teachers is the general decline in adult literacy and the reading public. Other significant contextual issues include the institutional constraints on teaching inherent in the devaluation of teaching in the tenure and promotion reward system, the broader labour process of the academic, the issue of resources and student enrolments, and the particular burdens of time and expectations placed on female and feminist teachers. My discussion is not meant in any way to suggest definitive answers to the questions that I raise. I wade into these issues from a stance of humility, experimentation, frustration, and often fatigue in reading and mining the students' silences, as well as evoking both sadly uninspired and wildly capricious interventions.

Whose Knowledge(s)?

The politics of student voice and representation in teaching and classroom practices have become a focus within critical and feminist pedagogical debates. Within critical pedagogy, the clarion call for progressive teachers to promote participatory learning and emancipatory self- and social empowerment among students is linked to projects of radical or 'creative' democracy (Giroux 1988, 202; see also Apple 1986; Aronowitz and Giroux 1985; Giroux 1983, 1992; McLaren, 1988). Thus, Giroux views the most important questions confronting liberal arts reform as those 'reformulating the meaning and purpose of higher education in ways that contribute to the cultivation and regeneration of an informed critical citizenry capable of actively participating in the shaping and governing of a democratic society' (1992, 100).

Recently, critical pedagogy's goal in empowering students has been critiqued by feminist poststructuralists for its failure to come to terms with feminist analysis and the contradictory and heterogeneous character of the subject(s) of empowerment. Luke (1992, 29–32), for instance, points to the retention in critical pedagogy of limiting liberal and androcentric assumptions. Thus, the appeal of critical pedagogues to promote citizenship education retains the private/public dichotomy of classic theories of citizenship that, as Pateman (1988) so brilliantly discloses, elevated male activities associated with the public sphere and public duties, and consigned women to the private and denigrated sphere of non-citizenship.[6]

Orner (1992) and Gore (1992) view the demands for student voice and empowerment in the educational writings of critical and Anglo-American feminist theorists as 'highly suspect' and as perpetuating 'relations of domination in the name of liberation' (Orner 1992, 75). The calls for 'authentic student voice' are problematic on two grounds. First, they absolve 'liberatory' teachers from their own complicity and conscription in oppressive power dynamics that characterize the university (Orner 1992, 84, 87; Gore 1992, 62). As Gore (1992, 68) points out, the conceptions of power in both Foucauldian and radical feminist analysis, which seek to replace notions of negative repressive power with notions of agency and positive, productive power, must come to terms with the institutional location of the classroom. The power relations within the classroom may militate against strategies of empowerment. 'The pedagogical relation of teacher to students is, at some fundamental level, one in which the teacher is able to exercise power in ways unavailable to students. Teaching remains embedded within a history of moral and cultural regulation' (Gore 1992, 68).

The claims for 'liberatory praxis' attribute extraordinary abilities to the committed teacher and hold a view that seems woefully out of touch with the context(s) in which most academics work. 'It is sometimes necessary,' cautions Henry Louis Gates Jr (1992, 192) 'to remind ourselves of the distance from the classroom to the streets.'[7] As educators, writers, and intellectuals, we would like to claim efficacy for our labours. Yet it is important to distinguish the reality and limitations of teaching and academic work from the 'hyper-reality' of texts, where reality has collapsed, all becomes image, illusion, or simulation, and the possibilities for liberating the oppressed are limitless (Rosenau 1992, xii). The context in which progressive teaching occurs, and which brings into view larger material constraints and forces in shaping both student and teacher subjectivities, is a vital, yet neglected, consideration in the debates about the possibilities of radical pedagogy, and will be addressed at a later point in this paper.

A second ground for scepticism with calls for 'student voice' raised by some feminist writers draws from feminist poststructuralist understandings of the subject and subjectivity (Fuss 1989; Gore 1992; Orner 1992; Weedon 1987). As delineated by Weedon,

> Humanist discourses presuppose an essence at the heart of the individual which is unique, fixed and coherent and which makes her what she is ... Against this irreducible humanist essence of subjectivity, poststructuralism proposes a subjectivity which is precarious, contradictory and in process, constantly being reconstituted in discourse each time we think or speak. (1987, 32–3)

Poststructuralist feminism assumes that 'experience has no inherent essential meaning' but rather must be invested with meaning through language (Weedon 1987, 34), and further that language is a 'site of struggle where subjectivity and consciousness are produced' (Orner 1992, 80). Hence, all calls for 'authentic (student) voice' are unfeasible. The discourses on 'authentic student voice' 'are premised on the [unrealistic] assumption of a fully conscious, fully speaking, "unique, fixed and coherent" self' (Orner 992, 79). As Rosenthal writes, 'in general, postmodernism and identity politics conflict in ways not easily resolved. The assertion of identity necessarily involves the drawing of boundaries around that identity, while postmodernism is dedicated to the transgressing of boundaries' (1992, 96).[8]

How is one to reconcile the poststructuralist and postmodernist representation of identity as fragmented and heterogeneous *within* as well as among subjects with the assertion of suppressed identities and the authority of experience made within some strands of feminist pedagogy and identity student politics? As Linda Carty (1991, 22) writes, 'The resistance of ... marginalized groups of individuals comes from an "outside knowledge" gained through experience, and a refusal to discard this, though it is not given legitimacy in the academic environment.' The poststructuralist scepticism of the 'cult of raw experience' (Loomba 1989, 3), runs counter to the demands for representation by women and men of colour, white women, lesbians, gays, disabled students, and other collectivities within institutions and curricula that traditionally have rendered them invisible, marginal, or deviant.

In light of such resistance by students asserting subaltern status, it is imperative to probe further the implications of such claims for authority based on experience in informing classroom practices. Within most university classrooms, there are typically students who are heterogeneous along lines of race, ethnicity, gender, sexuality, religion, often class, and a host of other more-or-less significant social relations and identities. As Fuss (1990, 116) argues, the politics of experience draws upon these identities, which then become a set of convenient pegs upon which to hang analysis, legitimize the moral authority to speak, screen out 'inappropriate' differences, and silence the voices of those deemed hegemonic, oppressing, or less oppressed.

> Identities are itemized, appreciated, and ranked on the basis of which identity holds the greatest currency at a particular historical moment and in a particular institutional setting. Thus, in an Afro-American Studies classroom, race and ethnicity are likely to emerge as the privileged items of intellectual exchange, or, in a Gay Studies classroom, sexual 'preference' may hold the top notch on the scale of oppressions. (Fuss 1990, 116)

Parallel to the hierarchy of identities among individuals and groups is the emergence of a 'hierarchy of identities ... *within* each speaking subject' (Fuss 1990, 116). One outcome identified by Fuss (116) of the ordering of identities within as well as across subjects is to see subjects only in terms of one part of their identities (for example, white male professors only in terms of their 'maleness,' Asian male or female professors only in terms of their Asian-ness). This frequently leads to the conferral of authority to particular subjects only on the basis of the most salient identities. Thus, Black female students or instructors are assumed to be experts on 'women of colour' issues but are assumed to have nothing to offer in areas that pertain to other identities, experiences, or acquired knowledges.

Fuss also suggests that the privileging of experience in classroom discussions may have the unforeseen, and for the progressive teacher, undesired, outcome of *depoliticizing* oppression and exploitation. Oppression may be viewed as explained or accounted for in personal experiences, thus leading to tendencies to 'psychologize and ... personalize questions of oppression, *at the expense of* strong materalist analyses of the structural and institutional bases' of oppression (Fuss 1990, 117).

Similarly, as argued by Sivanandan (1989, 15), the personalizing and individualizing of *resistance* in identity politics deflects struggles against institutions and practices onto struggles against individuals and attitudes. The logical outcome of identity politics is to suggest that to be a woman is to be feminist, to be Black is to be anti-racist, and that that is politics enough.[9] Without leaving the comfort of one's living-room or bedroom, the certainty of personal politics further transmogrifies 'I know and therefore I am' into 'I am, [and] therefore I resist' (Sivanandan 1989, 15). As Fuss further elaborates,

> the problem with attributing political significance to every personal action is that the political is soon voided of any meaning or specificity at all, and the personal is paradoxically de-personalized ... A severe reduction of the political to the personal leads to a telescoping of goals, a limiting of revolutionary activity to the project of self-discovery and personal transformation. (1989, 101)

The devaluation of scholarly knowledge directed at comprehending the underpinnings of racism, sexism, and other forms of oppression is an ironical outcome of the 'politics of experience' within the university setting whose chief purpose is purportedly to facilitate the construction, transmission, and exchange of such knowledge. A corollary of the process by which personal experiences of students are privileged can be an abdication on the part of the teacher of responsibility to use her voice to provide or facilitate the transmission of this other kind of knowledge – derived from the teacher/researcher's activities. This abdication is apparent in the account by Ellsworth (1992) of an experimental course (called 'Media and Anti-Racist Pedagogies') she had designed as a political intervention against campus racism at the University of Wisconsin–Madison in spring 1988. Ellsworth asserts that as the teacher, she 'understood racism no better than my students did, especially those students of color coming into class after six months (or more) of campus activism and whole lives of experience and struggle against racism – nor could I ever hope to ... My understanding and experience of racism will always be constrained by my white skin and middle-class privilage' (1992, 100).

While Ellsworth's assumption that the experience of white-skinned people of racism (especially of racism evoked by skin colour) is likely to be different than for people of colour is reasonable, her definition of 'understandings' of racism is one based purely on personal experience. There is no sense where there may be a 'difference' in understanding racism between the anti-racist teacher and her students based upon the academic's scholarly research, and distillation of debates about the nature of racism. This different kind of understanding might, for instance, address itself to the cultural, institutional (legal-juridical), and systemic bases of racism, drawing connections between histories of imperialism and colonialism, the restructuring strategies of international capital, and the influence of state policies in the emergence of racialized hierarchies of rights, inequities, and discourses. Such knowledge, derived from research and intellectual work, in a process where past knowledge is constantly challenged and reformulated, is not readily accessible to individuals and collectivities in their encounter with racism, even as activists in struggles against racism. Instead, Ellsworth advocates a pedagogy in which teachers do not teach but take the stance of talk show hosts – sprinting Donahues and Winfreys placing microphones in front of students who wish to express their experiences, and making the occasional 'comment' (based on what knowledge, one wonders?).

In Ellsworth's account of 'facilitating' a course on anti-racist pedagogies, knowledge gained through research and theorizing is labelled conservative, associated with the discredited 'rationalism and scientism' of the 'master's tools' (1992, 97). While Ellsworth acknowledges that 'all knowings are partial,' the provisional solution is 'the pooling of partial, socially constructed knowledges in classrooms' (102). Such a stance of anti-intellectualism, which only valorizes 'subcultural' exchanges among carriers of subcultures and identities, constructs a classroom infused with Manichean dualisms – oppressors versus oppressed, unclean Western rationalism versus untainted experience. It denies students the opportunity to learn from or be guided in their learning about racism, and about the means of eliminating racism through materials and analyses that are normally less accessible or available to students.

Both the pedagogical methods built around identity politics suggested by Ellsworth, and the outcomes, including the construction of racialized stereotypes built on dualisms – such as the implied construction of the 'Other (student of colour, etc.) lacking in Western rationalism' (97) would appear to be antithetical to any anti-racist pedagogy. Such anti-racist education is in danger of becoming what Phil Cohen has called 'a morality tale,' 'immortalis[ing] the struggles of the oppressed [transforming historiography into hagiography], only with the role of goodies and baddies reversed' (1991, 29, 38–9).

Ellsworth draws from poststructuralism to argue that rationalism and 'scientism' have constructed women and people of colour as irrational (1992, 96–7). She then asserts that students of colour ought not to be called upon to use 'tools such as rationalism' equated with the 'master's tools' to 'justify and explicate their claims' (97). This formulation divides subjects into those who are prone to rational deliberation (male, white, able-bodied, heterosexual men?) and subjects 'of difference' whose 'normal' discourse avoids the tainted ground of rational deliberation. Presumably, we are all affected by desire, fear, and other 'irrational' emotions. Critical reason retains a place in the analysis of the influence of such 'irrational' emotional investments in the construction of our thought.[10]

One further issue in addressing questions of student voice, identity, and experience that inevitably presents itself in teaching courses that focus on racism and feminism is the relationship of the curriculum and teacher to the students who are constructed and vilified as part of the 'oppressor' or 'privileged' categories – for example, white students in an anti-racist course, or male students in a feminist course. As Sivanandan (1989, 14) puts it, 'by personalising power, "the personal is the political" personalises the enemy: the enemy of the Black is the white as the enemy of the woman is the man. And all whites are racist like all men are sexist.' If the intent of an anti-racist or feminist course with students in the 'oppressor' categories is to teach, engage, and politicize students in anti-racist or feminist directions, then the latter are unlikely to engage with the 'morality tale' model 'in which their "side" are always and already the baddies' (Cohen 1991, 29).[11]

Cohen, who draws on experiences of teaching white, British, working-class pupils, also analyses the limitations of pedagogical methods wherein the teacher resorts to disciplinary measures in dealing with overt expressions of racist belief. 'The priority is rightly to protect [racial and] ethnic minorities from verbal and physical attack' (Cohen 1991, 43), a priority with which I wholeheartedly agree. Nonetheless, merely silencing and censoring racist remarks is inadequate, as it may in fact fuel resentment and reinforce and promote such views outside the classroom (43–4). Moreover, it is at such times when racist utterances seem to sting the ears of some listeners while reinforcing the entrenched prejudices of others, that it becomes apparent that racism is far from transparent. Language expressing and naming racism is socially contested (as much within oppressed groups as within the hegemonic culture) and in constant process of historical revision.[12]

This brings us to a consideration of one trend in anti-racist education that adopted the approach in many anti-sexist policies of reforming speech codes. There is a tendency to confuse 'verbal purification' with real anti-racist, anti-sexist, or other forms of progressive change.[13] While changes in discourse *may* be a reflection of changes in either the condition of a collectivity, or mobilization and collective consciousness preceding and accompanying changes in social conditions, this is not necessarily the case. Anti-racist activists and educators need to be attentive to the possibility that the only change that results from reforming speech codes is that of 'correct' language, providing racism and other forms of oppression with novel and more subtle forms of ideological codes, representations, and practices. Moreover, it is often the self-righteous attitude of some toward the use of the 'correct' terms that has gained them the images of the 'loony left' or the 'politically correct.' A sole concern with 'verbal uplift' has too often led to analytical and political paralysis.[14]

It is the responsibility of anti-racist teachers to confront and critique expressions of racism, but in a spirit that acknowledges the complexity of such tasks, and the necessity to negotiate the fraught but necessary distinction between destructive views and respectful dissent. The need to provide 'safe spaces' for students to critically engage both teachers and other students is addressed by Giroux, who writes, 'Put simply, students must be encouraged to cross ideological and political borders as a way of furthering the limits of their own understanding in a setting that is pedagogically safe and socially nurturing rather than authoritarian and infused with the suffocating smugness of a certain political correctness' (1992, 33). The teacher's skills in creating such a safe yet critical environment are particularly put to the test in dealing with the myriad of verbal and non-verbal gestures constituting the 'unconscious' and learned racism, sexism, and homophobia of individuals that serve to define and circumscribe some people not just as 'other' or different, but as unequal.

In critiquing pedagogical methods that rely almost exclusively on the authority of experience and identities, I am *not* suggesting that one exclude the expression of personal experiences in the classroom. On the contrary, such expressions can be empowering for students who voice them, as well as illuminating and challenging for those who are the listeners. While the progressive teacher can reject the fiction that truth equates with experience, it is precisely the 'immense power of that fiction' that 'prompts many students, who would not ... speak otherwise to enter energetically into those debates they perceive as pertaining directly to them' (Fuss 1990, 118). Rather, the point I am making is that there is a need to achieve some balance in the authority and time bestowed to both experiential and scholarly forms of knowledge, in a way that reflects the provisional, partial, and contradictory nature of *both* forms. The complexity of these tasks is compounded when the course tackles multiple and intersecting social relations, as is increasingly the trend in both social sciences and humanities courses that address the sociological trinity of race, class, and gender, and beyond.

How Much Complexity?

In the 1980s, much of social sciences can be seen to have gone the way of postmodernism, dedicating itself to dismantling the unifying traditions of modern Western though. Marxism, feminism, secular humanism, and modern science all became suspect *metanarratives* (totalizing systems of thought that assume the validity of their truth claims) whose assumptions held no more or less certainty 'than those of witchcraft, astrology, or primitive cults' (Rosenthal 1992, 6). The project of the metanarratives, hallmarks of modern thought, was to find order within the 'fragmented, chaotic, ruptured character of the modern experience' (Rosenthal 1992, 89). In contrast, postmodernism 'responds to, represents, or tries to embrace that part of modern experience that modernism tries to suppress – the decentred, the contingent, the unstable, the fragmentary' (89).

A positive outcome of the delegitimation of all 'master codes' has been to recognize that relations of class, race, ethnicity, gender, and sexuality could not simply be subsumed under each other's frameworks of analyses – that oppressions based on gender or race were not 'really' about class exploitation, or that class inequities could not simply be folded into patriarchy. The political implications of postmodernism, theorized by 'new social movement' theorists, was that radical social movements could not be 'assimilated to each other without smothering and denying their differences and uniqueness' (Rosenthal 1992, 95; see Boggs 1986; Melucci 1989; Touraine 1988).

The postmodern call within feminist discourse, taken up recently within some feminist pedagogy (Ellsworth 1992; Rothenberg 1992), has been to move away from analyses that focus exclusively on gender; prioritize gender over race, ethnicity, class, and sexuality; and generalize from the experiences of white, middle-class women (Mohanty 1991; Spelman 1988). This call originated from the struggles within feminist movements to deal with their own racist histories and exclusionary politics, from publicization of long histories of autonomous organizing by Aboriginal, racial, and ethnic minority women, and from a growing corpus of anti-racist feminist scholarship produced by women of colour and other anti-racist feminists in many different ('first' and 'third world') countries. Collectively, the impact of this work has been to point out the dangers in formulating generalizations about 'women,' 'racial minorities,' or other collectivities (with the possible exception of 'white men').

Such generalizations were viewed as rendering differences and contradictions among women/racial minorities invisible, differences that are at least as important as similarities. In contrast, anti-racist feminist scholarship has opened up an understanding of the plurality of women's experiences and oppressions, and the embeddedness of all women not simply in gender relations, but in a variety of other intersecting social relations organized by race, ethnicity, class, sexuality, and so on. These relations have placed different racial/ethnic groups of women in positions that are simultaneously hierarchical and interdependent (e.g., as in the relationship between female domestic workers and employers).

Frequently, however, the response to moving away from the essentialism inherent in a single theory of women's oppression has been to operate within a series of dichotomies: female/male, Black/white, lesbian/heterosexual, middle class/working class, and so on. As Vron Ware argues, 'the dichotomies are seemingly endless, and gender, race and class do not always fit so neatly on one or other side of the dividing line' (1992, 237). Many early writings that explored the relationship of race to gender, treated 'Black women' or 'women of colour' as homogeneous categories, and avoided the issue of how class mediated the effects of race and gender. This continues to be a significant issue in Canada, where class divisions have emerged within Caribbean, Chinese, and other racial categories of women as the result of a selective postwar immigration policy favouring the importation of capital and professional skills, as well as cheap labour.

One problem in addressing the diversity among women is that in moving away from an essentialist definition of 'woman,' through making specific reference to 'Black women,' 'white women,' 'Asian women,' and so forth, new forms of essentialism are constructed. Thus, the 'constructionist'[15] impulse present in much recent anti-racist feminist work, which seeks to 'specify, rather than definitively counteracting essentialism, often simply redeploys it ... through a number of ... sub-categorical classifications, each presupposing its own unique interior composition or metaphysical core' (Fuss 1989, 20).[16]

Another problem in the current postmodern celebration of 'difference' has resulted from the rush to embrace a form of politics that incorporates different social divisions and dynamics of power, without adequate analyses of these social divisions and their interconnections. Notwithstanding efforts to incorporate the categories of race and class into feminist theory and practice, much feminist writing and pedagogy has succumbed to a superficial and even rhetorical inclusion of race/class/gender axes of domination. Thus, one study of feminist organizing in Canada declared that 'socialist feminism is simultaneously about a transformation in the relations of domination between men and women and about a redistribution of political and economic power between classes and races' (Adamson, Briskin, and McPhail 1988, 98). This definition of socialist feminism is not subsequently supported by analyses of racism, either separately or in its complex relation with class and gender. Similarly, with reference to feminist pedagogy, Briskin (1990, 11) asserts that 'by extension, an anti-sexist strategy takes up race, class and sexual orientation,' without sustaining this assertion through arguments or evidence.

Such statements are problematic, obscuring as they do the long absence of white feminist involvement in the struggles of Aboriginal women, women of colour, and immigrant women, and the resistance of white feminists to seeing the implication of their practices in the context of racist structures. The authority and political import given in feminist frameworks to 'personal experience' have also forestalled the development of epistemological frameworks within which to connect race, gender, and class. The connections between the structures of 'triple oppression' – racism, sexism, and class – have remained abstract and not part of the lived experience of members of the largely white, middle-class women's movement. Thus, it has *not* been self-evident for many white feminists why racism is a feminist issue. Neither has it been self-evident for many Aboriginal women and women of colour why feminism, as it had been constructed by white, largely academic women, with different experiences and lives, should inform *their* lives. These separate realities are slowly being bridged, as apparent in the recent politics of the National Action Committee on the Status of Women (NAC). NAC, the largest coalition of women's organizations in Canada, has recently intervened in constitutional and immigration politics in ways that are supportive of the rights of Aboriginal women and refugee women, respectively. It has, however, taken active political engagement, often on issues that had previously not been defined as 'feminist,' to forge some sense of affinity among racially and ethnically diverse groups of women, and to assist women in seeing the connections between racist and sexist structures, discourses, and processes (Fuss 1989, 36–7; Stasiulis 1987, 1990, 1993).

The search for general theories of interconnections among racism, gender, and class has been less fruitful than analyses that illuminate these connections within historically contingent and regionally specific sites (Brah 1991, 68). Through detailed case studies examining particular women's conditions or representations in particular sites (colonialism, state, workplace, family household, discourses, etc.), there has emerged a more complex and nuanced sense of how material and discursive conditions shaping women's lives have been inscribed simultaneously by various (capitalist, racist, sexist, heterosexist) logics and interests (Stasiulis and Yuval-Davis forthcoming).

But the search for ever more complexity and inclusiveness in analyses and transmission of knowledge has also had some unfortunate consequences. It is a supreme irony that critical pedagogy (Giroux) and poststructuralist feminism, both premised upon the opening up of academic discourse 'in a way that contributes to the politics of difference' (Lather 1992, 132), should so closely guard access to the keys of progressive educational theory through resort to convoluted and inaccessible language. An instance of such tortured language occurs in an article aptly entitled '*Post*-Critical Pedagogies: A Feminist Reading,' whose opening sentence begs for red-pencil treatment. The author writes: 'This paper foregrounds the conflicts between the emancipatory projects and deconstruction by attempting a constructive displacement of the emancipatory impulse at work in the discourses of "critical pedagogy" ' (Lather 1992, 120)! My suspicion is that such game-playing verbal gyrations are a cover for an absence of lucid analytical complexity. Such writing is most certainly not a source of empowerment for students. Obtuseness of language, and sometimes (though not in the above instance) playful and ironic word-plays, have substituted for analytical richness or rigour.

A second lamentable outcome of the impulse to introduce heterogeneity to social analysis is the mechanistic, additive, and non-relational methods through which various categories have been introduced. In additive models of race, gender, and class, for instance, white women are viewed solely in terms of their gender, while women of colour are 'doubly' or 'triply' oppressed by the cumulative effects of race and gender, or race, class, and gender. Such additive models are resistant to acknowledging the relational nature of each social division, the fact that each is positioned and gains meaning in relation to the other (Glenn 1992; Stasiulis 1990). 'Black womanhood,' as Hazel Carby has shown in her study of the U.S. Antebellum South, though constructed through several intersecting scientific, psychosexual, and aesthetic discourses, must be seen as the refracted, opposite image of 'true' (i.e., white) womanhood. Glenn (1992, 35) similarly argues that 'white womanhood has been constructed ... in relation to that of women of colour. Therefore, race is integral to white women's gender identities.' In each instance, the interdependence and influence of one type of social relation on the other, the reformulation of one concept ('gender') in light of the influence of another ('race') is supported by evidence and arguments, rather than simply asserted. The notion that certain 'gains for women' could in fact be 'white, middle-class women's gains' and 'Third World women's losses,' while dismaying, could be strategically significant. Such a realization could, for instance, lead to political activism on more than one front – dismantling barriers that disadvantaged women positioned differently and unequally in relations of race, class, and gender.[17]

The capacity to uncover the relational nature of categories becomes diminished with the addition of ever more categories of 'difference,' particularly when one considers that each of these categories has undergone and is subject to a constant process of reconceptualization. Consider, for instance, the re-evaluation of the concept of class that began with E.P. Thompson's *Making of the English Working Class*, joined with Joan Scott's reconsideration of gender, which challenges Thompson's definition of class. Consider also the endless reconceptualizations of 'race' in relation to reformulated notions of biology and culture (Omi and Winant 1986; West 1987), which have had the effect of questioning 'race-free' notions of class, and more belatedly, gender. Similarly, debates about sexuality, including Foucault's de-essentializing efforts, and contributions by various gay, lesbian, and bisexual theorists have all profoundly contested the concepts of homosexuality, lesbianism, and heterosexuality (Fuss 1990, 97–112; Valverde 1985; Weeks 1977; Wittig 1980).

Ellsworth, in her aforementioned course on anti-racism, proposes that various 'differences meant that each strategy we considered for fighting racism on campus had to be interrogated for the implications it held for struggles against sexism, ableism, elitism, fat oppression, and so forth' (1992, 11). At both the levels of analysis and politics, this additive model of endless 'isms' undermines any sense by which different social divisions are relational and interlocking. Furthermore, there is a political danger in privileging heterogeneity and fragmentation to a point 'where the very possibility of understanding, formulation, and therefore resistance and change is questioned' (Loomba 1989, 4). Ellsworth's prescribed strategy of coalition-building conjures up images of endless agonizing about countless numbers of constituencies that would need to be consulted in order to be inclusive of all those things 'we did not share' (1992, 110). Both theory and politics are dead-ended when 'political "theory" becomes a list of all the groups, issues, and concerns you must remember to check off lest you offend somebody with no larger perspective connecting them' (Ehrenreich 1992, 337).

An uncritical, under-analysed model of power relations can serve to disguise the relations that consolidate rather than fragment power. This problem is endemic in many analyses that use the 'p' words – postmodernism, poststructuralism, and post-Marxism. The broader canvas for decentred identities, identity politics, and the new social movements involves the fundamental restructuring in the international organization of production, directed by multinational corporations and financial organizations such as the International Monetary Fund, and debt politics as played out between and within nation-states and class relations. Where these are most explicitly acknowledged in postmodernism, writers seem transfixed on the innovations and altered perceptions of time and space permitted by new, more flexible information technologies, computers, and robotics, and the new commodification of signs and images. Postmodernism ignores how integral the new information technologies are to the global restructuring projects of capital. The pre-eminence given to culture, symbols, and discourse in postmodernism means that economic causation is explicitly rejected (Laclau and Mouffe 1985) or paid only lip-service in a manner that 'typically takes the form of an ersatz and astonishingly crude political economy' (Rosenthal 1992, 104). As Sivanandan notes with respect to 'New Times,' a British version of postmodernism that emerged in the late 1980s, 'the economic was ... given only a walk-on part on to the "post-Fordist" stage' (1989, 5).

As Helvacioglu (1992, 15, 19) observes, even among postmodern Marxist writers who ground their analyses in the context of global capitalist restructuring,[18] there is a conspicuous silence about the ways in which the new contingent and 'schizophrenic' tendencies in postmodern culture and identities can be counteracted to transcend the pervasive power of transnational capital. There is a crying need to understand the 'sea-changes' in economic and social life, in global and national power structures, aided by the new technologies, that underlie the new miscellany of movements and identities. There is a need to comprehend the fragmentation that has resulted also from the new post–Cold War configurations in national boundaries, mass migrations, and sense of displacement among increasing numbers of people. This sense of displacement is especially acute among refugees and exiles ('the unwanted product of Third World modernization'), and among the homeless and the permanently unemployed (Helvacioglu 1992, 21–3). But the sense of dislocation is growing even among populations who have never moved away from their old neighbourhoods. Increasingly, these established populations attempt to make sense of their declining living standards and the increasing and threatening heterogeneous character of their societies by resuscitating often narrow and racist definitions of community. However, this analysis of the larger contexts for fragmentation and heterogeneity – which continues to be done by other scholars and activists – is ignored in frameworks that equate fragmentation and heterogeneity with progressive politics.[19]

The importance of context seems also largely to be ignored or provided with passing and highly abstracted reference within critical and feminist pedagogy. This is true even for the poststructuralist feminists who express scepticism about discourses on 'student voice' (Gore 1992, 67–8; Orner 1992, 80–2). In the next section of the paper, I will address some of the features of the context that have structured my own possibilities and limits for engaging in and achieving some success in progressive pedagogy.

Whose Classroom?

Most days when I teach I am aware that the students taking my courses are living in times vastly different from when I was a university student in the 1970s, following subjects that interested me and professors who engaged me. In the 1960s and 1970s, university students reaped the benefits of an expanding economy and had the luxury to be blithely unconcerned about their future in the labour market. In contrast, students in the 1990s are painfully aware of a scary new future of 'jobless growth.' Growing up during an epoch of massive structural change marked by the sudden convergence of new technology, new global patterns of production and de-industrialization, contemporary students recognize that competition for decreasing numbers of 'good,' or 'gold-collar,' jobs[20] will intensify. More frequently, new (or returning) entrants into the labour market face an expanded service sector dominated by degraded, dead-end 'Mc-Jobs.' This experiential knowledge inculcates among current university students an acutely instrumental view to education, results, and grades, in marked contrast to the view in critical and some feminist pedagogies of suppressed but eager subaltern subjectivities.[21] Moreover, the predominantly instrumental view taken by students toward their education may predispose them to actively resist the politicizing objectives or efforts at creating alternative forms of teaching of critical pedagogies.

The current writings about pedagogy in higher education also seem to avoid the problem of teaching Canadian students with generally low and declining literacy (as well as numeracy and science) skills, a situation that has sparked a debate among those educators who favour a 'return to basics.' When 29 per cent of Canadians between the ages of 16 and 24 lack the basic skills to read a newspaper, and universities do not necessarily screen out those lacking such rudimentary learning skills,[22] what does it mean for teachers who enter the classroom wishing to teach rich and nuanced analyses?

Regardless of the reasons for the low level of development among students of reading, writing, and analytical skills, the fact that few students develop these skills through an independent reading life throws the whole debate about curriculum, 'difference,' and the canon into an entirely different light. In view of the fact that leisure-time pursuits for all ages are more likely to include television and video viewing than reading, it is the 'medicinal' attributes of reading that become stressed by those of various ideological leanings in the canon debates (Pollitt 1992, 209):

> The chief end of reading is to produce a desirable kind of person and a desirable kind of society – a respectful high-minded citizen of a unified society for the conservatives, an up-to-date and flexible sort for the liberals, a subgroup-identified, robustly confident one for the radicals ... Read the conservatives' list and produce a nation of sexists or racists – or a nation of philosopher kings. Read the liberals' list and produce a nation of spineless relativists – or a nation of open-minded world citizens. Read the radicals' list, and produce a nation of psychobabblers and ancestor-worshippers – or a nation of stalwart proud-to-be me pluralists. (Pollitt 1992, 209–10)

As Kate Pollitt further argues, this 'simple, one-to-one correlation between books and behaviour' is premised on the belief that whatever books are put on course syllabi are the only ones that students are going to read. In Pollitt's imaginary 'country in which reading was a popular voluntary activity,' the choice of placing this or that book on a course list would 'be more like putting oatmeal and not noodles on the breakfast menu' (206–7). As it stands, many educators assume that 'if the list is dropped, *no* books are going to be read; thus, 'becoming a textbook is a book's only chance' (207).

This absence of a reading culture for most students is a critical feature in shaping how a textbook that introduces 'difference' will be read. Himani Bannerji's observations are here apposite: 'A text which is coherent with my experience as a non-white woman ... when inserted into the tentacles of an alienating interpretive device, loses its original reference points and meaning, and becomes inert and inverted' (1991, 76). For 'alien' audiences, texts speaking to particular Third World women's experiences will more likely be read through the glossy, orientalist, and distorted images of Third World women conveyed by television, Hollywood, and the tourist industry, than through connections with other related (unread) texts.

Moving from the context of the larger political economy and popular culture to the institutional context of the university, there are major constraints to provision of a critical education. These pertain to the funding crisis in higher education. With a thirteen per cent drop in operational spending on Canadian universities over the past fifteen years, the signs of decay, especially in universities lacking large private endowments, are visible everywhere – overcrowded classes, reduced support staff, outmoded equipment, 'ill' and unaesthetic buildings, and gutted libraries.

The cuts in funds percolating through the institution have particular effects on those who teach. In aiding the universities to cope with these cuts, academics are asked to spend more time on the following activities: pursuing large contracts and grants; conducting and publicizing cutting-edge research (that might attract both headlines and outside funds); increasing the number of contact hours with greater numbers of students both inside and outside classrooms; supervising thesis work and apprenticing student researchers; typing correspondence, research papers, and course material; photocopying; handling all equipment; and performing administrative work. In addition to the plethora of new and intensified demands on academics that work against stellar and innovative teaching, the tenure and promotion reward system operating in most universities shows an overriding commitment to research and publication, overshadowing the value of teaching (Smith 1991, 42). When one adds that in teaching, academics are expected to execute professionally something for which they have had little or no training, it becomes evident why teaching for many is increasingly experienced as punishment.

Feminist (or perhaps most female) teachers experience some additional burdens. The pressures of working in a male-dominated occupation and within an institution whose rules, modes of operation, discourse, and networks are androcentric have been extensively addressed in the feminist pedagogy literature (Luke and Gore 1992, 202). What I wish to highlight here are some connected issues that I have shared and heard communicated among networks of feminist academics and that connect with the politics of 'difference.'

While most female university teachers have been socialized into male models of academic argumentation, debate, and general conduct, there is an expectation among many students that female professors should be nurturing in traditional feminine ways, and offer different forms of emotional and tangible support. This means that students expect women academics to be available in a way that would never be presumed of male professors. Women professors are caught in a bind with respect to their conduct in the classroom: not wishing to replicate certain styles of male, hierarchical discourse within which they have, however, been thoroughly trained, but simultaneously fearing a loss of control and authority if their style is grounded in *their* sense of what it means to be a feminist. This fear is heightened by a new atmosphere of anxiety constructed out of the threat of male violence.

Especially since the mass murder of fourteen female engineering students at the Université de Montréal in 1989, there has been a growing perception across Canadian universities that the campus is not a safe place for women. I have had women students convey that they experience heart palpitations whenever they enter the engineering building on campus in order to attend my class. I have also had a student who reported that she had been raped, was further threatened and stalked on campus, and with whom I subsequently spent many hours navigating through inadequate avenues of security and investigation. The knowledge that sexual assault is a frequent occurrence on campus now forms part of female professors' calculations about whether or not to offer evening courses, work at night in one's office, and so on. It also introduces a new cautionary attitude in conduct with male students, and new challenges in dealing with female students' anxieties and confrontation with sexual violence (see Lewis 1992).

Conclusion

As teachers, we need to stay attentive to the context that structures the possibilities of doing progressive pedagogy in the classroom. As I have indicated above, this context pertains both to larger material and cultural realities, as well as the institutional context of the university. Together, these shape resources, student and instructor expectations, and the labour process of the teacher/academic. There is less and less time and resources available today for teachers to design courses that incorporate the basic attributes of progressive pedagogy, such as one-to-one contact between students and instructors. Moreover, the understandably instrumental attitude of many students toward their university education can subvert efforts of teachers to 'empower' them according to the tenets of critical pedagogy. Given these constraints, what lessons can be drawn about the two interconnected challenges I have here addressed: responding to issues of student voice and diversity, and teaching about diversity?

First, in dealing with questions of voice and student empowerment, I have indicated that one must not abandon the teaching of specific knowledges about aspects of the organization of the world gained through scholarship, conveying at the same time the provisional, partial, and contested nature of this type of knowledge. In understanding oppression and effective strategies for change, such knowledge is vital, and at least potentially empowering for students. Second, instructors cannot cast a blind eye to the declining levels in the most basic writing and analytical skills, as well as the absence of a reading public among students entering universities. It is incumbent upon university teachers to be realistic about the level of complexity in analyses that can be meaningfully absorbed by students, and to take opportunities to inculcate not only the art of critical inquiry and substantive knowledge, but basic skills such as essay writing as well.

In my discussion of student voice and identity politics, I have pointed out the dangers of re-essentializing new categories, and assuming authority based on experiential knowledge. However, I believe that the deconstructionist impulse taken too far can similarly be paralysing for the teaching process and for progressive political ends. Fuss suggests that the 'adherence to essentialism is a measure of the degree to which a particular political group has been culturally oppressed,' and further that 'in the hands of the subaltern,' essentialism can have politically strategic value (1990, 98, 32). Thus, when minority students speak as if the categories of Black women, lesbians, and so on are in fact internally homogeneous, I have learned to strategically choose to avoid undermining the sense expressed by students of a shared experience of oppression or resistance.

The question of 'how much complexity' is possible and desirable in doing progressive teaching cannot be answered in the abstract, just as a general theory combining all forms of oppression is pointless. To argue otherwise would be to ignore the intense contestation about the social meanings of each concept and the intricate debates regarding their intersections.

Each teacher, in each new course, classroom, seminar, or lecture, will have to navigate her own path between the shoals of closure effected by unifying discourses, and the dangers of endless, unanchored, and depoliticized 'difference.' Most universities have become more diverse in their student populations and, slowly, in their teaching and administrative personnel as well – along lines of class, race, ethnicity, gender, and age; there are also increased efforts to redesign physical space to facilitate access to disabled students and staff. Both formal curricula and the hidden curriculum require challenge and reformulation in responding to the greater heterogeneity of students' needs, understandings, and interests.

But this must occur in a manner that refuses to wallow in postmodernism's contingency and fragmentation, or to succumb to the tortured verbal gymnastics of poststructuralism.

Pluralism is not in itself progressive or defining of a political or ethical outlook. While there are endless possibilities of namings of significant relations and forms of oppression in any given analysis, there are real practical, political, and policy limits to the level of complexity in types of social relations and processes that can be considered at any one time. Gender oppression, race oppression, and class oppression are frequently experienced simultaneously. But few laws and public policies, and precious few politics (as fought by contemporary social movements), reflect the complexity of simultaneously experienced oppressions. This suggests that in each analysis, the complexity of what can be named must be chosen carefully, by selectively representing only those social divisions, relations, and representations that can lucidly be demonstrated to hold significance in comprehending particular phenomena.

Notes

I am grateful to Stephen Richer for his helpful comments on this paper. An earlier rendition was delivered to the Annual Conference of the British Association of Canadian Studies, University of Cambridge, 26–8 March 1993.

1 Of 45 universities surveyed by *Maclean's* magazine in 1992, more than 90 per cent reported that they had a sexual-harassment officer on staff. The presence or absence of race relations and employment equity policies was not questioned in this survey (*Maclean's*, 9 November 1992: 61).

2 While sharing some common goals (such as 'emancipation') with critical pedagogy, feminist pedagogy has also been critical of the latter's absence of meaningful inclusion of women and gender issues. In particular, feminist educational theorists have critiqued critical (male-authored) pedagogy for its tendency to replicate the 'rationalism and scientism' (Ellsworth 1992, 97), unreflexivity (Gore 1992, 62), and 'revalorization of ... patriarchal metanarratives' (Luke 1992, 25) typical of traditional educational discourses.

3 These include racial and ethnic minorities, women, disabled, poor and working class, lesbian and gay, and older students (Luke and Gore 1992, 192).

4 Ehrenreich further argues: 'We're not going to be able to defend multiculturalism without addressing its silly and obnoxious side, the phenomenon of political correctness. I have seen P.C. culture on college campuses, chiefly

among relatively elite college students and on relatively elite college campuses. It amounts to a form of snobbery that is easily made fun of by the right and even by students who are not on the right' (1992, 335).

5 Here I am paraphrasing Diana Fuss, who perceives the role of identity politics in the classroom as authorizing and de-authorizing speech. ' "Experience" emerges as the essential truth of the individual subject, and personal "identity" metamorphoses into knowledge. *Who we are becomes what we know;* ontology shades into epistemology' (Fuss 1989, 113).

6 Luke further argues that 'the Greek political ideal for citizenship education [supported by Giroux] is not a sufficient scaffold to support a feminist pedagogy. Citizenship, the good and just life – according to a presumably Aristotlean, "classical Greek definition" ... – was public life, the life of male community and citizenship which celebrated public speech in the pursuit of knowledge and truth. Aristotle (and Plato) silenced and privatized women and slaves in the *idion* (the private) of the *oikos* or household' (1992, 34).

7 Gates is addressing the recent turn toward politics and history in literary studies, but his remarks might be as applicable to the current interest in literary criticism and cultural studies within the social sciences. 'Academic critics write essays, "readings" of literature, where the bad guys (you know, racism or patriarchy) lose, where the forces of oppression are subverted by the boundless powers of irony and allegory that no prison can contain, and we glow with hard-won triumph. We pay homage to the marginalized and demonized, and it feels almost as if we've righted an actual injustice' (1992, 192–3).

8 While postmodernism and poststructuralism are not identical, the treatment by both approaches of the subject and subjectivity seem to be very similar (see Fuss 1989, 33, 34; Rosenau 1992, 3n; Rosenthal 1992, 96).

9 Sivanandan writes: 'The "personal is the political" has also the effect of shifting the gravitational pull of Black struggle from the community to the individual ... It gave the individual an out not to take part in issues that affected the community: immigration raids, deportations, deaths in custody, racial violence, the rise of fascism ... housing and schooling ... There was now another venue for politics: oneself, and another politics: of one's sexuality, ethnicity, gender – a politics of identity as opposed to a politics of identification' (1989, 15).

10 My argument here is similar to Habermas' defence of 'communicative rationality,' which treats as virtues certain rules of clarity, force of argument, and efforts at mutual understanding (Habermas 1982, 29).

11 This sentiment of being treated as oppressor and irredeemable is well expressed in a student poem entitled 'Silence.' It reads: 'I am sexist, heterosex-

ist and racist / I am middle class, an oppressor ... / I am silent. / I came to be challenged, to test and explore, But ... I am silent. / I disintegrate, / Isolated and alone among all those perfect people ... (Anonymous).

12 The constant revision of concepts used to name ethnic and racialized groups reveals the plasticity of racist discourse. In Canada, many individuals or groups who are so designated object to the term 'visible minorities,' arguing that it is a creation of the state (Carty and Brand 1988).

13 As Barbara Ehrenreich expresses, 'I like being called Ms. I don't want people saying 'man' when they mean me too. I'm willing to make an issue of these things. But I know that even when all women are Ms., we'll still get sixty-five cents for every dollar earned by a man. Minorities by any other name – people of color ... – will still bear a huge burden of poverty, discrimination, and racial harassment. Verbal uplift is not the revolution' (1992, 336).

14 Sivanandan (1989, 14–15) relates an incident whereby students in a racism awareness training class 'were so sensitized to the pejorative use of the term "black" that they baulked at asking for black coffee.'

15 Fuss (1992, 2) defines 'constructionism' as a perspective that is articulated 'in opposition to essentialism and concerned with its philosophical refutation [and which] insists that essence is itself a historical construction.'

16 Rosenthal (1992, 95) makes a similar argument. 'Identity politics can also work to smother difference and diversity within each particular group, by implying that there is one "essential" African-American experience, for example, or purer and less pure forms of Asian-American culture.'

17 This type of analysis has emerged in my research with Abigail Bakan on foreign domestic worker policy in Canada (Bakan and Stasiulis 1994, 1995). Currently, this policy provides a means of alleviating the double burden of domestic and paid labour for those (middle-class and mostly white) women who have the financial resources to hire live-in domestics. For women of colour domestics, it enforces a situation of bonded servitude in exchange for the *possibility* of future gains in rights and options. The foreign domestic policy, embedded as it is in certain global, racial, gender, and class inequities, fails to challenge the gender division of labour or the patriarchal assumptions of the organization of the state and civil society. It would seem that any effective strategy of redress for the inequities experienced by domestic workers would have to work simultaneously on various policy fronts, such as reforms to child care and immigration policies, as well as labour legislation and foreign aid to Third World countries.

18 Helvacioglu is here referring to the work of Fredric Jameson (1989) and Scott Lash and John Urry (1987).

19 See Helvacioglu (1992, 21), who argues that 'there is nothing inherently democratic about such fragmentation.'

20 In the new economy, the 'gold-collar worker' is computer literate, but also skilled in other critical corporate functions such as marketing or finance (*Maclean's*, 15 March 1993: 29).

21 In a November 1992 national poll, the differences in values between generations became apparent, these due to different relations to the labour market. When asked, 'If you had one wish, what would it be?' the baby boomers (aged 35 to 44), who have reaped the benefits of an expanding economy, were most likely to choose 'inner peace and happiness.' In contrast, Canadians between the ages of 18 and 24, facing dimmer job prospects, most often chose 'financial security' (*Maclean's*, 4 January 1993: 30–1).

22 My own university, for instance, is known for its 'open-door policy,' which in practice means that students with low grades and low levels of literacy are accepted.

References

Adamson, Nancy, Linda Briskin, and Margaret McPhail. 1988. *Feminist Organizing for Change: The Contemporary Women's Movement in Canada*. Toronto: Oxford University Press

Apple, M. 1986. *Teachers and Texts*. London: Routledge and Kegan Paul

Aronowitz, S., and H. Giroux. 1985. *Education under Siege*. South Hadley, MA: Bergin & Garvey

Bakan, Abigail B., and Daiva Stasiulis. 1994. 'Foreign Domestic Worker Policy in Canada and the Social Boundaries of Citizenship.' *Science and Society* 58 (1)(Spring): 7–33

Bakan, Abigail B., and Daiva K. Stasiulis. 1995. 'Making the Match: Domestic Placement Agencies and the Racialization of Housework.' *Signs* 20(1)(Winter): 1–33

Bannerji, Himani. 1991. 'But Who Speaks For Us? Experience and Agency in Conventional Feminist Paradigms.' In H. Bannerji, L. Carty, K. Dehli, S. Heald, and K. McKenna, eds., *Unsettling Relations: The University as a Site of Feminist Struggles*, 67–108. Toronto: Women's Press

Boggs, Carl. 1986. *Social Movements and Political Power: Emerging Forms of Radicalism in the West*. Philadelphia: Temple University Press

Brah, Avtar. 1991. 'Difference, Division, Differentiation.' *International Review of Sociology* 2: 53–72

Briskin, Linda. 1990. 'Feminist Pedagogy: Teaching and Learning Liberation.'

Feminist Perspectives (Canadian Research Institute for the Advancement of Women) 19 (Aug.)

Carty, Linda. 1991. 'Black Women in Academia: A Statement from the Periphery.' In H. Bannerji et al., eds., *Unsettling Relations*, 13–44. Toronto: Women's Press

Carty, Linda, and Dionne Brand. 1988. ' "Visible Minority" Women – A Creation of the Canadian State.' In *Resources for Feminist Research* 17(3)(Sept.): 39–42

Cohen, Philip. 1991. 'Monstrous Images, Perverse Reasons: Cultural Studies in Anti-Racist Education.' Working Paper No. 11. Centre for Multicultural Education, University of London Institute of Education

Ehrenreich, Barbara. 1992. 'The Challenge for the Left.' In P. Berman, ed., *Debating P.C.*, 33–8. New York: Laurel

Ellsworth, Elizabeth. 1992. 'Why Doesn't This Feel Empowering? Working Through the Repressive Myths of Critical Pedagogy.' In C. Luke and J. Gore, eds., *Feminisms and Critical Pedagogy*, 90–119. New York: Routledge

Fuss, Diana. 1990. *Essential Speaking: Feminism, Nature and Difference*. New York: Routledge

Gates, Henry Louis, Jr. 1992. 'Whose Canon Is It Anyway?' In P. Berman, ed., *Debating P.C.*, 190–200. New York: Laurel

Giroux, H. 1983. *Theory and Resistance in Education*. London: Heineman

– 1988. *Schooling and the Struggle for Public Life*. Minneapolis, MN: University of Minnesota Press

– 1992. *Border Crossings: Cultural Workers and the Politics of Education*. New York: Routledge

Glenn, Evelyn Nakano. 1992. 'From Servitude to Service Work: Historical Continuities in the Racial Division of Paid Reproductive Labor.' *Signs* 18(1): 1–43

Gore, Jennifer. 1992. 'What We Can Do for You! What *Can* We Do for "You"? Struggling over Empowerment in Critical and Feminist Pedagogy.' In C. Luke and J. Gore, eds., *Feminisms and Critical Pedagogy*, 54–73. New York: Routledge

Habermas, Jurgen. 1982. 'The Entwinement of Myth and Enlightenment.' *New German Critique* 9(3): 13–30

Helvacioglu, Banu. 1992. 'The Thrills and Chills of Postmodernism: The Western Intellectual Vertigo.' *Studies in Political Economy* 38 (Summer): 7–34

Jameson, Fredric. 1989. 'Postmodernism and Consumer Society.' *New Left Review* 176: 32–9

Laclau, Ernesto, and Chantal Mouffe. 1985. *Hegemony and Socialist Strategy*. London: Verso

Lash, Scott, and John Urry. 1987. *The End of Organized Capitalism*. Oxford: Polity Press

Lather, Patti. 1992. 'Post-Critical Pedagogies: A Feminist Reading.' In C. Luke and J. Gore, eds., *Feminisms and Critical Pedagogy*, 120–37. New York: Routledge

Lewis, Magda. 1992. 'Interrupting Patriarchy: Politics, Resistance and Transformation in the Feminist Classroom.' In C. Luke and J. Gore, eds., *Feminisms and Critical Pedagogy*, 167–91. New York: Routledge

Loomba, Ania. 1989. *Gender, Race, Renaissance Drama*. Manchester: Manchester University Press

Luke, Carmen. 1992. 'Feminist Politics in Radical Pedagogy.' In C. Luke and J. Gore, eds., *Feminisms and Critical Pedagogy*, 25–53. New York: Routledge

Luke, Carmen, and Jennifer Gore. 1992. 'Women in the Academy: Strategy, Struggle and Survival.' In C. Luke and J. Gore, eds., *Feminisms and Critical Pedagogy*, 192–210. New York: Routledge

Maclean's. 1993. 'Surf, Sand and Sex' (4 Jan.): 30–2

– 1993. 'Where the Jobs Are' (15 Mar.): 28–9

McLaren, P. 1988. 'Culture or Canon? Critical Pedagogy and the Politics of Literacy.' *Harvard Educational Review* 58(2): 213–34

Melucci, Alberto. 1989. *Nomads of the Present: Social Movements and Individual Needs in Contemporary Society*. Philadelphia: Temple University Press

Mohanty, Chandra Talpade. 1991. 'Under Western Eyes: Feminist Scholarship and Colonial Discourses.' In C.T. Mohanty, A. Russo, and L. Torres, eds., *Third World Women and the Politics of Feminism*, 51–80. Bloomington: Indiana University Press

Omi, Michael, and Howard Winant. 1986. *Racial Formation in the United States from the 1960s to the 1980s*. New York: Routledge

Orner, Mimi. 1992. 'Interrupting the Calls for Student Voice in "Liberatory" Education: A Feminist Poststructuralist Perspective.' In C. Luke and J. Gore, eds., *Feminisms and Critical Pedagogy*. New York: Routledge

Pateman, Carole. 1988. *The Sexual Contract*. Oxford: Polity Press

Pollitt, Kate. 1992. 'Why Do We Read?' In P. Berman, ed., *Debating P.C.*, 201–14. New York: Laurel

Rosenau, Pauline Marie. 1992. *Post-Modernism and the Social Sciences: Insights, Inroads, and Intrusions*. Princeton: Princeton University Press

Rosenthal, Michael. 1992. 'What Was Post-Modernism?' *Socialist Review* (Feb.): 83–105

Rothenberg, Paula. 1992. 'Critics of Attempts to Democratize the Curriculum Are Waging a Campaign to Misrepresent the Work of Responsible Professors.' In P. Berman, ed., *Debating P.C.*, 262–8. New York: Laurel

Said, Edward S. 1992. 'The Politics of Knowledge.' In P. Berman, ed., *Debating P.C.*, 172–89. New York: Laurel

Sivanandan, A. 1989. 'All That Melts into Air Is Solid: The Hokum of New Times.' *Race and Class* 31(3): 1–30

Smith, Stuart. 1991. *Report of the Commission of Inquiry on Canadian University Education*. Prepared for the Government of Ontario

Spelman, Elizabeth. 1988. *Inessential Woman: Problems of Exclusion in Feminist Thought*. Boston: Beacon Press

Stasiulis, Daiva. 1987. 'Rainbow Feminism: Perspectives on Minority Women in Canada.' *Resources in Feminist Research* 2: 97–112

– 1990. 'Theorizing Connections: Gender, Race, Ethnicity and Class.' In P.S. Li, ed., *Race and Ethnic Relations in Canada*. 269–305. Toronto: Oxford University Press

– 1993. ' "Authentic Voice": Anti-Racist Politics in Canadian Feminist Publishing and Literary Production.' In A. Yeatman and S. Gunew, eds., *Feminism and the Politics of Difference*, 35–60. Sydney: Allen and Unwin

Stasiulis, Daiva, and Nira Yuval-Davis. Forthcoming. *Unsettling Settler Societies: Articulations of Gender, Race, Ethnicity and Class*. London: Sage

Touraine, Alain. 1988. *Return to the Actor: Social Theory in Postindustrial Society*. Minneapolis: University of Minnesota Press

Valverde, Mariana. 1985. *Sex, Power and Pleasure*. Toronto: Women's Press

Ware, Vron. 1992. *Beyond the Pale: White Women, Racism and History*. London: Verso

Weedon, Chris. 1987. *Feminist Practice and Postructuralist Theory*. Oxford: Basil Blackwell

Weeks, Jeffrey. 1977. *Coming Out: Homosexual Politics in Britain from the Nineteenth Century to the Present*. London: Quartet

West, Cornel. 1987. 'Race and Social Theory: Towards a Genealogical Materialist Analysis.' In M. Davis et al., eds. *The Year Left 2: An American Socialist Yearbook*, 73–89. Stony Brook, NY: Verso

– 1992. 'Diverse New World.' In P. Berman, ed., *Debating P.C.*, 326–32. New York: Laurel

Wittig, Monique. 1980. 'The Straight Mind.' *Feminist Issues* (Summer): 103–11

Reaching the Men: Inclusion and Exclusion in Feminist Teaching

STEPHEN RICHER

I want in this paper to reflect on three years of introductory sociology teaching. I have actually taught introductory sociology on and off for over twenty years, but more recently I have explicitly incorporated a feminist perspective into the course. There were three factors that prompted this. First, I was convinced that feminist critiques of androcentric curricula in the arts and social sciences were tapping a major dimension of the power/knowledge connection. The rising importance of such scholarship, made all the more salient by my interaction with feminist colleagues and students, gave considerable impetus to my course revisions.

Second, these critiques dovetailed with the reality of striking changes in the gender and age composition of my classes. For several years I had witnessed the steady enrolment increase of women, but particularly 're-entry women' – older women who were coming back to education after years of prolonged absence. Their presence in the classroom gave daily material testimony to the more abstract conceptualizing of feminist discourse.

Finally, my own long-held commitment to critical teaching was an important mediating factor. In particular, the principle of taking classroom composition into account in one's teaching made it imperative that I provide space for issues of concern to these women. In addition, I do not subscribe to the notion that feminist approaches belong only in programs labelled 'women's studies.' The emphasis in critical pedagogy on holistic education (Richer 1981) rendered any such compartmentalization undesirable. I support the view that mainstreaming gender, and especially feminist thinking, is essential to mounting a serious challenge to traditional university curricula and pedagogy (see Aiken et al. 1988; Spanier 1984; Anderson 1988; Deegan 1988).

As the course developed over a three-year period, the issue of my own gender became a dominant one. First, I had to wrestle with the moral and political implications of a male teaching feminism. Out of this struggle emerged a shift from 'feminist male' to 'pro-feminist male,' a shift that was tacitly negotiated with feminist colleagues and students, and that contributed in no small way to whatever success I had in the course.

Second, I slowly realized that as a male I had a unique opportunity to reach the men, to make feminist thinking an appropriate male pursuit. At the same time it became clear that in order to take advantage of this opportunity, I would have to tread a delicate line, one that conveyed the legitimacy of the feminist challenge but did not *a priori* alienate men in the process. I should emphasize here that for me this objective of reaching the men was crucial. I became convinced after the Montreal Massacre that gender equality in all forms is impossible without the willing collaboration of men. Such horrendous and devastating violence, along with its deeply embedded structural roots, cannot with any impunity be defined as a 'women's issue': the issue is irrefutably *societal*. While men's exact place in the struggle has yet to be resolved, the necessity of our involvement is a given.

In the following pages I wish to address both aspects of the gender issue raised above. I begin, however, with a description of my personal view of critical teaching, set against some pertinent autobiographical background. I then indicate how I incorporated an explicit feminist pedagogy into this framework, and how this was a negotiated, emergent process. Finally, I spend the remainder of the paper discussing strategies for reaching the men.

Teaching and the Transformative Intellectual

As far back as I can remember, a concern with subordinate groups was a major part of my life. As one of only two Jewish kids on a block in Montreal's west end, I was acutely and sometimes painfully aware of the nature of dominant/subordinate relations. This awareness was fuelled by my upbringing in a patriarchal family, by my experience of two forms of authoritarian schooling (public school and afternoon Hebrew school), and by continual exclusion from peer play. (I was the overweight kid with glasses selected last for games of baseball and football, barely tolerated, relegated to the invisible fringes of activity groups.)

It was no accident, then, that I found myself in sociology, a discipline in which championing the underdog seemed a fundamental premise. It also followed that when I began teaching I would embrace 'transformative' education – 'a fundamental social project to help students develop a deep and abiding faith in the struggle to overcome injustices and to change themselves' (Aronowitz and Giroux 1985, 36). Central to this view of teaching is student empowerment – the creation of a classroom climate that optimizes student control over their own learning. Aided by discussions with colleagues and by key writers in critical education (Freire 1973; McLaren 1989; Shor 1980; Aronowitz and Giroux 1985, to name a few), I evolved a set of classroom practices that manifested this objective.

These practices were derived from one pivotal premise: that of the social construction of knowledge. The first third of my course is typically devoted to demonstrating the relativism of idea systems. I accomplish this in two ways: by placing the major sociological frameworks in historic, cultural, and biographical context, and by deconstructing my course syllabus in light of my own background. Marxism, for example, is discussed by allusion to major events of mid-nineteenth-century Europe, to values and ideologies prevalent at the time, and through an examination of aspects of Marx's personal life. The emphasis is on the role of such factors in the development of Marx's thinking about social life. The link is then made from dominant idea systems to their entrenchment in academic institutions as 'curricula.' This opens the door to an exploration of the knowledge/power connection – the issues of what is worth knowing, who says so, and why.

The above notions are reinforced when they are concretized and given immediacy by applying them to the construction of one's own course. This entails placing the material in autobiographical context, developing a multidisciplinary orientation, and extending legitimation to knowledge brought in from outside the hallowed halls. A good place to start is with a candid presentation indicating why particular items are on one's reading list, why certain texts are required and others not, and how these choices relate to your own socialization. Included here would be an indication of what is *not* on the reading list and why – i.e., the silences that are really constitutive of other perspectives within the field and of course those emerging from other disciplines.

The issue of discipline arbitrariness is relevant here. For me, critical pedagogy is inevitably multidisciplinary. But more than that, it is a critique of the very desirability of discipline boundaries. Esoteric specialization obscures the holistic nature of our experiences of the world, results in increasing dependence on experts, and is hence a major source of powerlessness. Revealing the arbitrariness of field specialization and its role in the credentials game is a salient feature of the pedagogy I'm advocating. Correcting silences thus means, among other things, creating courses that cross disciplines.

It also means a reversal of the process that gives exclusive legitimacy to knowledge acquired within educational organizations. This implies bringing community representatives into the classroom and making space for student voices.

Therborn (1980) has written about cultural power – 'the capacity of social groups to convey notions of actual, possible and preferable beliefs and practices to their own groups and throughout society as a whole' (quoted in Livingstone 1987). One's role as a critical pedagogue includes providing opportunities for the enhancement of cultural power. To this end I have frequently invited guest speakers to the class. The following have regularly shared their social and political views with my students: union leaders, farmers, members of parliament, native elders, members of the clergy, student activists from Third World countries, school teachers, high-school students, and ex-cons.[1]

Making space for these voices is important; however, making space for student voices is essential. One's own autobiographical revelations are, I believe, a necessary step in this direction. If one wishes students to engage in dialogue, to reveal something of themselves, their world views, the meanings they give to their experiences, one must do the same. This means revealing yourself as a whole person, someone who has a life outside the classroom. I refer here to providing students with glimpses into your private life – how long you've been teaching, where you did your training, what got you into sociology in the first place, leisure pursuits, hobbies. I refer also to any anecdotes culled from personal experience that could serve as relevant illustrations of social processes. For example, I find stories of my awkward adolescence (told with self-deprecatory humour) useful vehicles to illuminate phenomena such as gender relations, peer pressure, and symbolic interaction.

It is one thing to encourage students to speak; it is another to create classroom structures that facilitate this objective. I summarize below those particular practices I have found most useful:

Extensive Use of Discussion

Although discussion groups can work, their success depends on equipping teaching assistants with appropriate pedagogical techniques – 'appropriate' for me implying those techniques consistent with the tenets of transformative teaching. This in turn means sessions with one's teaching assistants discussing and practising the relevant elements.

It is an unfortunate current reality, however, that teaching assistant resources, as well as other teaching resources, are in short supply. This does not necessarily mean that we cannot involve our students in the learning process. The following strategies are ones I have found useful even in classes of well over 400 students.

Peer Introductions

During the first week or two of classes I have students introduce themselves to one person in the room they do not know, and to share a bit of their personal history. I do this again several weeks later. Expanding on this, I have these pairs form into groups of four, with each person introducing their partner to the other two. I find the frenetic activity and buzz that accompanies this process a welcome antidote to the usual passivity in lecture courses.

Students as 'Text'

Students can contribute directly to the curriculum by providing a range of demographic, attitudinal, and behavioural data. Some examples of each:

a) In discussing access to university, I ask students to indicate by a show of hands how many have at least one parent with a university education. This is invariably around 50 per cent of the class, significantly higher than the national average. A debate ensues over the connection between class and university attendance. In a similar vein, information on parents' national origin and length of time in Canada is a prelude to a lecture on multiculturalism and immigration policy.
b) Short, simple, self-administered surveys can elicit student attitudes toward abortion, capital punishment, Quebec separation, and a myriad of other issues. These can then be fed back to students to enrich and personalize lectures in these areas. Periodically gathering data on students' feelings about your lecturing, the course organization, preferred guest speakers is also appropriate. Most of us wait until the course is over to receive such feedback, clearly not helpful for our current students.[2]
c) Regarding behaviour, I typically weave my observations of student classroom conduct, as well as self-reported actions, into my lectures.

In a class on education I begin by asking the males to raise their hands, then the females, then those students over the age of 25. Invariably the younger males are seated toward the back of the room, the younger women in the middle and sides, and the older, returning women, near the front. I share this observation and ask the students to speculate on reasons for the pattern. This is a prelude to a sharing of various encounters with public schooling, and a more focused discussion on the gendered nature of education.

In the week before a lecture on deviance I distribute a short, anonymous survey on self-reported violations of the Criminal Code. During the ensuing deviance lecture I feed the results back, comparing them at the same time with national statistics. The focus is on class and gender correlations with commission, apprehension, and the formal entry into the justice system.

As a final behavioural example, a lecture on gender relations is preceded by a role-playing session in which a male and a female volunteer to stage an initial heterosexual encounter in a pick-up bar. Discussion centres on the normative structure guiding the interaction, including who initiates the encounter, the content of the conversation, and the messages encoded in non-verbal behaviour, particularly body language.

Listening to student voices is not confined to curriculum exploration, however. Classroom work practices and their products, including modes by which they are evaluated, are also fair game for student input. Collective work is always an option in my courses. Such work is at the root of political action and is hence a central empowerment process. Joint essays can therefore be negotiated. As well, I regularly offer a ten per cent bonus for involvement in an oral presentation with at least one other student. These are typically carried out in the discussion group hour and are approximately a half-hour long. A quarter of the class regularly participates.

None of the classroom practices alluded to above are likely to evoke resistance on the part of university administrators. A significant modification of traditional grading practices, however, *is* likely to produce resistance. Grades are the basic units of academic exchange, and the major device used to legitimize inequity in access to graduate school and scholarships. Failure to adhere to normative conventions regarding their construction and allocation, therefore, seriously threatens the institution of schooling. Indeed, eliminating grading altogether, although arguably consistent with the objective of empowerment, is virtually impossible, particularly in large undergraduate classes. As a radical pedagogue, then, one is forced to deal with the potential contradictions inherent in a goal of student empowerment on the one hand, and professorial control over grading on the other. As Kenway and Modra (1992) point out, borrowing a Freirian expression, 'the liberatory teacher can NOT "wither away" while she/he remains firmly in control of assessment of student work' (154). Yet neither critical nor feminist pedagogues have adequately dealt with this most basic of contradictions. My own solution to this dilemma is twofold: to deconstruct the 'grade' for students, and to encourage student involvement in the construction of their own grade.

The first solution entails a detailed explication of the criteria used to evaluate student performance. To illustrate, many of us in grading essays work with criteria based on the hypothetico-deductive model derived from the natural sciences. We therefore expect the essay to proceed in linear fashion from the general to the specific, with broad theoretical/ conceptual statements leading to and subsuming more concrete ones. Essays failing to embody this form are typically described as 'all over the map,' or in need of 'tightening up,' and do not fare well. How many of us, however, actually convey the expectations as to form, let alone explicitly instruct students on how to construct such essays? My own observations suggest that such criteria remain covert, part of the 'hidden curriculum' of schooling (Kennett 1973; Giroux 1983). I agree with Dence (1991): 'We should be prepared to teach and teach well whatever it is we claim to value in our grading practices' (15). The first few weeks of my course are thus typically given over to instruction on writing academic essays.[3]

Finally, although as professor I am the ultimate recorder and submitter of the grade, students can exert considerable control over its construction. Some practices I have used to this end are: take-home examinations, contract grading, and selective grading (encouraging students to decide for themselves the weights to be given to exams, essays, and group work).

Feminist Teaching as Transformative Pedagogy

As intimated earlier, a few years ago I decided to restructure my course along feminist lines. In thinking about it now, I can see two fairly distinct phases in the restructuring process: an initial period of relatively naïve enthusiasm, followed by a much more critical, reflexive examination of what I was up to.

Phase 1 – 'I Am a Male Feminist'

The first period, which lasted well into the second year of the course, was characterized by an innocence about what such work would entail. I saw the transition from a critical pedagogue to a feminist pedagogue as being accomplished simply by proclaiming myself a 'male feminist' and by infusing the course with a set of feminist lectures (focusing largely on the linkages among patriarchy, the social construction of gender, and gender inequality). That is, while I made changes in the content of the course, my classroom practices were left virtually intact. In brief, I believed my pedagogy to be perfectly compatible with a feminist agenda. Feminist writers on pedagogy borrowed liberally from the critical pedagogy of Paulo Freire, a writer who had considerably influenced my own thinking on education. The idea of empowerment underlies both the work of Freire *and* that of feminist scholars. Further, I was able to find ample support in feminist writing that the means to empowerment were consistent with classroom practices that I was already employing. The dominant ones include working toward non-hierarchical classroom relations; promoting the validity of divergent voices; taking a critical, deconstructionist approach to knowledge and truth claims; adopting a multidisciplinary emphasis; and encouraging collective work (Thompson 1987; Belenky et al. 1986; Shrewsbury 1987). What I did not consider at the time, however, was that these practices were predicated on the assumption of a woman teaching feminism to women. It was only in the second half of the second year that I began to reflect on how such practices might be quite differently read when the feminist teacher is a male. I return to this issue in the ensuing section.

The following highlights the salient curriculum changes in my revised course.

During the initial class I introduced myself, much in the manner I had in the past, sharing the elements of my biography that had led me to the discipline of sociology. In addition, however, I indicated that the course would proceed from a feminist orientation, and while the full meaning of this would emerge as the course proceeded, it could initially be understood as a perspective focusing on the extent and nature of gender inequality. For the next month and a half or so I did my usual thing: I introduced the forefathers (Durkheim, Weber, Marx) as exemplars of three dominant frameworks in sociology: functionalist, action, and conflict theory. In doing so, I put the men and their frameworks into historical, biographical context, thus using the idea systems in sociology as an illustration of the way in which knowledge is socially constructed. I then raised the question of why there were no founding 'foremothers' in sociology, which led to a two-pronged discussion of the differential access of nineteenth-century men and women to writing and intellectual activity in general, and of why women who did write (e.g., Rosa Luxembourg) were not accorded intellectual prominence. I asked whether much has changed, citing the national average of eighteen per cent women among the professoriate. This is the entry for a more prolonged treatment of the power/knowledge connection, exploring especially the possibility that much of our inherited knowledge is androcentric in both form and content.

Roughly six weeks into the course I explicitly introduced feminism as a framework by asking the students to take a minute and free associate. 'I'm going to mention a word,' I said, 'and I want you to write down the first thing that comes into your mind when you hear it. The word is *feminist*.' I then invited the students to read what they had written. Most of the responding voices belonged to older women; the following is a representative sample of their responses: change, confidence, equality, powerful, justice, sisterhood, liberation, strength. I then remarked that I had yet to hear a male voice, and asked the class why they thought this was the case. Much shifting in seats, until one young man at the back suggested that what some of the men had to say would not be well-received, particularly in a course taught by a self-acknowledged feminist. (I remember asking myself at the time whether the males would have held back if I was a female, deciding later that no, in all likelihood they would *not* have been reluctant to express discontent in this case – see McIntyre 1987.) I suggested that rather than voice their responses, they could leave them on my desk at the break, anonymously of course. Some did (including several younger women), and I read some of them to the class when we reconvened: man-hater, dyke, bra-burner, lesbian. I used the opportunity to introduce the notion of stereotypes, and challenged the class to reconcile the living, breathing, heterosexual male feminist standing before them with the attributes I had just read out. Laughter ensued and some of the tension dissipated. Yet I had not dealt directly with the general reluctance of men to make their views known in class. This was to resurface at various points in the course, but it wasn't until the third year of offering the course that I explicitly addressed the issue in my teaching.

The next step was to give them my definition of a feminist, which included three criteria: the belief that gender was a crucial axis of social inequality; a commitment to analysing and redressing this inequality; and a conviction that in both processes (analysis and change) the centrality of women's voices and experiences was essential. 'This means,' I pointed out, 'that, at least according to the definition I gave you, a male can be a feminist.' 'Indeed,' I emphasized, 'there's nothing in the definition that precludes this.' (The possible incongruity between this last statement and criterion three did not strike me at the time.) Having asserted this, I blithely continued with the course. I did not see then that merely proclaiming myself a 'male feminist' was insufficient. Indeed, I had violated my basic premise of teaching – I had not linked my feminist stance to my own biography. I had treated the male/feminist couplet as unproblematic, whereas for some students in the class it *was* problematic, and was, as I suggested above, a major source of the relative silence manifested by the younger men and women in the course.

I then indicated that the focus on analysis *and* change meant that feminism was *both* an intellectual framework and a political agenda. I emphasized that this was true of all sociological frameworks, although perhaps was more explicitly stated in feminism. After introducing patriarchy and the social construction of gender as the two key ideas in a feminist approach, I located the rise of second-wave feminism historically. Here I presented the contradictions in the role of women both during and after the Second World War, and in the left movements of the sixties, as the major catalysts for the renewal of feminism in the seventies and eighties. The rest of the course was devoted to a feminist analysis of traditional institutional areas – education, the family, the state, and, because of my own particular interests, a segment on children's play.

Phase 2 – 'I Am a Pro-Feminist'

Student course evaluations are institutionalized at Carleton, as they now are at most universities. These are administered at the end of a course and consist of a series of structured questions, as well as an open-ended comments sheet. In addition to this required instrument, I typically survey my students twice *during* the school year. I ask them to anonymously give me their perception of how the course is going, along with their gender and whether they are over 25 years of age. After the course, then, I have three sets of comments, with roughly 40 per cent of the students opting to participate in the process.

Before the transition to a feminist course my evaluations were very strong, with the critical comments focused largely on the text and readings. The content of my lectures and my teaching were rarely mentioned. With the change in my course, however, both aspects received student attention. I wish to present these by the three dominant gender/age groups – the over-25 women, the younger women, and the men. (There were very few males over 25 in my classes, insufficient to warrant a separate category.)

First, in all three years of the course the older women were by far the most receptive group. They were the most likely to speak in class, they contributed most to the evaluation process, and their comments on the evaluation sheets were the most positive. A favourite of mine: 'It's wonderful to see a male so committed to feminism. Are you teaching any second-year courses, and how do I sign up!?' There were several exceptions to this pattern, however, and one in the second year proved to be very significant to my own subsequent teaching. I reproduce the salient comments:

> First let me say I admire your attempts to convey feminist principles. I'm sure they are well-intentioned. As a feminist woman, however, I feel uneasy when a male tells me what is important in feminist thinking and what is not. I am particularly bothered when you talk about women as passive victims of patriarchic ideology – are we really so stupid as to buy into this stuff without thinking, without rejecting at least some of it? I think not ... Finally, you should ask yourself whether using the same type of evaluation techniques as non-feminist profs (e.g. essays, exams) is consistent with your feminist views.

The student's second point forced me to look more critically at my evaluation criteria. Through the work of one of my honours students (Duquette 1990), I was made aware of several works on gender and writing, particularly Daumer and Runzo (1987). In this piece the authors postulate the dominance of androcentric models of essay writing: 'We still primarily teach a style, whose distinctive features are detachment from others, suppression of emotion, a "logical" – i.e., hierarchical – organization, "appropriate" topic and word choice, persuasive strategies, and reliance on rules' (52). Since the essay form originated in Francis Bacon's scientific writings of the sixteenth century, these characteristics are hardly surprising. In the recent version of the course I therefore not only armed students with techniques to reproduce the dominant writing form, but also deconstructed this form as an individualistic, linear, rational, and objective view of the organization and dissemination of knowledge, with a beginning in early scientific writing. I contrasted this with other forms that would be equally acceptable in my class, forms such as the journal and the life history, both of which give validity to personal experience and to writing as process rather than product (Berthoff 1982; Elbow 1981; McCarthy 1987).[4]

It was the student's first point, however, that had the most impact on my teaching, as it forced me to examine the issues of empowerment and voice as they applied to my own situation – a male teaching feminism. She was bothered by both the lack of agency in the feminist models I had presented, and by my own gender. Further, these were mutually sustaining – the seeming impotence of women in the face of patriarchy was reinforced by the presence of a male authority figure espousing feminism!

As I worked this through I was aided in large measure by a 1990 article by Jennifer Gore (reprinted in Luke and Gore 1992), in which she looks at the implications of a Foucauldian conception of power for critical and feminist pedagogy. As she puts it, 'Rather than conceiving of power as a possession or commodity, a thing to be held or exchanged, Foucault (1980) argued instead that power is "exercised, and ... only exists in action" ' (58). Power is thus always immanent, and resides not in individuals but in deployment itself. Agency is thus ubiquitous – it only requires articulation as power. In the subsequent offering of my course, this conception of agency proved a welcome antidote to the predominantly structuralist view of patriarchal hegemony extant in the literature.

Perhaps more salient, the notion of *em*powerment takes on a completely different meaning. As Gore remarks, 'Given Foucault's conception of power ... empowerment cannot mean the giving of power. It could, however, mean the exercise of power *in an attempt ... to help others to exercise power*' (59, my emphasis). This reconceptualization of empowerment resonated with the conclusions recently arrived at by two of my feminist colleagues, both white women, who were struggling with the white feminist/women of colour issue so prevalent in discussions of 'authentic voice.' Daiva Stasiulis (1993), in her analysis of the Canada Council's emergent policy on fiction writing, commends the Writer's Union's Ad-hoc Committee on Racism in Writing and Publishing for shifting the voice debate 'away from the paralysing issue of "authenticity" to focus on political and economic issues of *access* to print of new or excluded voices' (my emphasis). Addressing the issue in a teaching context, Lorna Weir (1991) alludes to the sensitivity required in classroom treatments of the race/gender couplet:

Race-gender analysis undertaken by a white woman in the presence of women of colour comes dangerously close to speaking for people of colour, displacing these voices, replicating the form of racist knowledge production and circulation ... the question is one of fashioning a teaching practice which *creates openings for women of colour to speak* their understanding and experience of racism. (25, my emphasis)

The above works aided me in redefining my role as pedagogue – from one who used *his* power to speak on behalf of and about feminism, to one who *provided classroom access* to women's feminist voices. Translating this into classroom practice embodied four elements: continuing to encourage women in the class to share their experiences; including on my reading list a wide range of feminist material; inviting guest speakers with feminist views (recent guests included a lesbian rights activist and a rape crisis worker); and the extensive use of feminist-inspired films and videos. Two films I shall now regularly use in my course are Jeanne Kilborne's *Still Killing Us Softly*, a well-crafted critique of the use of women's images in advertising, and the National Film Board's *Not a Love Story*, a raw and engrossing look at the pornography industry. As I shall indicate shortly, the former work has been especially valuable in reaching the males in the class.

The above practices are consistent with a pro-feminist rather than a male feminist position. Adopting such a position entails a shift from my presenting feminist frameworks and women's experiences to conveying them through feminist writings, guest speakers, and film. This does not mean that I cease integrating and synthesizing ideas or engaging in critical analysis. It does mean, however, that I consciously provide classroom access to female feminist voices. An important element of my teaching is therefore that of facilitating such access, to ensure space for women to claim feminism as their own. With this shift came the insight that as I stepped back a bit, providing more breathing room for women, I simultaneously positioned myself more clearly as a masculine subject, providing the impetus for the men to come closer. Indeed, I have come to the conclusion that the most useful contribution male pedagogues can make to the feminist cause is to mobilize the support of their male students.

Reaching the Men

Although the reactions of the older women to the first two years of my revised course were very positive, there were signs of unease. These came mostly from the younger men, but also from some young women. Their resistance was manifested in three forms: they (particularly the young men) were the least likely to speak up in class, they disproportionately opted out of the evaluation process, and, when they did opt in, they were more likely to express negative comments. In contrast, in my pre-feminist years the negative comments were not correlated with particular age–gender groups, nor were they focused on lecture content, but were concerned largely with the readings and assignments.

Two major themes now dominated the negative comments: the privileging of gender as the organizing theme in the course, and the perception that the course inordinately blamed men for the oppression of women. Here is a sample of these from the first two years of the revised course, the first four from young women, the latter five from men:

My only criticism is perhaps allowing too much time for class discussions, therefore allowing the class to sometimes go off on a tangent re *feminism*! (even though I am a female!)

Need more balanced presentation, e.g. because pro-feminism, anti-male feeling set in class for a few weeks. What about 'real women' groups and other women who are not feminist?

Classes were interesting but I felt too much time was spent male-bashing. Perhaps discussions could've been organized so that a wide variety of things were touched upon, not just feminism. I understand, being a female, feminist issues are important but this is sociology, not women's studies.

The course itself is interesting, however I am getting a bit sick of the repetitive monotony of 'gender.' Surely there must be more to sociology.

The view of feminist inequality was too major a concern in class and was always too often referred to. The view of the professor as a feminist was too strong in my opinion to be objective.

As a male, I feel alienated in the class due to gender-specific focus. Male-bashing discourages equitable male participation.

There is more to life than gender differences, and sometimes things are pushed.

Too narrow-minded on the concept of gender. According to S. Richer, the world would be a better place if everyone was a woman.

As a male student I feel that the way the teacher *steers* the subject matter towards a feminist slant gets to be a bit too much *sometimes*. I paid my fees to get both sides of the story, and both sides in a fair manner, I feel this is not being done *fairly* in this class. (As the prof said, after all he is a *male feminist*.)

By the second half of the second year of the course I had developed a set of renewed teaching practices aimed at addressing the above concerns. I incorporated them into my most recent offering of the course, with encouraging results: the feedback from the younger students was generally more positive, and, perhaps more important, the men were noticeably more active in classroom discussion. The salient change, symbolized by the 'pro-feminist' lexicon, was clearly positioning myself as a masculine subject. This was essential to the success of the other course changes: emphasizing the historical roots of patriarchy and its *structural* characteristics; adopting a non-essentialist position regarding the impact of one's gender on the reproduction of patriarchy; resisting the temptation to 'over-privilege' gender; and reconstructing my own discovery of the importance of feminist analysis. I discuss these in turn.

As I suggested earlier, my original declaration as male feminist impeded the development of a relationship with the men in the class and, by implication, impeded their identification with feminism as an intellectual and political framework. Essentially, the male feminist proclamation evoked closure, final conversion. The term did not readily allow for an exploration of what many men in the class were experiencing – the ambivalence inherent in a male embracing feminism. I was absolved from addressing this problem by collapsing the two components into one expression. This proved a successful gloss and, reinforced by my formal authority, left no openings for the men to explore their ambivalence.

This ambivalence, I believe, was rooted at least partially in tensions around sexuality. In a society such as ours, males manifesting female traits are typically viewed with suspicion, particularly by other males. A male calling himself a feminist runs the risk of homophobic reactions, of being labelled a 'wimp,' 'wussy,' or 'fag,' and of thereby being discounted by heterosexual peers. My own positioning as a heterosexual made it safer for the heterosexual males to entertain a feminist perspective.

This in turn made it safer for the young heterosexual *women* in the class to contemplate a feminist position. Magda Lewis (1992) offers an insight into the dilemma feminism poses for such women:

For many young women the concern about the compatibility of feminist politics with marriage and family is the concrete realization that making public what our feminist consciousness reveals about women's experiences of patriarchy can result in potential limits on desire. (185)

In a class where the men are relatively open to feminist thinking, such concerns are somewhat allayed. Indeed, during my most recent offering of the course, there was a noticeable increase in the participation of young women in classroom discussion.

Exactly what concrete classroom practices are implied by 'positioning oneself as a masculine subject'? For me, there are two related implications: acknowledging and reflecting on one's privileged status in a patriarchal order, and on one's complicity in the reproduction of that order; and acknowledging and reflecting on the construction of masculinity in exclusively heterosexual terms.

First, as Lewis (1992) argues, men in the class must be required to 'own their social location by exploring the parameters of their own privilege' (188). I begin this exploration by explicitly asking the men in the class to reflect on these benefits. This was greeted with much head-turning (to see who would begin) and considerable unease. No one speaks. I take the initiative by noting that both myself and my brother went on to Ph.D.s while my sister acquired an elementary teaching certificate. I then link this to recent national data on the disproportionate presence of males in graduate school, and ask for similar examples. Someone comments that most public school administrators (principals and vice-principals) are males, while the 'front line' teaching force remains largely female. A general discussion ensues of the gendered nature of opportunity, and of the policies currently being explored to address the issue.[5]

In the next class, an older woman tentatively raises the issue of women's constant fear of violence, a fear she suggests is simply not a part of men's daily existence. I was hoping this issue would be raised (and would have raised it myself if a member of the class had not), and offered some data on the prevalence of acts of violence against women, and on women's attitudes regarding fear of public places and of walking alone at night. Several of the women were eloquent in expressing their own fears – 'always in the back of your mind'; 'a part of what it *means* to be a woman' – and it was generally agreed that the *absence* of such fear was indeed a major privilege enjoyed by men.[6]

The acknowledgment of complicity in the reproduction of patriarchy, however, was not as easily explored. Sensitive to the critique of 'male-bashing' that arose in the first two years of the course, I prefaced the discussion with two observations: that patriarchy is a *structural* phenomenon, in that it is encoded in discourses, images, and practices not of our own making; and that its roots are embedded in the long history of human society. Patriarchy, I emphasize, is at least 3500 years old. I then illustrate this with an analysis of the patriarchal nature of Judaism and Christianity, tracing them both to a male godhead and to a common creation myth accentuating the moral and material inferiority of women. I found that contextualizing patriarchy in this manner served to alleviate somewhat the perception that men, and in particular contemporary men, are directly to blame for the misogynist aspects of gender relations.

I go on, however, to indicate that although social structure pre-dates us, we are *all*, in our daily lives, responsible to some extent for its reproduction. As an example I make the point that masculinity in our society has been conflated with heterosexuality, and that as men we are subjected to considerable social pressure to perpetuate this connection. Resisting the temptation of the critical teacher (so well described by Lather 1992, 131) to 'demonize some "other" ' while positioning oneself as 'innocent,' I refer to my own struggle to resist constructing women predominantly as sexual objects. 'We men,' I begin, 'are very good at this.' (I must point out that the 'we' is very important here. It serves not only to transcend somewhat the professor–student distinction, but works as well to remove a major obstacle to men's classroom participation: the *individual* guilt that is often felt about the victimization of women.)

I proceed to recount growing up with a group of male friends: the prevalence of discourse around 'tits' and 'ass,' the sexist humour that was a regular part of our interaction, and how one's masculinity was constructed at least in part in terms of one's success at 'scoring' with the opposite sex. A reluctance to yield to this pressure, I go on, produced assorted homophobic reactions (taunts like 'homo' and 'wussy' were typical). I point out that such homophobia simultaneously accomplishes three things: it reinforces the sexual objectification of women, it reinforces male heterosexual desire, and it serves to subordinate homosexual men. In this daily heterosexual discourse, I conclude, we all make and re-make relations of power and domination. 'Even I, for example, still catch myself sometimes defining women primarily as sexual objects – me, your profeminist prof! What does *that* tell you about the power of patriarchy?'

I then ask the men in the class whether their experiences resonated at least in part with my own. 'Sure,' one ventured, 'but it's natural, are you saying it's wrong to like a nice body?' A supportive young woman points out that she and her friends all like 'a nice butt' on a man, and so men weren't alone in focusing on physical characteristics. What followed was a lengthy and vociferous discussion of the 'naturalness' of sexual constructions of others, the moral status of such behaviour, and the societal and personal consequences for the objects of such constructions. There was general agreement that being sexually attracted to someone was certainly not immoral, but that if that was 'all you saw in a person,' this was problematic. Several women reinforced this conclusion by describing what they felt like being continually assessed physically ('visually undressed' as one woman put it) by strange men – 'work gangs, construction workers, truck drivers, professors – you name it.' She connected this to the unease in public places that was expressed earlier, and alluded to fear, anger, and helplessness as dominant emotions in such situations.

'You make it sound like all men are potential rapists,' commented a male in a tone that conveyed both hurt and righteous indignation.

This seemed the appropriate time to address the essentialist issue underlying his comment, and after a moment of silence I pointed out that, extrapolating from recent statistics, the majority of men in the class had not committed and would not ever commit an act of physical violence against women.[7] However, I continued, because such violence, when it does occur, is largely a male act, women's fear and sense of powerlessness is understandable. I suggested that men could at least partially empathize with the process by reflecting on experiences in our lives in which being labelled by others made us feel frustrated and impotent. As an example, I related my own encounters with anti-Semitism, and one male talked about how being labelled 'slow' by a grade-school teacher negatively affected his self-perception and classroom participation throughout elementary school.

This provided an opening for me to again make the point (made several times earlier in the year) that gender was only one source, albeit a crucial one, of inequity and oppression. Others included race, ethnicity, class, and a variety of other social relations. I reminded the class of the two Ph.D.s and a teaching certificate held by the children in my own family, and pointed out that one could not fully understand this without taking *both* familial social class and gender into account in the analysis. This was an explicit response to the privileging of gender critique I had received in the previous two years, and in the revised course I made a conscious effort to 'balance' the treatment of gender with a consideration of how other factors, both independently and in interaction with gender, contributed to systems of inequity.

At the same time, precisely *because* of its focus on gender, I made it clear throughout the course that for me feminist analysis held great promise as a basis for understanding *all* forms of inequity. Indeed, I found that recounting how I came to this belief, how I personally 'discovered' the importance of gender and hence of feminist analysis, was a very useful device to reach the men in the course. In essence I took them on a journey that made some sense of questions many of the males were implicitly asking: What's this guy up there on about? Why should a *man* support feminism? What's in it for him? (And by implication, what's in it for *us*?)

Dorothy Smith (1992) talks about a 'regime of rationality' that pervades academia, and that works to maintain patriarchal control of knowledge and knowledge production. While this is conceptualized as a structural property of institutions, it was quite clear to me that the epistemological premises underlying the 'regime' resonated closely with the world view of many of the men I was teaching. In retracing my own steps in the discovery of feminism, I therefore found it useful in my teaching to emphasize at the outset that I was not *born* a pro-feminist, but that my adoption of the framework emerged from considerations of the personal and social *benefits* of a feminist agenda, and of the *empirical* significance of gender in human relationships.

Regarding the first, I suggest to the class that men as well as women pay the price of patriarchy. I lean forward, hands clasped, elbows on the lectern: 'Tell me if this sounds familiar (I'm talking to the guys here). You're sitting in a movie theatre and there's a scene of profound sadness, and you have an overwhelming urge to cry, or at least sob a bit. The familiar ache is in the back of the throat, tears are welling up ... but you can't cry, or, to be more accurate, you *won't* cry. A little macho character, chest out, manly swagger, whispers in your ear: "Whoa buddy, get a grip – you don't wanna *do* that." And by God you don't! You swallow that ache, you blink back the tears, you stare straight ahead – "Doesn't bother you, no siree!" Much laughter, nods of the head. 'We're locked in," I continue, 'We're in a box called "masculinity" and we sometimes find we can't express who we really are or want to be. We think the cost is too great. But the cost of staying locked in may be much higher than the cost of breaking out.' We talk about the stress inherent in attempting to live up to stereotypical definitions of masculinity, specifically competitive individualism and the appropriateness of violence in conflict resolution. I make the tentative link to male heart disease and lower longevity. 'There are possible social costs, as well,' I continue, 'of adhering to such expectations. What might these be?' A discussion follows of the effects of competition on the environment. The celebration of physical violence in masculine culture is linked to the Gulf War and to the posturing of Bush and

Hussein. Wc speculate on the kind of society that would accrue from the adoption of values emphasized in feminist circles, such as communalism and cooperation. Throughout the discussion I take care to avoid an essentialist position by emphasizing the institutional basis of patriarchy and the variation in attitudes and behaviour that exists *within* gender categories.

Regarding the *empirical* dimension, I tell the class that there are four pieces of data that have been instrumental in my own conversion to feminist thinking. The first, I say, involves the salience of gender in my own childhood. I begin with a personal anecdote about being discovered by my second-grade male classmates playing skipping with a group of girls. 'I still remember the taunts – "wussy face"; "homo"; "sissy pants"; "girlie" – the embarrassment, the shock, the feeling that somehow I had crossed a line I didn't even know existed.' I point out that insulting a male by the attribution of feminine characteristics is a major social control device among male peers, and serves inevitably to convey the message of female inferiority. I introduce the notion of gendered identities, how as children we socially construct others primarily in terms of biological sex, how these constructions are hierarchical (in that males are accorded greater value than females), and how they work to shape our self-conceptions and our interpersonal relationships. I conclude by presenting some material from my recent research on sexism in children's play (Richer 1990), balancing the recounting of personal experience with more 'objective' data.

In the next lecture I suggest that the negation of things feminine begun in early childhood is replicated in continual messages that objectify and commodify women. 'A very important influence on me in this regard,' I continue, 'was the following film, which I first saw about five years ago. It's on the images of women in advertising, and is entitled *Killing Us Softly*. I'm going to show it now, and then we'll discuss your reactions.' The film (and it's sequel, *Still Killing Us Softly*) is a well-presented and persuasive analysis, and the class is attentive throughout. Considerable discussion follows, ending with speculation on the possible links between such media imagery and acts of sexual harassment and violence against women. The men are active in the discussion and on the whole accept the film's analysis. One male approached me after the class and commented that the film 'really opened my eyes,' and that 'I will never look at commercials in the same way again.' Part of the reason for the film's success, I think, is that it emphasizes the structural embeddedness of misogyny rather than the personal acts of particular men.

In the next class I hold up a table on respondent's education, gender, average salary from wage labour, and father's occupation. 'The third piece of data,' I say, 'is this – some data on Canadian salaries. I'm going to hand copies out, and I want you to look at the table closely.' (The table is reproduced below.)

Annual Income from Salaries, Full-Time Canadian Labour Force, by Gender, Father's Occupation, and Education of Respondent
(Quality of Life Study, Institute for Behavioural Research, York University, 1981)

	Less than high school		Graduated from high school		University degree	
	Male	Female	Male	Female	Male	Female
Professionals, managers	24,938	14,077	21,509	15,486	31,957	23,901
Clerical, sales, service	20,807	11,762	21,358	14,808	30,076	20,759
Manual	20,076	11,781	22,148	15,801	28,951	21,841

'I put this table together about four years ago,' I continue when the copies have been distributed. 'I was doing a paper on the connection between social class background (crudely measured here by father's occupation), the respondent's education and salaries. I decided to refine the analysis by including gender as well.' Cognizant of the 'power of teaching as dramatic performance' (Lewis 1992), I pause and lean forward. 'While I expected a class origin effect and a gender effect, I did *not* expect the patterns evident in this table. Can someone tell me what the table says about how salaries connect to these factors?'

It doesn't take long for several students to point out that gender is a much better predictor of salaries than father's occupation. It takes even less time for students to detect the table's major anomaly – that women university graduates possess less earning power than male high-school dropouts. I conclude with the comment that these data forced me to develop a more complex societal analysis than I had previously developed, an analysis that featured gender as the central concept.

'And the last piece of data that convinced me of the validity of feminist analysis,' I pause, 'is evident in the pattern of support for the framework. Look around this class for example – which students are most conspicuous in their support of feminism?' A young woman correctly alludes to the older women in the class: 'It's the same in all my classes,' she observes. 'Right,' I acknowledge, 'and why would this give me additional faith in the relevance of feminist analysis?' An older single mother, front row centre, turns and faces the class. Her four-word answer makes the point in a way I never could: 'Because we've been there.'

Conclusion

The critical classroom manifests a continually emergent dynamic. There are opportunities to be culled, moments to be seized, by abstracting salient theoretical and substantive issues from the give-and-take of professor/student and student/student interaction. The above, therefore, cannot be a recipe for teaching in a mixed-gender setting. There is a contrived dimension to the preceding discussion due to the necessity of retrospectively imposing sequence and coherence on a complex, multilayered process. Nevertheless, it is offered in the hope that some part or parts may be useful for others in their own teaching.

As I reflect on it, whatever success I had in the course was due in large measure to my recognition of the importance to the teaching process of my own gender. As I suggested earlier, the most ironic testimony to the power of patriarchy is that I, a male, experience less difficulty introducing students to feminism than my female colleagues. This is not to say that there is no resistance, but it is less pervasive and more benign than that encountered by women teaching virtually the same material. My classes are not systematically disrupted (McIntyre 1987), I do not receive obscene phone calls or death threats (Coulter 1991), and I do not have to re-establish my legitimacy every time I encounter a new class.

This academic double standard, repugnant in its injustice, can be turned on itself. Our greater perceived legitimacy and comfort as male academics require us to work to create spaces for the emergence of feminism and other 'subjugated knowledges' (Foucault 1980). In doing so, our greatest strength may be in reaching those who are arguably the major obstacles to transformative feminist teaching – our male students.

Notes

I am grateful to Jared Keil, Heather Kitchin, Rob MacLeod, Val Norlen, Edith Smith, Daiva Stasiulis, and Lorna Weir for their thoughtful and helpful comments.

1 Bringing community representatives into the classroom is important, but a truly radical pedagogy implies student involvement in the wider society – an expansion of 'classroom' activity to include political action. In a large class,

though, accomplishing this via projects of one kind or another is virtually impossible. As a critical teacher, however, one hopes that processes of empowerment within the classroom might translate into *extra*-classroom political activity.

2 An unexpected finding I obtained from one of these surveys was that students wanted me to convey information about university services, particularly counselling services related to entering majors and honours programs. This request came largely from part-time students, some of whom felt alienated from the mainstream of university life. It struck me that such information was a source of empowerment in the most direct sense – it gave students some control over a large and often confusing bureaucracy. It also made sense to me that they saw the classroom as a reasonable place to receive this knowledge. This is the one place where students regularly gather, and is hence a logical focal point for questions about institutional rules and regulations. As a result I now habitually devote two hours during the first month of classes to a free-flowing question-and-answer period about university 'survival.' Members of the registrar's office and other administrative officials are invited and participate actively in the discussions.

3 Some texts I have found useful in this regard are Heather Avery et al. (1989), *Thinking It Through: A Practical Guide to Academic Essay Writing*, and Joanne Buckley (1987), *Fit to Print*.

4 I do not wish to leave the impression here that I espouse a totally gendered writing style dualism. One need not adopt an essentialist position in pointing out that writing style varies, and that particular forms are more compatible with feminist principles.

5 This discussion, focusing largely on affirmative action, produces the most concentrated burst of male participation in the entire course. Some are sympathetic to the need for such policies, but others express anger and frustration that they must pay the price of past injustice. The term 'backlash' is used by one young man, who argued, with some support, that women may be going 'too far, too fast.' It was clear to me that this issue was at the heart of much of the male resistance to feminism, and had to be resolved in some fashion to consolidate the gains made thus far in the course. I invited the students to construct a policy they felt would be a fair one in the light of past discriminatory practices. We eventually reached a compromise that maintained intact the meritocratic principles that were so central to the value systems of the majority of students in the class. This entailed a set of strategies to increase the pool of women applying for various jobs, while basing the final selection on 'ability.' In the interests of moving the course along, I resisted the temptation to deconstruct the term 'ability.' In my next offering of the course, I plan to formally devote a major section to affirmative-action and employment-eq-

uity issues, particularly in relation to the 'backlash' metaphor. (In this connection I shall make considerable use of Janice Newson's 1991 paper, ' "Backlash" against Feminism: A Disempowering Metaphor.' I recommend it to the reader.)

6 Gay men are clearly not exempt from such fears. The concerns of gay men and lesbians, however, were left largely unexpressed in the course. Their relative silence may have been due to my use of anecdotes and illustrations drawn from my experiences as a heterosexual male. As indicated periodically in the text, these included several homophobic references used to illustrate the heterosexual grip on the construction of sexuality. Given my assumption that male resistance to feminism is largely heterosexual resistance, I focused on reaching these men at the possible cost of neglecting their gay counterparts.

7 From the perspective of the women who spoke in this issue, all men indeed *were* potential rapists. My comment was meant to soften this implication.

References

Aiken, Susan Hardy, Karen Anderson, Myra Dinnerstein, Judy Lensink, and Patricia MacCorquodale. 1988. 'Trying Transformations: Curriculum Integration and the Problem of Resistance.' In Elizabeth Minnich, Jean O'Barr, and Rachel Rosenfeld, eds, *Reconstructing the Academy*, 104–24. Chicago: University of Chicago Press

Anderson, Margaret L. 1988. 'Moving Our Minds: Studying Women of Color and Reconstructing Sociology.' *Teaching Sociology* 16 (April): 123–32

Aronowitz, Stanley, and Henry A. Giroux. 1985. *Education under Siege*. South Hadley, MA: Bergin and Garvey

Avery, Heather, et al. 1989. *Thinking It Through: A Practical Guide to Academic Essay Writing*. Peterborough: Trent University

Belenky, Mary Field, Blythe McVicker Clinchy, Nancy Rule Goldberger, and Jill Mattuck Tarule. 1986. *Women's Ways of Knowing: The Development of Self, Voice, and Mind*. New York: Basic Books

Berthoff, A. 1982. *Forming/Thinking/Writing: The Composing Imagination*. Rochelle Park, NJ: Hayden

Buckley, Joanne. 1987. *Fit to Print: The Canadian Student's Guide to Essay Writing*. Toronto: Harcourt Brace Jovanovich.

Coulter, Rebecca. 1991. 'Integrating Feminist Scholarship into Teacher Education.' Paper presented at session on *Women in Universities*. Learned Societies, Kingston, Ontario

Daumer, Elisabeth, and Sandra Runzo. 1987. 'Transforming the Composition

Classroom.' In Cynthia Caywood and Gillian Overing, eds, *Teaching Writing: Pedagogy, Gender and Equity*, 45–62. Albany: State University of New York Press

Deegan, Mary Jo. 1988. 'Transcending a Patriarchal Past: Teaching the History of Women in Sociology.' *Teaching Sociology* 16 (April): 141–50

Dence, Carole. 1991. 'The Tyranny of Grading.' Paper presented at the Canadian Sociology and Anthropology Association meetings. Queen's University, Kingston, Ontario

Duquette, Tammy M. 1990. 'Women and Academic Writing: An Analysis of Writing Theory and Its Implications for Women's Education.' Honours Essay, Department of Sociology and Anthropology, Carleton University, Ottawa

Elbow, Peter. 1981. *Writing with Power*. New York: Oxford University Press

Foucault, Michel. 1980. *Power/Knowledge: Selected Interviews and Other Writings, 1972–1977*. Edited by Colin Gordon. New York: Pantheon Books

Freire, Paulo. 1973. *Pedagogy of the Oppressed*. New York: Seabury Press

Giroux, Henry A. 1983. *Theory and Resistance in Education*. South Hadley, MA: Bergin and Garvey

Gore, Jennifer. 1992. 'What We Can Do For You! What *Can* "We" Do for "You"? Struggling Over Empowerment in Critical and Feminist Pedagogy.' In Carmen Luke and Jennifer Gore, eds, *Feminism and Critical Pedagogy*, 54–73. New York: Routledge

Institute for Behavioural Research. 1981. Quality of Life Study. York University

Kennett, John. 1973. 'The Sociology of Pierre Bourdieu.' *Educational Review* 25

Kenway, Jane, and Helen Modra. 1992. 'Feminist Pedagogy and Emancipatory Possibilities.' In Carmen Luke and Jennifer Gore, eds, *Feminisms and Critical Pedagogy*, 138–66. New York: Routledge

Kilbourne, Jean. 1979. *Killing Us Softly: Advertising's Image of Women*. Cambridge: Cambridge Documentary Films

– 1987. *Still Killing Us Softly: Advertising's Image of Women*. Cambridge: Cambridge Documentary Films

Lather, Patti. 1992. 'Post-Critical Pedagogies: A Feminist Reading.' In Carmen Luke and Jennifer Gore, eds, *Feminisms and Critical Pedagogy*, 120–37. New York: Routledge

Lewis, Magda. 1992. 'Interrupting Patriarchy: Politics, Resistance and Transformation in the Feminist Classroom.' In Carmen Luke and Jennifer Gore, eds, *Feminisms and Critical Pedagogy*, 167–91. New York: Routledge

Livingstone, David, et al. 1987. *Critical Pedagogy and Cultural Power*. Toronto: Garamond Press

Luke, Carmen, and Jennifer Gore. 1992. *Feminisms and Critical Pedagogy*. New York: Routledge

McCarthy, Lucille Parkinson. 1987. 'A Stranger in Strange Lands: A College Student Writing Across the Curriculum.' *Research in the Teaching of English* 21(3) (Oct.)

McIntyre, Sheila. 1987. 'Gender Bias within a Canadian Law School.' Canadian Association of University Teachers *Bulletin* (Jan.): 7–11

McLaren, Peter. 1989. *Life in Schools: An Introduction to Critical Pedagogy in the Foundations of Education*. New York and London: Longman

Newson, Janice. 1991. ' "Backlash" against Feminism: A Disempowering Metaphor.' Paper presented at a joint session of the Canadian Association of Sociology and Anthropology, and the Socialist Studies Society, Queen's University, Kingston, Ontario

Richer, Stephen. 1981. 'Toward a Radical Pedagogy.' *Interchange* 12(4): 46–53

– 1990. *Boys and Girls Apart*. Ottawa: Carleton University Press

Shor, Ira. 1980. *Critical Teaching and Everyday Life*. Boston: South End Press

Shrewsbury, Carolyn M. 1987. 'What Is Feminist Pedagogy?' *Women's Studies Quarterly* 15(3, 4): 6–14

Smith, Dorothy. 1992. 'Whistling Women: Reflections on Rage and Rationality.' In William K. Carroll, Linda Christiansen-Ruffman, Raymond F. Currie, and Deborah Harrison, eds, *Fragile Truths: 25 Years of Sociology and Anthropology in Canada*, 207–26. Ottawa: Carleton University Press

Spanier, Bonnie. 1984. 'Inside an Integration Project: A Case Study of the Relationship between Balancing the Curriculum and Women's Studies.' *Women's Studies International Forum* 7(3): 153–9

Stasiulis, Daiva. 1993. ' "Authentic Voice": Anti-Racist Politics in Canadian Feminist Publishing and Literary Production.' In Anna Yeatman and Sneja Gunew, eds, *Feminism and the Politics of Difference*, 35–60. Boston: Allen and Unwin

Therborn, G. 1980. *The Ideology of Power/Power of Ideology*. London: Verso Books

Thompson, Martha. 1987. 'Diversity in the Classroom: Creating Opportunities for Learning Feminist Theory.' *Women's Studies Quarterly* 15(3, 4): 81–9

Weir, Lorna. 1991. 'Anti-Racist Feminist Pedagogy, Self-Observed.' *Resources for Feminist Research* 20(3/4) (Fall/Winter)

Re: Turning the Gaze[1]

HIMANI BANNERJI

An Act of Dissociation: The Private and the Public Self

The native's challenge to the Colonial World is not a rational conformation of points of view. It is not a treatise on the universal, but the untidy affirmation of an original idea propounded as an absolute. The colonial world is a Manichean World. (Frantz Fanon 1963)

Usually I write quickly. Usually I like writing. It's like fishing with a net, it's flung far, pulled in and gathered to a point, gathering me together into thoughts and images. This time, months of false starts, procrastinations, a nerveless dead centre. My mind turns its back on the project. I want to/have to and I don't want to/cannot forget/remember my years of teaching, of being perhaps one of the oldest non-white women teachers in Ontario universities, on what has become simultaneously trivialized and sanctified as the 'mantra,' or perhaps a hegemonic device for teaching a certain kind of feminist theory in the universities, namely 'Gender, Race and Class.'

What I want to write about finally is this not wanting to, of a persistent refusal by me, the writer, an Indian woman, to write about me, the Indian woman teacher, in a classroom at York University and in many public spaces for lectures. The private and the public parts of me refuse to connect in a meaningful formulation, and actually simply even to recount. Being a 'black' woman in the classrooms of universities should have been an 'empowering,' 'enriching' experience, but alas my stubborn mind even refuses to face that moment, that act of teaching, many years ago, continued for many years, 1975, 76, 77, 78, 79 ... My gestures of communication, defiance, knowledge, submission, humility, rage – the complex totality of my being and politics on display, through these years. The only politics other than writing that I have done in a *systematic* way in my years of residence here.

But what constitutes my private and my public? What cut off the nerves that connect them, or obscured from the self, my particular self, the elemental constitutive relations between them? Why is remembering so hard, and doing so 'natural,' so necessary a gesture?

These questions flooded my mind for a few days after a friend had lovingly, congratulatingly pointed out the fact that out there, there were many women, non-white and white, to whom my 'work' matters, who say this or that good thing about it – for example, that what I say influences how they think – or who even make a film. That is, I am taken seriously, I exist in others' minds as a real political presence, standing for a certain type of feminism. In hours of despondency my friend was trying to connect me with my 'achievements,' helping me to take strength from what I built, to appropriate what I have alienated. I have heard similar 'good' things from others and could never summon a response.

I tried seriously to 'feel' what she said. But the nerve was dead again. What I came up with instead was an image, like Oscar Wilde's *The Picture of Dorian Gray*, a splintered, public self, wandering the city, doing its work, growing as a perception 'for others,' echoing, projecting, developing what I daily inchoately think, feel, live, and read. She takes away from 'me.' I do not grow in or through her. The fruits of my labour, my public persona, are not my satisfaction. She does what has to be done and goes away. When the occasion vanishes she does too; she does not come 'home' with me.

Why is this? I ask myself. My 'acting' self, writing and teaching and talking self, is queried by my 'being' self. Am I lying? Are these empty words? Do I really not have a politics and simply utter noises whose meaning comes only from some outer combinations of words and meaning? and I go over what I said/say, what I teach, what I write and read, and there is no duplicity. If these are not *what* I am, *who* I am, then I have no idea who I might be except an empty signifier. The content of my public utterances are also the reflexes, impulses, emotions of my private self. What is coded as patriarchal, or 'racist' is felt/discernible, in the deepest emotional interchange. And yet, and yet, that 'other' of my 'self,' my public 'me' remains frozen in the public space where she was called forth by the occasion while I take the subway and go home ...

A Body in a Space – or the Social Relations of Production of 'Knowledge' in the Universities and Classroom

> I think of my daughter. I grow afraid. I see designs against her deep-set into their concrete structures or embossed into their Education Act. The blue of the sky, the gold of the sun, become me Aryan-eyed blonde and her spiked heels dig into my bowels. Fear lurks in the trees and gives the leaves their sharp precision. I sit in the Queen's Park, in the shadow of King George the Fifth, I am under his horse's hooves! I realize what Karl Marx once meant by being subject to the violence of things – a violence, an oppression, so successfully realized that it has no separate life. It lives, no longer in itself, contained like a cop's dog tied to leash, but in us, multiplied by our million cells, in our retina, eardrums, nostrils or goose flesh of the skin, lives this terror, at once an effect and cause. (Bannerji 1986, 25)

The other night I tried to describe what is going on to two of my students in a course on 'Race and Racism' that I am currently teaching. I tried to speak to them as thoughtfully and honestly as I can, trying to bring across the 'essence,' as it were, of this teaching experience. And what comes out of my mouth is not 'pedagogic' or 'conceptual'; I am recounting, I notice, about being a body in a space. And since it is *a* body, in *a* space, I am speaking particularly of my own non-white Indian woman's body, in a classroom where the other occupants are mostly white, and in a classroom in Canada. The space I occupy is the pit of an amphitheatre, a semicircle of faces and bodies occupying chairs that recede all the way to the ceiling. The room is high, fluorescent, a green board, a film screen that can be pulled down, a table, a desk, a lectern, sometimes a microphone. The hour is here, I am present, I am standing next to the table, they are waiting. Our class must begin. I am a non-white, five-foot-one woman. I am the teacher. They are the students. I must open my mouth, speak and grow to fill that room to the top. A hundred and fifty students will start taking notes. They will be restless and cause 'discipline problems' if I cannot sufficiently command the space by holding their attention. I am surrounded by their eyes, their ears, their pencils, papers, reluctance, scepticism, incipient boredom, the preconceptions that they bring to the class. But I must teach them. The spacing of our bodies indicates that is my 'job'; and their 'job' is to be a 'student body.' These bodies, mine and theirs, are antithetically placed. They think I have power, all this space is for me to fill with voices and ideas. They are a *captive audience*, they *have to be* there, fulfil course requirements, get the grade they need to be successful. They think I will stand in their way of getting it, I and my course material that they will have to get past, tackle, dominate in the name of 'learning.'

There is no need for arms, physical violence, material constraints. Just a gaze. (Foucault 1980, 155)

The course material is about racism. We are going through books that critique sociobiological theories about 'race,' the political economy of slavery, colonialism and imperialism, we are discussing histories of pillages, plunders and conquests, we are watching classes forming in Canada and other 'western countries,' we are decoding images of bodies that are not 'right,' not 'normal,' grossly noticeable as 'visible minorities.' We are reading all this through class and gender. But my lecture and the readings are touching the edges of disbelief of many of these students, going against years of their living and institutional education. The method and the content are alien, and they hug the upper edge of the class as though getting away from the centre, from me from whom these sounds float up and spray the edges of their consciousness. But their disbelief, discomfort or downright anger, float down to me as well. They confront me. They look at me. Their look tells me volumes. They stop on the outer edges of my skin, they pick out my colour, height, clothes, and I am aware of this look, 'the gaze' that both comes from and produces fixity. And I am teaching about bodies and how they are constructed into signs of differences tinged with inferiority. How histories, cultures, ideologies of Europe constructed a 'European = White self,' in relation to whom the 'others,' now called 'people of colour,' 'visible minorities,' 'immigrants,' 'Third World people,' are 'different,' the inferiority of whose 'difference' is signalled physically – materially, by skin colour, a nose shape, a mouth, a yellow star, leg irons, or other symbols of danger and domination. The 'hottentot venus' tells it all. And while I am lecturing on 'bodies' in history, in social organization of relations and spaces, constructed by the gaze of power, I am actually projecting my own body forward through my words. I am in/scribing rather than erasing it. First I must draw attention to it, focus this gaze, let it develop me into a construct. Then I take this construct, this 'South Asian' woman and break it up piece by piece. In every sense they are learning on my body. I am the teacher, my body is offered up to them to learn from, the room is an arena, a stage, an amphitheatre, I am an actor in a theatre of cruelty.

> The history which bears and determines us has the form of a war rather than that of a language: relations of power, not relations of meaning. (Foucault 1980, 114)

The social relations of teaching and learning are relations of violence for us, those who are not white, who teach courses on 'Gender, "Race" and Class,' to a 'white' body of students in a 'white' university. I want to hide from his gaze. I don't want to be fixed, pinned with a meaning. I hear comments about a Jamaican woman with thirteen children being 'related to rabbits or something.' It hurts me, I don't want to have to prove the obvious to explain, argue, give examples, images from everyday life, from history, from apartheid, from concentration camps, from reserves. And my body from which all this information emanates, fixed, pinned and afraid, hiding from the gaze.

And I dissociate.

I dissociate from my own presence in the room. But I signify, symbolize, embody a construct and teach on it. But I would rather not, I am tied to a stake and would rather not be – a 'Paki,' a 'visible minority woman,' an 'immigrant woman,' a 'they,' an 'other' – but be 'I' among many. But this body, along with centuries of 'knowing,' of existential and historical racism, is my 'teaching' presence and tool.

And I dissociate. My own voice rings in my ears, my anecdotes of the street feel hollow, I am offering up piece by piece my experience, body, intellect, so others can learn. Unless I am to die from this violence of the daily social relations of being a non-white, South Asian woman, in a white Ontario, Canada classroom – I have to dissociate. I hold a part of myself in reserve. All has not been offered up. A part is saved. That is mine. I step out of the half circle of the teaching space; here and there I meet 'students.' They say 'You're great'; the teaching assistants say, 'That was a good lecture.' Some student wishes to speak after class, she is young, white, and good natured. She is asking very basic questions, I can see that the course is working. But I, the 'I' of me that has been preserved feels no connection with what is being said. But asks instead, 'What has this to do with me?'

> An inspecting gaze, a gaze which each individual under its weight will end by interiorising, to the point that he [she] is his [her] own overseer, each individual thus exercising this surveillance over, and against himself [herself]. (Foucault 1980, 115)

I finish quickly and leave. My own work, the fruits of my labour, are alienated from me. Someone took them. I gave them away. Social relations of alienation, violence. I am dissociated. In one sense I am schizophrenic. I am inauthentic. And that is what I teach about, embody, respond to the violent social relations, forms and images that create my division and self-removal. So, of course, that I am a 'good' teacher; the impact I have on people is far away, dead or lost to me.

De-Colonization Is a Violent Process: Anger, Authenticity, and De-Colonization

De-colonization is always a violent phenomenon. (Fanon 1963)

But there is another way to understand my distress, my dissociation. Fear of the gaze, my presence in the theatre of cruelty, the sacrifice of my body to a white pedagogic god, is not the entire story. I am an object. But also I am a subject. My dissociation has also much to do with that. My pedagogic choice to teach at all, in this country, and what I insistently teach about, have something to do with de-colonization of myself and others, my innermost need to fight patriarchal, imperialist racism. And existentially, with my anger, to make it visible for myself, for others, to make it political. It is a long-drawn, patient, stubborn, persistent anger transformed into curriculum, into lectures brought centre stage into the theatre of cruelty. Every day a self dies, and a self gathers solidity. Every day an anger is shaped into a weapon through the hours, and every day its sharp edges are polished away by the rules of pedagogy. Every day I come home with somebody, and every day I leave somebody behind in the public space. But she does not perhaps just disappear at the end of the act. She is carried away in the eyes and mind of others, albeit frightening, the picture of Dorian Gray.

Teaching does not permit or perform anger, but real life, meanings, grievances, and injustices are daily brought into the room where I teach, a real relation of violence obtains in the room itself. I am a real person who is angry at having to prove to real people grown accustomed to racism, that it has a history, political economy, culture, a daily existential dimension. Sceptical, brutal, shame-faced questions dart out at me; a white woman defends the killing of a black young man, herself a part-time member of the police force, her husband implicated in the killing. I hear her, I see the stony faces of the black students in the class, the uncomfortable body motions of some white students, I hear a few hisses. My body feels tense and hot, I want to shout at her, just plain scream –

'you fucking racist idiot,' 'you killer' – but I cannot. The theatre of teaching, its script, does not permit me to do that. If I have to say it, I have to say it pedagogically; exact a teaching moment out of it. I must build up a body of opinions and explanations here, which will challenge and crush her racism. Carefully, cunningly, smoothly I create with comments and statements and debates an ambush for her racism. I begin to summon up previous police killings, the work of the police in general, I invoke Sophia Cook, I remind her of the essays on the state, the police and commonsense racism ... on and on. I am teaching. The point is coming across, the meaning of racism is becoming evident and wider; but in the meanwhile there is me, there is she. My anger seeking the release of name-calling, a slap across the face, not this mediated rage. Of course I dissociate. My work and I part company. I am aware of doing violence to myself by choosing this pedagogic path.

> I should not have to hope. I should not have to care, about the multiplying, white interpretations of me, of Black people. We should have an equal chance to express ourselves directly. (Jordan 1989, 7)

And yet I chose to do this violence to myself. Because I choose to decolonize, to teach anti-racism, not only for myself but for others as well. This slow long extended anger of a method, perspective, theories, ideology, instances, political economy, and history – these hours of lectures, examinations, and essays, are my spontaneity, my anger, formalized, expanded, and contained, occasioned and stymied by the regulations of a white university. Subversion, protest, not revolutionary yet, or perhaps will never be. Yet a stream moving on its way, a little tributary to join what I dream of – a real socialist revolution, feminist, anti-racist, Marxist, anti-imperialist. The voices, the logic, the politics of my students, who are also my fellow beings, may become a little clearer, more convinced. An anger motivates me. I work on the anger of others with reason, so that somehow it will take shape of a sustained politics, of strategy and goal.

Fanon said, legitimizing violence against violence, de-colonization is a violent act. Daily I perform it with others.

> No matter what position she decides to take, she will sooner or later find herself driven into situations where she is made to feel she must choose from among three conflicting identities. Writer [teacher] of colour? Woman writer [teacher]? Or woman of colour? Which comes first? (Minh-ha 1989, 6)

Yes, it distorts me or us. Because anger against the daily ordinary violence and anger of racism distorts us. But there is no out, no clean hands. Undoing history soils us, cuts us up. We are in the front line. Others are coming along with and behind us, someday we will be whole.

So, yes, I dissociate. The mediation of my anger cuts me into two. But here in my actual, immediate work of teaching, I am not silent. At least not that.

Silence and Fury: Time among the Pedagogues

Who will educate the educators? (Karl Marx)

Where am I silenced then? By whom? And how? My existence is most powerless among those who are most supposed to be in the know. And there are stages of their knowledge and ways in which they wield the power of this. I have been both a student and a teacher for a long time. If I have felt dismissed and irrelevant among my student colleagues, and the faculty, arguing in private reading courses about the legitimacy of the Third World armed struggles, with European professors sworn to violent pacifism, among my bosses/colleagues both male and female (I was a part-time instructor for nineteen years at Atkinson College), my denial and dismissal felt total. This was curious because I was among male Marxists and female feminist professors, who were in some instances female Marxists.

What is the curriculum? What are the standards that only human life threatens to define and lower? (Jordan 1989, 27)

There were the first few years of apprenticeship at a feminist course and teaching 'concepts of male and female in western civilization.' A teaching assistant, lecturing in the course when the necessity arose for one lecture on marxism and feminism. For this reason called by the course director, jokingly, 'the male in residence'; marxism being a male sign, the concept of class a male social space, the worker a male. Curious I thought, this abdication by feminists of the role of women as producers, except in early matrilocal agricultural societies. Having proved that women created pottery, weaving, gathered and cultivated – we retreated into interior, into the home, into the psychology of a Jungian self, with intact masculine/feminine stereotypes – anima/animus – now added into 'androgyny.' We did 'culture' without any notion of labour, we did the goddess.

And our goddesses were white, from Crete, from Robert Graves. Our goddesses never went to the east of Asia Minor. They were the foremothers of the white women whose lives and experiences we discussed, who were iconized in Virginia Woolf, Gertrude Stein, and Vita Sackville-West. And through this act of omission racism and class lent no inflexion to white bourgeois feminism. Non-white goddesses and non-white women were absent together and working-class white women were their close companions. No one of the feminists I taught with, in those heydays of the discovery of patriarchy, thought that 'race and class' mattered. And this 'no one' was not me. It was 'them,' the shapers of courses and the destiny of something called Women's Studies, a little club of white women, otherwise kind to me, who never thought about my absence from their courses, along with non-white cultures (implying there were none, appropriating the Middle East as 'western'). The shame and anger of the days when I sat among these women, being women together, tongue-tied, becoming smaller with my irrelevance. And a self-hatred growing inside me along with a firm resolve to fight growing as I walked home in the snowy evenings, through slushy streets. Their self-ness made them so unself-conscious. They never considered their ideas irrelevant, their lives marginal, because they so happily were the centre, the creators/subjects of their discourse. When I raised, as I did stubbornly, the importance of race and class I was told that these notions belonged to another realm of politics. 'The personal was political,' but the political never became personal. I continued to make a living in this and other courses, drawing on my knowledge of European history and literature I provided a token presence.

These were two modes of consciousness that could not coexist with one another. (Smith 1987, 7)

And I felt ashamed and silent. Of course I spoke and argued, created curriculum but I became two selves. 'They' never touched my 'private' self with which, with my own voice, I wrote poetry, short stories, spoke with those who held no power. In those days of happy, unself-conscious cultural racism, my white feminist colleague did not even know that she was being racist! I wonder if there is one female white academic left anymore in Ontario, with such ignorant innocence. These feisty white maidens have become middle-aged academics who are now anxious about being called 'racist.' So under-politicized they still are that they don't yet know why they are questioned when they *are* being racist.

These are some of the forms in which silencing and exclusion of women have been practised, some have arisen inadvertently as a concomitant of [non-white] women's location in the world, some have been a process of active repression or strong social disapproval of the exercise by [non-white] women of a role of intellectual or political leadership; others have been the product of an organizational process. (Smith 1987, 25)

My first attempt to discuss 'race' with patriarchy was actually in shaping-up a course called 'male-female relations,' with a male Marxist colleague. His 'race' awareness came from the civil rights movement in the States, in which he participated. As he was quite forthright about racism, and anxious to learn feminism, and equally anxious not to seem racist, I was able to introduce the occasional text or idea that would point to the special situation of black or non-white women. When Angela Davis's book came out and articles appeared in Britain and the United States the task became easier. In Toronto, however, we only had ephemeral, empirical untheorized material which we put out, such as an issue of *Fireweed* on 'immigrant women.' It was much used. A journal/magazine called *Connexions* in the United States even reprinted our rather hasty, casually taped conversation that passed as the introduction.

There was no one to my knowledge, even in the late seventies, who taught feminist literature in the universities of Ontario from an anti-racist standpoint other than myself. Outside the academia, white young women, some of whom were Trotskyists, through the late seventies and early eighties practised an all-white 'class' feminism without any awareness of 'race' as a category of ruling or racism as an integral part of Canadian political economy. They evolved toward some control of print media but never considered 'solidarity' or 'sisterhood' (they straddled both concepts) with non-white women. They spoke about 'the working-class women' in Canada and never considered their peculiar racist formation and oppression. The birth and development of the Canadian state and economy from a white settler colony never entered their writing or organizing. They wrote books about domestic labour, but they never wrote about non-white domestic workers. They spoke of factory labour but their talk was devoid of racism toward non-white women or contained barest allusions to 'other' workers. When they did wake up to 'immigrant women' they expanded their horizons to Italian and Portuguese women. Subsequently, however, a few of these women went on to teach courses on 'gender and class.' Held to question by the non-white women's movement in the city, which had spilled over into the universities, these women woke up to the need of introducing the question of 'race' and racism. Never, however, did they communicate with us, who were non-white women, some of whom wrote, edited 'issues' of magazines, organized and generally lived around them, who marched with them, or with me, who taught courses on 'Gender, Race and Class.' On the few occasions I encountered them, when I was being summoned to embody, illustrate 'immigrant women' and eventually 'women of colour,' they were uneasy, withdrawn and even hostile. I felt surrounded, alone and in need for retreat.

In curriculum meetings, in designing courses white men and women automatically spoke about 'theory' and marxism and feminism as their preserve. I was allowed to speak to an 'issue,' racism not being seen as a fundamental form of social organization of what is called 'Canada' and thus not an entry point into social analysis. To this day I get invited to lecture on this 'issue' of racism once or twice in courses on feminist or social theory. Not even feminist theorists of the left seem to know how to build in this 'issue' as an integral aspect of their theoretical/analytical enterprise. I still notice how I, and a few more of 'us' who work at the university, have to teach these 'issue' courses, or better still how our courses even when they have a highly theoretical organization are considered as being 'issue' based. We continue to work in separate streams, white women and us, engaged in producing different kinds of knowledges.

> I am white, English-speaking, a paid member of the Canadian intelligentsia. I have my place in this same organization of relations that generates the experience of the world of those I observed. Such considerations as these suggest yet other possibilities in the relationship [between white and native people of Canada] ...
>
> Then a young native woman came down the tracks and, sitting beside us on the ground, cried and screamed at us in a language we did not understand. We had no idea what she was saying to us or why she was screaming at us – after all we were not driving the train; we were not in control ... We can only see what this might have been about if we shift from the immediate level of the relationship to the underlying historically determined structure of relations. (Smith 1987, 113–14)

To this day I have never, with one solid exception, heard a white woman academic speak honestly about her own work, problems of change with respect to inner and outer racism. It is not surprising therefore that I dissociate when I am with them. I find it very hard to remember names and faces of white women I encounter on these occasions. The response on their side is mostly guilty silence or guilty confessions, need for encouragement or congratulations because they are finally able to see; belligerence for exclusion from our lives and experiences because they can see. I once more dissociate from my performance. I don't want to speak any more than what I had to say in the meeting or my talk. I hate the bad faith of being 'nice' about something as brutal. I would have welcomed a real questioning conversation. Instead I'm given platitudes, passive aggression, and evasions. I have to be careful with the physical nature of my anger. So once more I dissociate. I don't care who is listening to what, what they carry away, mostly I concentrate on what I have to say – and leave the rest alone. Anger and repeated disappointment have taught me a depersonalization of myself and my audience. Rarely I meet a white woman who speaks from neither guilt nor patronage, who does not turn vicious and power tripping when pointed out in her racism, whose politics demands that 'racism' be more than an add-on to the main agenda of feminism.

> Women's liberationists did not invite a wholistic analysis of women's status in society that would take into consideration the varied aspects of our experience. In their eagerness to promote the idea of Sisterhood, they ignored the complexity of women's experience. While claiming to liberate women from biological determinism, they denied women an existence out of that determined by our sexuality. It did not serve the interest of the upper and middle class feminist to discuss race and class. (hooks 1982, 190)

The issue of adding brings me back once more to the strictly academic enterprise of designing curriculum for the classroom and criteria for the hiring of teachers. It has to be admitted that whatever anti-racist initiative I was initially encouraged or allowed to make came through teaching marxist courses or Women's Studies. It is under this project of 'adding women' that I proposed to add 'racism' and carried through one of the first courses at York University on 'Immigrant Women in Canada.' The course had two parts, on where the women came from and why, and where they came to and how they responded to their new situation. By stating that the course covered Canadian immigration from the 1950s to the mid '80s, I was able to demonstrate the fact that class formation in Canada has always relied on race and ethnicity and the Canadian state conducted its politics on that basis. This social zoning and political economy of the subaltern classes in Canada, the segmentation of its labour market, its refugee policies, its human rights records were connected to

Canada's white settler heritage and economic dependency on the United States. The last part of the course dealt with issues of subjectivities and agencies, and spoke about 'immigrant women's' own initiatives, their political organizing and cultural resistance. Of course we began by problematizing the notion of 'immigrant women' itself, soon to be joined by 'visible minority women' and 'women of colour.'

While designing this course I noticed how this category of 'other women' was added on, because times were changing through agitation of non-white people, and I believe, because some faculty members saw them as 'relevant' to their left perspective. But I also saw how I, an 'immigrant woman,' became invisible to them as such or lost my sociocultural identity. Nothing was changed in the main frame of the perspectives and methods of Humanities and Social Sciences used thus far. Genderizing racism and using this to think about class as a part of rethinking the methods of Social Science and Humanities was yet to come. These courses were to be added as a 'political' gesture. Both marxist males and females, members of the department, continued to hold a perspective of economistic political economy. They were content with a political arithmetic. And I felt intellectually cheated, politically negated and existentially invisible.

> The problem isn't to make third world women a topic within a feminist political economy, nor yet to invite third world women to speak in this zone of discourse. Of course they have already seized that initiative. The problem I am explicating is of a different kind; it is a problem of the concealed standpoint, the position in the relations of ruling that is taken for granted in how we speak and that bounds and constrains how a political economy of women can speak to [*sic*] women let alone third world women. It is a problem of the invisible centre that is concealed in the objectification of discourse, seeming to speak of the world dispassionately, objectively, as it is. For third world women, nothing is gained by being entered as a topic into the circumscriptions of white, male grounded or white female grounded discourse. The theoretical expansions of political economy introduced by white women remains, the standpoint within ruling is stably if invisibly present. Nothing will serve but the dissolution of objectified discourse, the decentring of standpoint and the discovery of another consciousness of society systematically developed from the standpoint of women of colour and exploring the relations of political economy or sociology from a ground in that experience. (Smith 1989, 55)

Designing courses for new Women's Studies was a more complex problem. A thorough critique of gender or patriarchy was obviously the reason for the existence of the program. The general cast of the program was what could be called 'white feminist.' This decoded meant that a racist gender essentialism pervaded the atmosphere. A 'Canada' was constructed where Native, Black, Chinese, South Asian, or Japanese people never existed as integral to its development or formation. But for the women's movement in the city of Toronto, arguments in the International Women's Day Committee touched Atkinson's more responsive program. A new course was to be devised and it was to be devised by me. And on its own merit, within its own scope, appreciated; but also bracketed, not connected with other courses, themes carried or traced from one to the other. To my knowledge, other than introducing 'racism' as a topic, or 'women of colour' and Black women as added topics or a faint gesturing toward anti-racist or 'Black feminism,' there was no discussion among the educators as to how to link the courses in the overall program. We never thought of exciting possibilities of reading feminist texts through the lens of gender, race, and class. For example, if Kate Millet's classic text, *Sexual Politics*, were to be rewritten or read inscribing 'race'/'ethnicity,' along with class, how phenomenally different a text or reading it would be. Or, for that matter, what the history of the British labour movement would look like if Sheila Rowbotham had another dimension to the picture of British working-class women, namely that they were Black and Asian. No reflexive, integrative analysis could be arrived at because in actual terms social power and social organization were not problematized.

> In contemporary works, like *The Remembered Gate: Origins of American Feminism* by Barbara Berg, *Herstory* by Jane Sochen, *Hidden from History* by Sheila Rowbothan [*sic*], *The Women's Movement* by Barbara Deckard, to name a few, the role black women played as advocates for women's rights in the 19th century is never mentioned. (hooks 1982, 161)

Instead of days spent in discussions about the common sense of racism, mostly with white women, and a white man or two, I heard from white people their concerns about 'ghettoization' and 'tokenization' of non-white people as teachers in the universities of Canada. But I, who was the 'token,' pointed out the inevitability of that phenomenon, in the general absence of non-white faculty and the impossibility in any case of creating a ghetto with one or two dark skins. Arguments then rose to the issue of representation, testimonials put forward as to how this or that white woman learned about her non-white lover or friend's pain by 'sharing' their thoughts or experiences, this was meant to advance claims about 'knowing' how it feels to be in her shoes. But this necessary empathy of friendship stood in for 'knowledge' and stood in the way of understanding the need for affirmative action in hiring. 'Progressive' men and women saw nothing wrong with almost total absence of non-white people in postsecondary teaching positions. The discussion gravitated instead to the question, 'Why can't white people teach about racism, particularly if they have a good politics and social analysis?'

It amazed me that such people of 'good politics' and social analysis could not see the fact that the exclusion of non-white people was not accidental, that the social organization of Canada actually expressed itself in the social organization/relations of the academic world and general production of knowledge as well. Nor were they, so eager to represent those who cannot represent themselves, questioning the situation on the basis of denial of subjectivities and agencies of non-white people. They never for a moment questioned their own motives nor saw as marxists that a 'good marxist analysis' includes praxis, recognizes the material, social relations, and conditions of knowledge.

Sitting there with a rage inside me, feeling both intellectually and existentially thwarted, I realized again the perils of being alone in a political struggle. It was apparent again that we, non-white women, have to be there in large numbers to make our point. The problem, so tendentiously constructed as 'Why can't whites teach *about* racism?' after all should be phrased as 'Why aren't non-white people teaching at all in the university about racism or anything else?' Why do our children not go on in their intellectual professional work in large numbers? Where do they go after their BAs? What do the faculty expect of them intellectually?

And sitting there, hearing claims about sharing 'experience,' having empathy, a nausea rose in me. Why do they, I thought, only talk about racism, as understanding us, doing good to 'us'? Why don't they move from the experience of sharing our pain, to narrating the experience of afflicting it on us? Why do they not question their own cultures, childhoods, unbringings, and ask how they could live so 'naturally' in this 'white' environment, never noticing that fact until we brought it home to them? Where is their good marxist feminist analysis in their everyday living? I imagined a land of marxist feminist apartheid, run by these people like Plato's philosopher-kings as our guardians speaking about us, without us. Of course all the right things are said about and for us, we live in a happy utopia of non-age, and never having the privilege of speaking for ourselves, making gains, making mistakes, learning from them, in short in not being agents of our own socialist revolution.

In the classroom of that 'Gender, Race and Class' course some white women students cringed every time I mentioned slavery, racism, and colonialism. They were affronted by the possibility of their consciousness being constructed through a white, male, middle-class culture. They could not or would not see that they had to question their common sense, knowledge apparatuses, and politics. They complained about my smoking instead, with ten letters, extending from the university president's office to that of the janitors. They did not have the decency to talk to me once before they embarked on this move. They accused me of being 'masculine' for teaching Marx and other male theorists, or having power over them because I lectured in the class and graded them, even though they accepted equally male Hegelian, Foucauldian, Derridian bases for postmodernist, post-marxist feminist theories and also knew that they were in an institution that runs on the very basis of competitive evaluation. In every way they seemed threatened and made efforts to undermine or de-authorize me. The worst was to have to sit through listening to their confessions of past racism, and present coming to light. An aura of guilt emanated from these empathetic white women rather than questions, criticisms, and politics. I felt suffocated and fled to those students in the class both Black and white, who had a less 'feminine' feminism, who 'masculinely' read theorists, argued with me for hours as to how exactly 'gender race class' mediated the social organization of each of us. The victim posture of many white women with regard to their men was seriously jolted by non-white women pointing out the racism of white women and their feminist movement.

The world has not changed very much since the days of my 'gender, race and class' course. The denial, the nausea, the feeling of bad faith – of others not mine – the offering up of guilty confessions, the many ways of creating exclusion, an in-built thwarted sense of distrust, an arrogant claim to theory, these and much more are still with and around me. How can I not dissociate? How can I in any serious way appropriate or incorporate the creations of my labour when the social relations amidst which, through and for which I create them, namely institutional and everyday practices of conceptual cultural racism, have pre-organized the conditions of my alienation and reification.

And yet, the last word in politics has not been said. Our options are limited, we can either engage or not engage in this struggle for de-colonization, for challenging various solid relations of power. If we do, the dualism, the manicheism of our world initially cuts us into two. If we don't there is no safe space to withdraw into, except a shadowy, confused, self-denying existence. But waging a struggle of anti-racist marxist feminism, might move us beyond a simplistic 'Black/white' manichean politics into one where we think in terms of social relations and ideology, rather than in myths and metaphors. As the formative relations between the public and the private become evident, my disassociation, my almost-schizophrenia might yield to a sense of a whole self – a little bruised perhaps at the end of the battle.

Notes

This article is reprinted with permission from *Resources for Feminist Research* 20 (3/4) (Fall/Winter), 1991.

1 Thanks to Robert Gill who suggested the title.

References

Bannerji, Himani. 1986. *A Separate Sky*. Toronto: Domestic Bliss Press

Fanon, Frantz. 1963. *The Wretched of the Earth*. New York: Grove Weidenfeld

Foucault, Michel. 1980. *Power/Knowledge*. Trans. Collin Gordin. New York: Pantheon

Gates, Henry, Jr, ed. 1986. *'Race,' Writing and Difference*. Chicago: The University of Chicago Press

hooks, bell. 1982. *Ain't I a Woman: Black Women and Feminism*. New York: South End Press

Jordon, June. 1989. *Moving Towards Home: Political Essays*. London: Virago

Minh-ha, Trin T. 1989. *Woman Native Other*. Bloomington: Indiana University Press

Smith, Dorothy E. 1987. *The Everyday World as Problematic: A Feminist Sociology*. Toronto: University of Toronto Press

– 1989. 'Feminist Reflections on Political Economy.' *Studies in Political Economy* 30: 37–59

Understanding and Solidarity

GERALDINE MORIBA-MEADOWS AND JENNIFER DALE TILLER

'Understanding and Solidarity' is a creative dialogue that resulted from the authors' collaboration of personal diary notes based on the shared experience of meeting bell hooks – a feminist writer and teacher who speaks widely on issues of race, class, and gender.

The conference 'Women in the Struggle for Liberation' has been quite a project. Chaos, frenzy, frustration but it is almost ready. This is my story: Now was my chance. She was sitting alone. I timidly asked her if she would sign my book. She smiled, said yes, and talked with me about the conference. I was proud to tell her that I was one of the organizers. I was so excited that bell hooks was showing an interest in me. I felt special, almost proud that she considered me someone worth speaking to. Because of everything she stands for, I wanted her recognition of my values. That I do not tolerate sexism or racism, or any other ism or phobia. Not that I think I know, or understand everything, but that I 'respect' and I want to learn.

the audience that i am addressing as i write / consists of white female academics / students and professors * in a sea of about 200 pigmentless faces i counted only 8 beautiful naturally pigmented faces * december 1 1989 * centre * for the first time in my university career have my BLACK sisters and i ever been so deliberately and joltingly placed at centre * not really the centre of attention / or a geographical centre * a new centre which did not make us object * this new centre made us the subject * not the audiences subject / but our own subject * we were without warning put at the vocal centre * someone was trying to give us a voice

On stage bell hooks was radiant. Her powerful words and gestures sent chills up and down my spine. I FELT a unity of purpose. I RESPECTED and admired her for her articulation of humanistic goals and standards. Most notably, I RESPONDED to her call for women to express their experiences. For women to learn to VOICE and document their lives. To stop outsiders (men with regards to women and whites with regards to Blacks) from interpreting and objectifying non-realities. My mental focus was on the issue of violence against women. I have waited, patiently to hear the muffled, silent voices of survivors. Every word a survivor whispers is pulled from deep inside, painfully. The experiences are real, not imaginary and they must be acknowledged, not analysed or explained. Please, just listen.

our realities * our voices were suddenly at centre * bell hooks spoke to us directly * she did this in the midst of white people who could do little more than observe * this brief moment will remain with me forever * how brave * she moved us from margin to centre literally * language is so powerful * with words as her weapon she / if even only momentarily / empowered us and silenced the rest * she was wonderful * wow * i knew that i would never be satisfied unless i spoke to her one on one * i had to meet this BLACK woman

* i wanted to learn more

You could have heard a pin drop while she spoke but as she finished, the room shook with passion. My passions were confused. I was in a euphoric state; in silent tears. I believed every word she said and I understood why she said it. She discussed white racism in historical literature and feminist theories. She emphasized that as a researcher or writer one must think about who they are and what context they are coming from. I wasn't offended because I am white. I was excited because she was providing me with new tools to build my ideal humanity.

as people began to leave i began to move in her direction * i wanted to run over and hug her and thank her * i was stopped * white people always think that they understand everything and everyone * the white people that i knew in the audience started coming up to me to get some reassurance that they were okay * piss me off * what they wanted was a BLACK person to tell them that they were good people and that they shouldn't take bell's message personally * too damn bad * i wanted to gloat and tell them that they should feel ashamed and guilty * i wanted to tell them that i didn't care how they felt at that particular point in time * i wanted to tell them that the slight discomfort that they were experiencing was only that / slight discomfort * while BLACK people have been involuntarily enduring pure pain for centuries

Wow, I am so excited to be invited to the dinner party held in her honour. I can't wait to talk to her some more. There is so much she can teach me. There is so much I want to learn.

my impatience and annoyance was not malicious * i wanted to be rude * i wanted to insult * but my socialization dictated politeness and diplomacy * i would have rather been congratulating bell / instead / i talked to them * i remained behind to play a role of adviser / and unwilling therapist * they must learn that reclaiming women's voices / means the voices of all women / not just white women or middle-class women who seem to do all the speaking * white feminists have to be made aware of their position * this one lecture certainly was not enough / but it was a beginning * in retrospect i think that maybe i should have revelled in the moment and been constructively verbally abusive * but this probably makes no sense to you anyways

wait * i'm not quite finished yet * i still have more to say * i don't feel entirely comfortable sitting here, describing my most intimate personal thoughts and opinions * i am vulnerable * my womanhood makes me vulnerable * my BLACKNESS makes me vulnerable * i don't want to further expose myself * i don't want to be misinterpreted * i don't want to be misunderstood * although i know it will happen / it always does * and most importantly i am damn well not looking for your sympathy * don't you dare look at me with pity in your eyes * i am a human being not an animal * if i sound angry / it is because i am * i am fed up and you disgust me * if this last statement bothers you / good * i am tired of qualifying my beliefs and disguising my true feelings in order to avoid offence * because of my growing impatience and desire to see a change / i don't care if i offend you * i must tell you the truth * this is not bitterness * this is an expression of anger * anger can be healthy * anger can be directed * the expression of anger is an indication of growing consciousness and dissatisfaction * the refusal to stifle your opinion is an indication of confidence / the desire for change / refusal to be tolerant or submissive / and the refusal to have your actions controlled or dictated by the status quo

At the dinner party I felt tension in the room. It was a strong atmosphere with very strong women present. I felt shy but immensely curious as I listened in on the conversations of various groups.

i finally had my opportunity to speak to bell but instead of approaching her i hesitated and spoke to people i already knew * i was a little scared * this physically petite woman had so much power and meant so much to me and i lacked the confidence to just walk up to her

The room was segregated. In particular I noticed the group of white middle-class academic women that seemed to dominate the living room floor. Their topic of conversation was not the conference but of personal and political ideals and dilemmas. I wanted to talk to bell who was sitting on the couch, but I felt shy and nervous. I wondered if she would remember me from the conference?

deloras / jennifer / and i / stood together and talked to people who came over to us * i didn't want to be engaged in comparatively trivial conversations / i wanted to talk to bell * finally the three of us walked over

When my friend Geraldine went to speak with bell I anxiously tagged along.

she held my hands and directed me to sit beside her on the couch * bell / deloras / jennifer / lyn / and i / sat together in a tight closed circle and began to share our thoughts

Geraldine, with her friend Deloras, sat beside bell on the couch. I felt as comfortable as a puppy by the fireplace at bell's feet. I probably looked like a little puppy sitting there because I felt so much admiration for this woman. I idolized her.

she smiled * her eyes twinkled * her warmth did not feel artificial or condescending * it was refreshing to talk to someone who didn't have a hidden agenda * someone whose actions were independent and not controlled by the status quo or their desire for tenure * i was still nervous / but oh so excited

The conversation really began when bell turned to Geraldine and asked: 'What are you doing now and what do you want to do with your life?' After Geraldine had answered, Deloras was asked the same question. By this point I had stopped listening. I was anticipating my turn to respond. I was actively conjuring up the best words, phrases, and examples to use to express my humanitarian ideals and goals. I wanted so badly to be impressive. I wanted to impress bell.

at one point a white woman / i don't really remember who / came over / sat near bell and tried to join in * to my amazement and pleasure bell subtly turned her back to this woman without ever once looking in that direction * what was initially so subtle became blatantly obvious

... Deloras had finished answering. My pulse was racing with anticipation and stage fright ... but ... it wasn't my turn yet. bell asked the woman to the left of me first. So, I continued to recite my lines in my head.

aside from one other BLACK woman present / who doesn't really count because she is a wannabe with a whitettitude / we were the only BLACK women present * bell had gathered us around her symbolically closing us off from contact with any of the other women present * she had again created a new centre * a BLACK focal point in the midst of a white environment

Oh, the anticipation ...
Then ... the conversation changed.
My heart rang in my ears.
Wait a minute.
What about me?!
You forgot me, bell.
I want to tell you about my life and my goals too ...
I could hear nothing.
I could focus on nothing else in the room but bell.
I searched her face for an answer.
Had she skipped me on purpose?
Was this a test?
A lesson?

Why does she think I need to be tested or taught a lesson?
What did I do wrong?
Is it because I am a white woman?
Does she think I am insensitive to Black women?
A fake. A fraud. Pretending to want to sit in this circle.
NO! 'I want to be here, I want to listen, I want to learn, I want to be a member of this circle of women who do not tolerate sexism or racism. I wish to fight these evils too. I always have.'
Why have you excluded me?
It hurts so bad, I want to cry.

it was so wonderful * bell spoke to us * we spoke to each other * we communicated * her character was so positive and warm * she listened and she understood where we were coming from * i wanted to scream out * make everyone conscious of what was going on * i wanted them to feel peripheral and excluded * 'not so nice eh / better get a sweater if you are feeling chilly'

I keep the smile on my face. Everyone else is so happy. I am so confused. My heart and my head are battling inside me. My head says 'Don't worry about it, Jennifer. Don't take it personally. These women are talking about their life as Black women. You can't participate.' ... I know, I understand that, and I enjoy listening ... but ... my heart says: 'I want to be accepted into this group of Black feminists. I may not share all of their experiences but I do share their concerns. I am willing to learn if they will teach me. I don't want to fight their battles for them but I do want to fight beside them.' Is this so impossible?
Why am I being shut out?

as we close ourselves off we were creating a reflection of what western society does to all who don't fit into the status quo mould * as we sat together the image created was similar to that of a photograph negative / the colours reversed

I am hurting. I am alone. Then ... Geraldine asks me a question and bell speaks to me. She put her hand on my knee when she spoke and she looked directly at me. What a relief. Perhaps I am over-reacting. I am not being ignored!

But am I really here.

as i grew conscious of how bell was deliberately putting her theory into action / i also grew conscious of how jennifer was physically sitting in our circle but was left out * i knew that she was being marginalized * i was sensitive to it * jennifer was silent * i could not tell if her silence meant that she was aware of her alienation and she was hurting / or if her silence meant that everything that was happening was going right over her head

Do they know what I am thinking? Do they know that I hurt?
Do they care?
I am so sure that bell knows.
I stare at her but she doesn't respond.
I have to speak with her alone.

i didn't want to care how jennifer felt but because i am sensitive to how one feels when silenced / i did care * shit * if she hadn't come over here with me this wouldn't even be a dilemma * 'jennifer why don't you go away * give us a chance to rejoice in our sisterhood / and our BLACKNESS / amongst ourselves / by ourselves'

i couldn't bear it any longer * if jennifer was going to be a part of this group i would try to incorporate her * i deliberately posed a question that bell had asked me to jennifer * i deliberately gave her an opportunity to speak * at that point in time i didn't really care what she had to say * not because i don't value her opinion / but because i could hear her opinions anytime * this was our only opportunity to speak to bell and i am the one who altered our focal point * BLACK people always do this / no one changes their agenda for us

I must talk to her alone.
They keep her so occupied.
I must get a chance to talk to her alone.
I am pulled back from my personal solitude and mental conflicts when I hear the discussion turn to the topic of marital integration. Deloras has strong opinions. Negative opinions. I have heard these feelings and fears before, but not while I was sitting as the only white woman in a circle of powerful, articulate, Black feminists. I don't want to run though. I want to hear their honest opinions on the issue. Deloras comments that Black men only want white women for one thing. She hisses that a Black–white relationship is based on anything but love.
I am incensed.

Angry.
Scared, as usual, to debate this perspective.
Especially in this circle.
I want to speak so badly this time, but I am sure that I won't.
Geraldine is looking at me in a funny way. She doesn't have to warn me. I have been in this position many times before. I know when it is not a good time to announce to a crowd that my ex-boyfriend is Jamaican. I was young when we met and I honestly didn't notice that he was Black and I was white. It didn't matter to me at the time, I fell in love with the man. As I grew, I became conscious of our differences. I learned through loving experiences with his family and through racist confrontations with strangers. I became aware that I loved a Black man.
But I felt no different.

I am angry at Deloras' overgeneralizations and insinuations. I so badly want to speak this time. Deloras is stereotyping me and the man I do love. A man I have loved for the past nine years. But I don't really care what Deloras thinks, and I know what Geraldine thinks. What I care about is what bell thinks.
I must speak with her alone.
I remain silent.

the topic eventually came around to the issue of interracial relationships * immediately i knew that jennifer would want to speak * the topic didn't bother me / everybody's got an opinion * what bothers me is that i feel that jennifer thinks that she understands BLACK people because she has gone out with a BLACK jamaican man for something like seven years * 'give it up jennifer' * i know that she loves her ex-boyfriend * i do not doubt this * what i didn't want to hear was a generalization of her experience to the entire race or how she now understands us * of course there is significance to her relationship / but only within the context of her relationship * white people always think that they understand everything * send a white person to any AFRICAN country for a year / a month / a week / and they come back experts on every issue related to the entire AFRICAN continent * BLACK people need space * we must stop allowing ourselves to compromise

The party is over. We are all leaving. I followed bell into the bedroom. Others followed too. I helped to find her leather coat. I wanted to speak, but others were constantly around us. I wanted to ask her why she had

skipped me. I wanted to tell her that I really was in love with a Black man and that he loved me too. I wanted to know what she would say. I needed to know what she would say. I have never needed any stranger's approval of my relationship before. Friends and relations who initially showed reservation, always came around when they met us both. But I need bell's approval, badly.
I must talk with her alone.

we prepared to leave * bell signed my book * we spoke some more * i really wanted to ask her for her address but i didn't think that anything i wrote to her would be of any value to her * i didn't want to waste her time * this is what my culture has taught me / self-doubt

Geraldine is so happy. She hugs bell good-bye.
I am so jealous.
I want to hug her too. Maybe I could quickly whisper my questions in her ear ...
But I can't.

we all walked out to our cars together * being the kind of person that she is / bell hugged a few people * then she hugged me and gave me some last words of inspiration

Every step I take closer to my car my heart and soul SCREAMS
'GO BACK AND TALK WITH HER ALONE!'
This is my last chance.
She drives away.
I will never, ever know.
I can't hold back the tears any longer.
I cry uncontrollably in my car. I don't feel silly.
I just can't stop. It hurts so bad but I don't know why.

jubilation * inspiration
i feel so happy * i wish my mother was here * i wish my sister was here * i want all BLACK people to experience something like tonight * if only there was some way to capture this feeling / this experience

I can't hide my emotions. At home I tell a friend what happened. His immediate reaction is that I have been a victim of reverse discrimination. No. I know that wasn't what happened. I am not angry. I am upset. I know that I wasn't ignored. I just wasn't given special attention. Now I feel silly and selfish. Am I upset because I didn't get special attention and the Black women did? Well, why shouldn't they? I respect this. It makes sense to me that this famous Black woman would be more interested in the life and goals of young Black women than in mine. So why does it still hurt me?

deloras and i immediately embarked on a conversation that ended up continuing well into the morning even though we went to a christmas party * we tried to be sociable / but we really wanted only to speak to each other / so we did * we reflected * we
analysed * we passed judgments * we laughed * we grew

Weeks / months go by. Every time I see Geraldine, I want to tell her my feelings and confused questions from that night with bell hooks. But I am afraid to. What if she said it was all my imagination, or that I was being over sensitive, or that she thought I deserved it. I don't really know her. Sometimes I am not sure what really did happen. Why was I feeling so insecure that evening? Why did I feel like I needed recognition and approval from bell? I want to do my Masters degree on anti-sexism and anti-racism. I want to learn how to educate individuals to value and respect diversity. I want to learn how to combat all the ism's and phobia's our world thrives on. These are my goals. This is me. I wanted bell to know ME. I didn't get the chance to speak with her alone.
It still hurts deep inside and the pain is a memory I can't shake.

i still think about that night * i always will * our experiences shape us * i have been moulded * every paper i write / i incorporate that night into it * every public event i speak at / i incorporate that night into it * i have always had a voice / it is stronger now

Two months later I found my explanation. I felt as if bell hooks wrote directly to me in her book *Talking Back*. This is why I, the only white woman in the circle, was not asked to describe my life and goals.

bell explains:

To make the liberated voice, one must confront the issue of audience – we must know to whom we speak. When I began writing my first book, *Ain't I a Woman: black women and feminism*, the initial completed manuscript was excessively long and very repetitious. Reading it critically, I saw that I was trying not only to address each different potential audience – black men, white women, white men, etc. – but that my words were written to explain, to placate, to appease. They contained the fear of speaking that often characterizes the way those in a lower position within a hierarchy address those in a higher position of authority. Those passages where I was speaking most directly to black women contained the voice I felt to be most truly mine – it was then that my voice was daring, courageous. When I thought about audience – the way in which the language we choose to use declares who it is we place at the centre of feminist discourse. I was transformed in consciousness and being.[1]

Again you have reduced me to tears, bell. This time I cry for joy. I knew that you had consciously skipped me in the discussion and I knew there had to be a real explanation. Now I know that it wasn't me. I was so insecure. I thought I personally had done something wrong, but I hadn't. You've taught me something very important, bell. By putting Black women at the speaking centre you gave them a voice and power and confidence. What I have learned is that I must find a way to allow all voices to be heard. To learn to educate others to genuinely value diversity. To monitor the strong voices and foster and nurture the timid ones. No one should be left out and no one should dominate. Perhaps an unrealistic ideal but one that I must strive for. Thanks bell.

i hope that i haven't sounded like i was delivering an ode to bell hooks * if i did i suppose that it is okay / she deserves it * i will not deny her a place in history * i am writing now because i feel that i have to * i have learned that before we can understand or be good to one another we must understand and be good to ourselves * and for those of us who are marginalized we must come together

I AM A WOMAN OF AFRICAN DESCENT
I AM A WOMAN WHO HAPPENS TO BE WHITE
RIGHT NOW WE ARE FEELING STRENGTH AND CONFIDENCE

Epilogue

Two months had passed before we discussed and reflected on our personal experiences from the evening with bell hooks. Our conversation was both exhilarating and exhausting and it inspired us to create this dialogue in conjunction with a longer theoretical paper that we researched and wrote together. The final product was submitted in a Women's Studies theory course and presented orally in class. In 1990, 'Understanding and Solidarity' was awarded the first Women's Studies Essay Award from the Department of Women's Studies and Feminist Research at the University of Western Ontario.

Retrospective Three Years Later

Geraldine

A funny thing happened to me the other day at work. I got a phone call from a friend of mine, an enraged friend on the verge of verbally slicing a classmate of hers to shreds. My friend is of African descent, and her classmate is of European descent.

They had been working on a joint video assignment, the topic was Black motherhood. From the very beginning of their project they battled over whose interpretation of Black family, whose interpretation of womanhood, and whose interpretation of motherhood they were going to use. And it didn't end there either. They also argued about the relevance of feminism to women who face multiple oppressions. They argued about culture. Most importantly they argued about standpoint.

It was a battle that climaxed in the editing room, when a portion of tape that my friend viewed as vital to achieving an appreciation of Black motherhood, was easily dismissed by her classmates as trivial details that should be edited out.

My friend called me to vent some of her anger. She needed to know that she wasn't over-reacting. As I consoled her, I remembered what it was like to write 'Understanding and Solidarity.'

To me, it was the ultimate exercise in patience and self-censorship. It was as rewarding as it was frustrating. To create something this personal with someone who can empathize, or identify with your standpoint is one thing. To do it with someone who, at best, has only a peripheral understanding, is another.

This assignment, as simple as it may appear, was a very effective way of allowing an introspective analysis of our personal convictions. Instead of focusing on the abstract we created a dialogue based on real experiences. Few academic assignments permit this type of personal growth. In the same way that films encourage audiences to become voyeurs, most academic assignments encourage students to separate themselves from the substance of their courses.

Exercises such as a journal by two people of different cultural, racial, sexual, or economic backgrounds encourages dialogue and self-reflection (the topics the students write on can deal with an assigned subject matter). For maximum effect, the journal should be written separately, not as a collaborative effort, and then combined as one (each student making sure that they don't compromise the uniqueness of their individual journals). The students should also be told that the objective isn't to agree or disagree with one another, but that they should analyse their differences and/or similarities.

In the end, after much compromise and frustration, I don't think that I changed Jennifer. (I never expected to or intended to.) And I know that she didn't change me. On the other hand, we were able to successfully follow the process we initiated through to completion, and we put theory into practice at a personal level. As far as I'm concerned, within the academy this is as close as you can get to reality.

Jennifer

Producing this paper was a true test of 'understanding and solidarity.' Both Geraldine and I were acutely aware of the potential for conflict that lingered on the surface because we were attempting to combine such emotional, personal experiences that were based in inherently different perspectives. It was a test of patience, compromise, and respect. To this day, we engage in critical discussions that are a reflection of the original exercise. And as frustrating as it may be, I hope we never stop. Learning is a critical process.

In retrospect, I find myself somewhat nervous about how you, the reader, will interpret the characters as presented in the dialogue. Over the past four years I have continually changed my interpretation of what I learned that evening with bell and what I learned through the process of creating this collaborative work with Geraldine. I expect that all readers will interpret the dialogue differently and some will find messages that relate to their personal identity and experience.

The dialogue is not presented as a theoretical essay to be analysed in traditional academic terms. It is our experience and a real-life example of praxis – theory in practice.

In terms of pedagogy, I learned that experience is an essential basis of education. An education that allows you to express and analyse personal experience is most enlightening. One must honestly and sincerely face the dilemmas of self-analysis – of standpoint – of bias – and prejudice. The 'process' is in fact the content.

There are no set rules or methods for facilitating critical/experiential learning within academic frameworks. However, some guidelines would include a strong commitment to dialogue and a reconceptualization of student/teacher roles and relationships so that both are recognized as active agents in the learning process. If more students were encouraged to assume control of their education, and consider their personal experience as valuable knowledge, then perhaps education could become a liberatory process that encourages critical thinking and social change.

We offer this dialogue as a guide, encouraging further commitment to radical pedagogy that utilizes experiential content and collaborative learning.

Note

1 bell hooks. *Talking Back: thinking feminist, thinking black.* Boston: South End Press, 15.

Joining the Dialogue

bell hooks

Rereading the dialogue between Geraldine Moriba-Meadows and Jennifer Dale Tiller, I was reminded of the enormous impact feminist teachers have when we speak and write. It is an awesome responsibility. I believe that it is in these moments of encounter with an anonymous feminist-thinking and/or feminist-seeking public that we work through, in experience and encounter, our understanding of feminist solidarity, of the ways we connect theory to practice. Consistently, I have felt over the years that a major obstacle to the development of feminist solidarity has been fear of conflict, and the even greater fear that our tenuous bonds and ties, especially if they are across differences, will not be sustained if we open ourselves to hearing one another speak rage, hostility, disappointment, and constructive critique along with all the positives. Working as a feminist teacher, I felt that my responsibility in this triangulated encounter did not end with just meeting the two women. I read this dialogue and I encouraged them to think of publishing it. I thought it was important because of the way it shows the different ways we perceive reality based on our needs, expectations, longings, etc.

When I first read it, I was struck by how differently I would 'read' the contact between me and Jennifer. I gave her attention but I never gave her the amount of attention she desired. My centring of black women/women of colour was informed in part by my understanding that there were indeed specific issues we would discuss relevant to our struggles to self-actualize in white supremacist patriarchal cultures. During the long stages of my development as feminist thinker and activist, I was initially very opposed to separate groups for women of colour not because I did not think those groups were important, but because it had not been my experience that we had moved past separatism. While I appreciated the need for separatism, a safe place, I also longed to see us move beyond separatism. And it seemed to me unless women worked as hard to arrive at a place where we could remain 'subjects,' not objects, whether we are in the majority or with people in a 'safe' place, there would be no real liberation. Context should not make us free or unfree. Women of colour who find it easier to speak among themselves must still struggle to come to voice in diverse settings. We live and work in a diverse world.

The tension between Geraldine, Jennifer, and myself highlights the difficulties that can arise in a context where white women are not excluded but where there is a process of decentring. That decentring was as much a space for Jennifer to learn about how it feels to be in the margins (that is not necessarily a space of exclusion or subordination) as it was about the decentring of whiteness. Concurrently, Geraldine was clearly working with interrogating the kind of power relations that can exist between a black woman and a white woman friend where the historical racist/sexist defined roles of servant–served are played out. Geraldine is throughout the encounter much more concerned about taking care of Jennifer than vice versa, even to be willing to subordinate her own needs for affirmation. Sometimes, I and other black women refer to this as a process of re-mammification. No longer maids and servants of white women, the covert demand is still often that we serve their needs. It is useful that Geraldine observes herself taking on this role whether Jennifer places it on her or not. This offers her the opportunity to reflect on the power of internalized racism.

I felt that this dialogue (similar to, yet different from, the discussion I have with my white woman friend and colleague, Mary Childers, in *Conflicts in Feminism*) enables us to bear witness to a feminist process of interaction where different perspectives, disagreements, and emotionalities like envy and jealousy can be acknowledged, yet we can grow stronger, closer together, toward that sweet communion that is sisterhood rooted in authentic solidarity. The more concrete examples we have of this process the more confident feminist women will be that there is hope for a mass-based feminist movement.

Anti-Racist Education and Practice in the Public School System

TIM McCASKELL

The attack against 'political correctness' has become a major ideological gambit of conservative forces over the last few years. Although the use of the term has reached the popular press, its usefulness in countering and disarticulating movements for progressive social change has primarily been restricted to university campuses. This is not accidental. The efficacy of 'political correctness' as an ideological frame is dependent on particular kinds of power relations, values, and assumptions that are perhaps most highly developed in the lofty terrain of academia.

Briefly, the gambit works in the following way. The conservative forces appear to give up their institutional or social power. They portray themselves as victims who are being silenced by those who feel their utterances around race or sex or whatever are unacceptable – 'politically incorrect.' They abandon the voice of authority they have traditionally assumed, and appeal to the 'people' for protection.

Notions of freedom of expression, speech, the press, and so on, have long been dear to progressive movements and the left. However, when the right deploys the notion of 'political correctness,' the left finds itself placed in the role of censor, arguing for limits on expression, speech, and so on. This is a very uncomfortable position for many. It tends to divide more libertarian elements from those most committed to anti-racist or anti-sexist work.

Conservative forces thereby wrap themselves in the flag of freedom of expression while their now-fragmented opposition appears doctrinaire, authoritarian, anti-democratic, even totalitarian. Traditionally progressive positions around free speech are articulated into the hegemonic discourse of the right.

It is obvious that what is necessary for the effectiveness of this gambit is a general consensus as to the value of free expression, the exchange of ideas, and so on. And it is just such notions that make up some of the central elements of the mythology our society holds about the nature of higher education.

But higher education is not the only area that has been undergoing a struggle for change around gender and race. The notion of 'equity' is also being increasingly raised in the publicly funded school system. A number of boards of education across the country have taken steps to meet the challenges of educating an increasingly diverse student body and overcoming well-documented disparities of educational outcome based on race, class, or gender. Their strategies have included the introduction of policies prohibiting racist and sexist speech, the promotion of more-inclusive curriculum, and establishing goals and timetables for the hiring and promotion of women and visible minorities. Yet we have not heard the same oppositional refrain outlining the dangers of totalitarian political correctness within public education that has been chorusing through university corridors.

The absence of these arguments certainly does not indicate that there has been no resistance to such changes within the public school system. But the arguments raised by conservative forces to block institutional change here are different because of differences in the institutional context.

The notion of freedom of speech has seldom been extended to include young people or children. And because they deal with young people and children, even teachers are expected to respect limits of permissible and acceptable speech. The goal of this article is to explore how and why conservative arguments against change in the public school system differ from the 'political correctness' gambit that has been so powerful in higher education.

Much of the content of this paper has been distilled from a decade of work in anti-racist education at the Toronto Board of Education. The Toronto Board is widely recognized as one of the leading boards in Canada in developing this type of policy. Since 1981 I have worked as a Student Programme Worker attached to the Toronto Board's Equal Opportunity Office. The bulk of this work has concentrated on anti-racist education but has also included issues of gender, class, and sexual orientation. My location in the system has been relatively unique. As a student worker I have had direct access to students and their concerns in environments that encourage honesty and disclosure. I have learned the undeniable reality of racism, sexism, homophobia, and other forms of brutality that make up the everyday experience of students in our educational system. Organizing students to fight for change has allowed me to experience the elation that comes from victories and the frustration that is the result of insurmountable institutional resistance.

The work has also involved training hundreds of teachers and administrators in in-service or professional development activities. Here, and as a result of my work with students, I have met many dedicated professionals struggling to deal with difficult issues. I have also encountered many varieties of resistance, blockage, and subterfuge, which this article attempts to analyse.

While I believe that much of what follows can be generalized for other boards, I would caution that just as the difference between the postsecondary and public institutions fundamentally affects the types of arguments that are mounted in each, so too the different demographic, political, and social contexts of different public boards may generate important differences.

A Note about Anti-Racist Education

There has been a far-ranging movement among progressive educators in Canada, the United States, and the United Kingdom to challenge racism and/or sexism and/or homophobia and/or class prejudice at one of their crucial points of reproduction – the education system. Anti-racist education has perhaps been the area to experience the most theoretical and practical development in recent years, especially in Canada and the United Kingdom. To a certain extent then, the problems and debates around anti-racist education are similar to those around other struggles for equity, although the specificity of these struggles must also be noted. It is therefore helpful to note some of the principles of anti-racist education in order to more clearly understand the nature of the resistances that such struggles often produce. The following six principles have been distilled from the work of anti-racist educators on both sides of the Atlantic (Francis 1984; Goody and Knight 1985; Lee 1985; McCaskell 1988, 1990; Mukherjee 1988; Mullard 1984; Thomas 1984).

- Anti-racist education starts from the assumption that observable differences in behaviour between human groups are *historical and cultural* in origin, not biological. Race is an arbitrary social category that makes use of somatic differences. It is not a biological reality. Anti-racist education therefore attempts to reveal the real institutional and social *power* relationships that underlie and produce 'race relations' and racism.

- The *motor force* in anti-racist education is seen as being those communities of people circumscribed by specific, socially constructed racial identities and their fight for justice. Institutional change is the result of political pressure.
- Anti-racist education cannot be an add-on. It requires changes *across the curriculum*. Since culture (and power) is ubiquitous, anti-racist education must affect the content of all subject areas.
- Anti-racist education must be *system-wide*. Personnel hiring and promotion policies, assessment, discipline, school community relations, social work, counselling, and symbolic value representations are all implicated in reproducing institutional racism, all reflect and engender racialized power relations, and all must be transformed.
- Anti-racist education requires a particular type of *pedagogy* that encourages and equips students and staff to understand power relations and challenge unjust systems. It must be based on learners' real social experience and it must be relevant to their lives. Teachers and students are therefore partners in an exploration of social reality that encourages responsibility and critical thinking.
- Anti-racist education must be willing to engage learners concerning *other relevant forms of oppression* (sexism, homophobia, class prejudice, etc.) as these arise in the educational process. Understanding a range of power relations will make our understanding of racism more acute.

The Nature of the Institution

The public school system operates quite differently from the marketplace of ideas that is supposed to characterize higher education. If the market is the quintessence of a capitalist economy, and the free flow of intellectual commodities the metaphor that rules higher education, the public school system can be better described with reference to feudal relations.

In a feudal arrangement we find the monarch and the court at the top of the hierarchy. The power of the monarch and the court is, however, often far more symbolic than actual. Real power lies with the barons out in the field where agricultural surplus is produced and confiscated. It is the barons who maintain the armies who assure that the peasants pay their dues. It is they who implement or ignore the rules and regulations that emanate from the court. Barons must swear their loyalty to the monarch, but woe to that monarch who incurs the wrath of his barons.

For the peasant, the basis of the system, the monarch is as far away as God. Real concrete power over life and death lies in the manor house.

As long as everybody observes their obligations – the peasant scratches surplus out of the soil, the baron collects it and pays a share to the king, and the court doesn't do anything so outlandish as to upset the barons – the system works smoothly and at least those at the top of the hierarchy are happy.

In the public school system, the top of the hierarchy includes boards of education, elected officials, and a bureaucratic apparatus of directors, superintendents, consultants, and departments. Policy is made at the board level after consultation with the appropriate layers of the bureaucracy.

Real power however lies in the actual school site. Each principal runs his or her school much as he or she sees fit. If principals feel a policy is unworkable, it goes nowhere. This pattern of decentralized real power within a nominally hierarchical structure is extended into the classroom. The classroom's activities take place behind closed doors. Each teacher then enjoys relative autonomy concerning what goes on in his or her classroom. Few boards of education will be willing to pass policies that may incure the opposition of their principals. Although principals display very different kinds of leadership, few will try to implement policy in the face of opposition from his or her teachers.

This organization also produces differences in the way knowledge and 'truth' are generated. While in the university the free market of ideas determines the value of any intellectual commodity, truth and knowledge in the public school system are more likely to be declared by fiat. They eminate from the authority of the teacher, the department, or the ministry-approved textbook.

As far as the student is concerned, the face of power is the teacher, or in more serious situations the vice-principal or the principal. It is they who make the decisions that affect the life a student leads on a day-to-day basis. It is they who decide what is to be learned and what the correct answers are.

Foucault (1980) has explored the development of knowledge and surveillance in the developing capitalist societies. In this respect our feudal analogy holds, for the public school system has few regular systems of 'accountability.' The institutional culture is 'collegial.' Practically, that means that we are all professionals and we are all doing our job unless the contrary is brought to someone's attention. This is a system that assumes that everything is working well unless it is informed otherwise.

Only when there is a crisis in the classroom that cannot be contained does the teacher seek higher authority. Only when there is a crisis in the school do higher authorities intervene (Hitner Starr Associates 1985, 12).

In 1985 the Toronto Board commissioned a study on the implementation of its race relations policy. This report, by consultants Hitner and Starr, pointed to a failure to prioritize, dysfunctional bureaucratic reporting lines, and ineffectual communication as responsible for the lack of implementation of the Toronto Board's 1979 race relations policy during its first seven years. More important, however, the Hitner Starr report discussed the impact of the *collegial system* on the process of institutional change. The effects of this system were twofold. First, it was impossible or difficult to actually monitor the implementation of, or compliance with, a given policy. Second, it is difficult for the system to generate institutional knowledge of what is actually happening to students and teachers in the schools on a daily basis. If that knowledge is unfavourable, each hermetic compartment, each classroom, each department, each school has an interest and an ability to suppress information (Hitner Starr 1985).

The culture of the education system is therefore a cautious and conservative one. Everyone tends to work hard at not antagonizing those above or below them. Everyone strives to maintain an appearance of normality so as not to occasion outside intervention. The need for such intervention is seen as an admission of failure.

The Culture of Paranoia

There is an added factor that magnifies this culture of caution into a culture of paranoia. In spite of the flexibility and autonomy of the collegial organization, teachers represent 'the state' in the classroom. In Ontario, for example, the main relationships of public education are regulated by the Education Act. Relations with other teachers and administrators are defined by the Teaching Professions Act. Accreditation is dispensed through provincially regulated institutions. Curriculum taught is defined by the Ministry of Education. Texts are selected from provincially generated lists. Salaries are paid from the public purse (and for the purposes of Ontario social contract cutbacks, teachers negotiate alongside other government employees). Evaluation of students is shaped by the demands of other accredited educational bodies. The job of teaching is therefore tightly regulated.

But, at the same time, teaching is 'front-line' work. Classrooms reflect the sum total of society's problems, stresses, and contradictions. Teachers therefore find themselves expected to teach, supervise, police, counsel, socialize with, and evaluate their students in closely regulated ways, while faced with conditions often hardly amenable to any of these functions. The demands put on the base of the system are extraordinary. These demands are to be handled by individual teachers in isolation in the context of a system that doesn't want to hear about their problems. Teachers often feel they are riding a tiger, and that no one is interested in, or understands their problems. Fear that something will go wrong, that someone will be blamed, that all hell will break loose, permeates the system.

This culture deeply affects the arguments that are made and not made in regards to change. If any change is seen as potentially upsetting a very precarious applecart, then even talk about change is dangerous. Rather than actually argue against it, it may be more effective to simply ignore it. Many of the barriers to progressive change do not take place at the level of discourse. They are structural and administrative. Those who are secure in their power structurally and administratively have no need to make arguments. Those who are secure in subverting policy have no need to contest it.

Mythologies of Public Education

Just as the feudal system rested on particular belief systems (the divine right of kings, the reflection of heavenly patriarchy and hierarchy on earth, rewards in the hereafter, and so on) so too does the public school system weave a mythology about itself that is brought to bear in debates about change. Foremost of these is the notion of professionalism – that the education system is party to specialized knowledge of the educational process – that it and its agents actually know some obscure secrets about children's minds that are key to how people learn and how to educate.

Out of this professionalism come further ideals of neutrality and objectivity. This belief in the neutrality and objectivity of the system is fundamental, since the system not only is required to educate, it must evaluate. Those evaluation procedures can only be legitimized to the extent that they are apparently neutral and unbiased.

Finally, the education system has a social role. It not only educates and evaluates, especially at the primary level, it socializes. It creates the kind of men and women that society needs and will need. Education therefore deals with instilling values in new generations. This widely accepted consensus that the public education system is about professionalism, neutrality, and socialization figures large in the debates around educational change.

Challenges and Resistances

The principles of anti-racist education mentioned above all suggest different kinds of changes and have generated different kinds of resistance.

The notion that 'racial' differences are historical and cultural, rather than biological, is a philosophical/scientific position that underpins the others. It defines what kinds of ideas are acceptable and what are not, and therefore what the boundaries are for appropriate classroom comment. While Philippe Rushton continues to hold forth at the University of Western Ontario on the 'biological' differences in intelligence, sexuality, and character between the 'races,' at least two high-school teachers who have expressed similarly racist or anti-Semitic views have been removed from their classrooms in different parts of the country. The ability to define what is appropriate speech reflects the very different set of relationships at work in the public school system compared with those found in postsecondary education.

'The Toronto Board of Education condemns, and will not tolerate the expression of racial/ethnic bias, or bias on the basis of sex or sexual orientation, in any form, by its trustees, administration, staff or students' (Minutes 28 June 1990). This statement prohibiting bias has been the cornerstone of the Toronto Board's anti-racist efforts since it was first adopted in 1978. With slight wording changes, this position has been reaffirmed on several occasions since that time. This statement not only limits what is acceptable as curriculum, it also defines what is acceptable speech between students, staff, or administration. It would clearly encompass any assertion of the biological superiority of any particular group.

The Community as the Motor Force

If disadvantaged communities are to be the motor of anti-racist change, then they must somehow be engaged wih the educational institutions and mobilized to exert pressure on them. Opposition then must concentrate on disconnecting that motor. In the Toronto Board a School Community Relations Department was set up in the late 1970s to mobilize disadvantaged and marginalized groups to ensure that their needs were being met by the educational system. This mobilization stressed the significance of the 'partnership' between home and school and its importance to children's school success.

When a more conservative Board was elected in 1986 one of its first moves was to disband this department and have School Community Advisors (SCAs) report not to an independent department but to area superintendents. SCAs were therefore much more tied into the system and less likely to be able to organize communities to exert pressure for change.

The arguments used to justify this roll-back of the advances of the previous administration were couched largely in terms of efficiency and cost savings. The non-economic arguments however referenced the notion of neutrality and objectivity, which, as we have seen, are fundamental myths of the educational system. The School Community Relations Department was portrayed as 'too political,' and therefore not congruent with the neutrality of the system. Instead of 'building bridges' between communities and the system, the School Community Relations Department was seen as inciting parents to complain, much to the discomfort of school authorities. The reorganization of school–community relations efforts sought to re-establish order and the traditional primacy of the school administration in managing these contacts.

Curriculum Changes

Progressive educators have used several arguments to call for curriculum changes. They maintain that children will learn better if curriculum reflects their home cultures and is thus more relevant to their lives. English literature therefore should also include works by authors other than the traditional 'dead white men'; history should include non-European perspectives; and science and math should also note the contributions of non-Europeans.

For minority students, it is argued, such curriculum materials are important in terms of 'self-image.' Students who learn about contributions of varying cultures including their own, will feel better about themselves and therefore will do better. A more inclusive curriculum will also correct the 'Eurocentric bias' of majority students, which is seen to be a major component in their susceptibility to racist ideas and practices (Consultative Committee 1988; Subcommittee on Race Relations 1978).

It is important to recognize that what is at stake here is not the prohibition of one sort of speech but rather the replacement of one speech content by another. It is therefore difficult to base one's opposition to curriculum change on the spectre of totalitarian orthodoxy (political correctness) since those in opposition are in fact clearly defending another orthodoxy. The debate does not engage the notion of political correctness but must focus on the supposed superiority of one orthodoxy over another.

There are three major lines of argument in the debate on curriculum change. The first has to do with the importance of the classics in the traditional curriculum and the notion of 'greatness.' There is great drama, great art, and great music, all of which are generally expected to be European in origin. But the 'greatness' of these works allows them to rise above their ethnic, racial, or cultural specificity to deal with 'human values' of equal relevance to everyone. Traditional curricula thereby attain the status of the universal, while the work of people of colour, for example, is locked into its ethnic, racial, or cultural specificity.

Once the greatness, and therefore the essential character, of the traditional curriculum content has been established, the introduction of 'additional' material becomes a question of practicality and time, since there can be no question of actually replacing the 'human and universal' curriculum with the fragmented and ethnicized curriculum.

A second tactic is to dress up standard curriculum in new clothes and in effect say, 'We are already doing it.' Thus Joseph Conrad's *Heart of Darkness* is given as proof that African literature is being dealt with. A twist is to say that teachers are not properly trained to deal with anything but the most orthodox curriculum, and therefore are not qualified to teach other material. This argument prefigures deeply held assumptions of the teacher as the fundamental and authorized source of knowledge, a topic that will be dealt with in more detail later.

The final element of the curriculum argument is the notion of 'reverse discrimination' – that talk about racism somehow disadvantages majority or 'white' students. It is sometimes argued that an inclusive curriculum ignores the 'majority' and that by 'bending over backwards' to meet the needs of minority students, we are in fact forgetting about the majority and are therefore undemocratic.

A slightly stronger variation on the theme of majority as victim maintains that dealing with racism only serves to make white people feel defensive and guilty. This is especially believed to be true in the case of history class, where looking at historical injustices and discrimination is said to 'just open up old wounds' and to disrupt the harmony of the modern classroom.

Then there is the position that anti-racist efforts are actually racist or discriminatory. When a notice was sent out to Toronto Board secondary English heads inviting young women of colour to contribute to an anthology of writings in 1990, a number of the heads were furious and refused to post the notice on the grounds that such an anthology was racist and sexist since it discriminated against white and male students. We can see here a strategy similar to that employed in the right-wing appropriation of 'political correctness' to portray the traditionally most advantages or power groups as victims. However, since teachers regularly tell students what they can or cannot write about, the concept deployed is 'discrimination' (a breakdown in neutrality) not 'freedom of speech' (which evokes issues of political correctness).

Some arguments against curriculum change are subject-based. While it may be granted that some areas such as English literature or history and the social sciences lend themselves to anti-racist work, those involved in the 'hard' sciences are more likely to see it as unrelated to their subject area. Although it is true that some subjects are more flexible in their content, concerned science and math teachers can go a long way toward providing an anti-racist classroom experience through different kinds of group work, examples, and problem content (Shan and Bailey 1991).

System-Wide Implications – Discipline

The most striking non-curriculum area that attempts to regulate speech is the area of discipline. As we have mentioned above, in the Toronto Board, particular kinds of speech have been prohibited – name calling, derogatory comments, racial, ethnic, and sexual slurs, and so on. Such a policy would be most problematic in a university setting, eliciting howls of 'politically correct' censorship. However this policy statement has probably been the least controversial part of the Toronto Board's Race Relations initiatives, and perhaps the one in which most progress has been made in the public school environment. A policy of disciplining particular kinds of speech has affected both teachers and students. Teachers have often told me that the most dramatic change in behaviour that has taken place in the fifteen years of the race relations policy at the Toronto Board is that the telling of racial jokes is no longer socially acceptable in the staff room. Among students, too, there has been a marked increase in sensitivity to racial name calling and a similar, but less dramatic, decrease in sexist and homophobic language.

There have been a number of reasons for the relative success of these efforts and the lack of opposition to them. One is institutional culture.

Language – including the production of appropriate language and the censoring of inappropriate language – has always been a function of the public school system. 'No swearing,' 'No sexual talk,' 'Proper grammar' – these have been central components of schooling in Canada for generations. The task is therefore not to set up dramatically new practices around language but rather to shift the categories of the inappropriate and unacceptable to include particular forms of racist, sexist, or homophobic speech.

The arguments used by those who have pushed for stronger measures against this kind of speech have also been congruent with the general cultural parameters of the institution. Teachers' expressions of racial prejudice undermine their position of neutrality in terms of student evaluation. Such expressions are 'unprofessional' and will generally be policed by peers and colleagues.

A second reason for the success in prohibiting certain kinds of speech is managerial in nature. It is evident that racist speech acts increase racial or ethnic tension and easily escalate into other kinds of confrontation that may be uncontrollable. The use of racist speech in personal arguments tends to transform personal confrontations into group confrontations. From the purely practical point of view of classroom or school management, logic dictates that certain forms of speech must be prohibited. The culture of paranoia and teachers' fears of losing control if volatile speech is permitted further encourage such measures, even among those who might not be normally expected to be sympathetic.

A third explanation, which is more appropriate to primary schools, rests on the consensus around the school's important role in socialization. Children are to be taught the social skills of sharing, cooperation, empathy, and so on – the foundations of being good human beings. Teaching children that 'it's not nice' to say hurtful things about other people is once again congruent with fundamental educational practices.

Two final explanations deal with students' capacity to participate in the learning environment. Once again 'self-image' is a key concept, along with 'safety.' Although research fails to show a significant correlation between a positive self-image and educational performance, the notion that children with poor self-images do poorly is an accepted and powerful myth among educators (Ogbu 1987; Solomon 1992, 24). Facing a barrage of negative names and connotations produces poor self-image, which then inhibits educational performance, goes the argument. Therefore, prohibition of certain kinds of speech is important to ensure that all students do well.

On firmer empirical ground is the concept of safety. Children who must face constant taunts and negative comments or harassment are more likely to be absent and preoccupied, to resist institutional demands, or to drop out, all of which ultimately affect their performances. When students feel that the school is a hostile place for themselves or their group, they are likely to develop what Ogbu (1987) terms 'cultures of resistance.' They resist cooperation with the system and thus success within it, because such success is seen as a sign of selling out and giving in to a hostile structure. The development of a culture of resistance will certainly affect the performance of anyone subscribing to the values of the resisting group.

Since all of these arguments are so firmly rooted in the basic assumptions of the culture of the institutions, the arguments mobilized to oppose them are relatively weak. Conservative sectors that oppose a range of other educational changes can hardly reject what amounts to stiffer discipline – the traditional institutional power relations are unchallenged.

A handful of educators will still quote, 'Sticks and stones will break my bones but names will never hurt me,' in an attempt to downplay the seriousness of racist speech. Still others will paraphrase Nietzsche's 'What doesn't kill you makes you strong.' The notion here is that facing adversity builds character and therefore those who are most harassed are actually most privileged. However, since this concept runs against the grain of the patronizing instincts of the majority of educators, who believe that their role is to help and guide their charges and keep them from harm, it tends not to carry much weight.

Perhaps the most effective argument against prohibiting racist speech is the spectre of false accusations. Teachers fear that students will use such policies in personal vendettas, accusing them of racism in order to escape discipline or settle scores. One Metro Toronto Board actually defines unsuccessfully accusing a teacher of racism as a racial incident, thereby making a complainant subject to discipline if the complaint is not accepted – a strategy guaranteed to make any student think twice about making a complaint (East York Board of Education, pamphlet, 'Judge Me Not'). Such a policy demonstrates fears that anti-racist policies will loose a torrent of accusations and disrupt the ordered power relations that are seen as essential to the smooth functioning of the educational project.

Pedagogy

Perhaps the area that produces most resistance and that best illuminates the differences in context between higher and 'public' education has to do with pedagogy. Here the question at issue is not what cannot be said, but what can be said and by whom.

We have seen how the question of discipline and the policing of language and action is perfectly compatible with the culture of public education. Changes in curriculum, while causing some discomfort and resistance, aim at transforming *what* is said but not *who* is doing the talking.

The pedagogy suggested by anti-racist education often causes most resistance since it runs against the grain of educational culture. At question here is both what is said and who is saying it. Anti-racist education demands a profound democratization of education. It calls for active community involvement. It presupposes that students have the ability to become experts in deconstructing the power dynamics that race, sex, sexual orientation, and so on, weave through their lives. Where students are encouraged to speak frankly about their experiences, the power relationships between teachers, administrators, and students may also be called into account. The power relationships of the school and how they are implicated in producing and reproducing racist ideas, practices, and conflicts may also be revealed.

The arguments against a pedagogy that encourages students to speak about race and other forms of oppression in their lives usually pivot around the question of power, articulated in terms of control. One particular form of resistance states: 'If you talk about racism, you cause racism.' Speech is seen as exacerbating racial tensions, potentially polarizing racial groupings and laying the groundwork for further conflict. A second line of defence is that teachers are not properly prepared to manage such discussions. Again the spectre of speech leading to a breakdown in control is used to avoid speech.

In 1986 the Toronto Board's Equal Opportunity Office organized a contest to encourage students to identify bias in their texts and library books. The contest offered a prize for the best student essay explaining why a particular passage was biased. Although the Board since 1979 had a policy encouraging students to identify bias, the response from teachers and principals was so dramatic that the contest had to be cancelled. The tone of some of the unsolicited letters from teachers opposing the contest illustrates the nature of these fears:

As a teacher-librarian, I am appalled at the implications of turning students into 'thought police.' I believe that all responsible educators must oppose prejudice but not by such means. They are totally unacceptable to me. Surely context and culture, time and place must be considered when reading any material. Are *The Bible*, Shakespeare, Twain and many other culturally significant writing to thus be targeted for bias by these latter-day Savonarolas?

The contest aspect of identifying bias is extremely ill-advised. I have received numerous telephone calls from secondary school teachers who are affronted by this extraordinary method of removing biased materials from our schools.

The attitude of these callers has been extreme anger that students should be encouraged by a prize (especially a monetary prize) to seek out biased material. Several teachers have asked if they should start by removing *The Holy Bible* from their shelves.

Students require careful guidance in *interpreting* bias; identifying it is the easy part. Guidance should come from someone with expertise in the curriculum which is being dealt with, that is, from the teacher.

Most of the writers took pains to point out that they were not opposed in principle to identifying biased materials or even removing them from school circulation (although the contest involved identification only, not removal). Their anger focused on the fact that students were encouraged to do this identification outside of their control or supervision. Once 'unqualified' students embarked on this task it would undoubtedly end in excess, even to the point of questioning the Bible.

These 'floodgates' arguments all rest on a bedrock of paranoia, the fear that student speech will be uncontrollable and will escape or challenge teacher's and administrator's authority in the school. The spectre of students 'out of control' then allows for the deployment of 'safety' arguments – 'If we talk about this they will riot and somebody will get hurt.' The assumption recalls a colonial fantasy in which only a thin red line (here of teachers and administrators) stands between civilization and the potential anarchy of the savages (i.e., students). Student speech is the spark that could ignite the tinderbox. Pedagogy that encourages such speech is seen as potentially dangerous.

Other Issues: Class, Sex, and Sexual Orientation

Because anti-racist education opens up the question of social power and therefore requires discussion of all forms of oppression, it often moves into areas that cause different kinds of discomfort. The arguments that attempt to block such explorations take various forms. Occasionally the conservative position is sophisticated enough to recognize that it is the exploration of power itself that poses the danger of a coherent social critique and brings into question a range of traditional relationships and values. The response then is often a kind of instinctive naïvety that would reduce anti-racist education to a call for tolerance and Christian love and abandon all this troublesome and complicated talk about power.

The exploration of specific areas of power can provoke different kinds of opposition. In terms of race, there is a general consensus in our society that racism is 'wrong.' That means that fundamental opposition is very conservative in nature and is generally unable to convince 'reasonable people.' For this reason most of the arguments noted above have been tactical in nature. They don't oppose the goals of anti-racist education, just the methods used to achieve those goals. Around other forms of power relations similar kinds of consensus do not always exist. Opposition will be more wide-ranging and even occasionally will take on a 'progressive' character.

Class is one of the most difficult areas of power relations to speak of in the public school system. The notion that we live in a classless society, or at least one where class is the result of individual merit, is deeply embedded in the values of a public education system that is expected to offer the same kinds of opportunities to everyone. The suggestion that the educational system may somehow be complicit in the reproduction of class difference is met with hostility. In practice the only acceptable way that class power can be talked about is with reference to its gender and racial indicators. We can talk about the power that certain groups of white males wield in our society, for example, but other forms of describing class will immediately be identified and discredited as Marxist, communist, or 'political.'

A more specific discussion of class runs into several difficulties. People can be enjoined to give up racist ideas and practices but they can hardly be enjoined to give up class privilege. The whole notion of equity calls for equal access to 'success' (i.e., class privilege) in spite of irrelevant characteristics such as race or sex. It does not question the notion of 'success' itself.

While the left is often ambivalent about talking about class, since class contradictions are seen as irresolvable in the educational setting, more hegemonic positions have either denied the existence of class or insisted on a model of mobility that allowed anyone who works hard equal access to the fruits of success. Whereas in mainstream thought racial inequality is generally tied to the concept of injustice, class inequalities are not. In a society that professes social mobility, one's class position is seen as the result of merit. In the practice of anti-racist work, I have found that talk of class is usually restricted to moments dealing with the objections of poor or working-class white students. The introduction of class into the conversation allows for the validation of experiences of oppression from this group, who, if race is the only operative category, find themselves unproblematically identified with and lumped in with the dominant white power group. Recognition of class oppression becomes a bridge that helps this group understand the racial oppression that others experience.

A second problem is that the racially defined communities that are central to anti-racist education, and the political organizing along these lines that are the motor pushing change, generate notions of racial solidarity that are challenged when other kinds of oppression come on to the floor. How does one talk about class, or the oppression of women, or lesbians and gay men in minority communities, without subverting the solidarity of those communities or perhaps reproducing racial stereotypes? In the same way, does talk about racial oppression not put into question such categories as 'women' or 'lesbian and gay community'? These difficulties generate parallel streams of work around different issues, with co-operation between them depending on a host of factors. Arguments about who is most oppressed, which area has had most resources, and what areas should take priority are generated under these conditions, all of which tend to block progressive work of various kinds.

Debates around homophobia for instance are closely related to these difficulties. The public school system does not easily deal with questions of sexuality and children. In spite of the schools' responsibility for sex education, this highly charged area is still felt to be the prerogative of the 'home,' and parents still exercise veto power over the participation of their children in sex education. If sexuality is highly charged, homosexuality is even more so. Opposition to dealing with homophobia then ranges from the right-wing position that the school is somehow subverting moral standards set in the home, to more 'progressive' fears that speech on this topic will endanger the ability of progressive people to conduct speech in other areas. 'It's hard enough to deal with sexual harassment of women without bringing the harassment of lesbians and gay men into it,' one progressive educator explained to me. The usual argument here revolves around 'time.' It's never 'time' to deal with issues of homophobia since the system 'isn't ready for it yet.' If we do talk about this, it might discredit us in terms of other, more important work.

This last principle of anti-racist education – its identification of the concept of social power and the subsequent logical step of dealing with other power relationships – therefore tends to generate a whole different family of oppositional arguments based on problems surrounding the tactics of dealing with more than one issue at a time. These arguments do not always come from traditionally conservative forces but from areas that may generally be considered progressive.

Conclusion

The debate around 'political correctness' has not taken on important proportions in the struggles around race and gender equity in the public school system. The right-wing use of political correctness presupposes the inviolability of the market (of ideas). It conceptually frames 'arbitrary' attempts to restrict speech in that market by linking them to the strategy of intervention or suppression of a market economy common to the 'now discredited' experience of the former socialist world. Attempts to restrict racist or sexist speech therefore become totalitarian.

The ideology of the public school system however has never encompassed the notion of the marketplace of ideas. Children have never been afforded freedom of speech or entry into that market. Their access to ideas and speech has always been closely controlled by higher powers. In the same way, children's rights have been restricted in most spheres, for 'good reason' (for example, children have been denied entry into the market economy by labour legislation in order to protect them from exploitation).

Opposition to changes in the rules of discourse around race, sex, sexual orientation, and so on, in the public schools therefore traditionally has not reflected the strategy of opposing political correctness. Rather, it bases itself on notions of the effect such changes might have on the system's ability to exercise control and manage its often captive and restless population.

Postscript

This article was originally written in the summer of 1992, looking back on the experience in the Toronto Board in the late 1980s and early 1990s when the debate on political correctness was raging in the universities. Since then, however, 'political correctness' has become a household concept, percolating down from the hights of academia into popular culture. In this respect it is today more commonly being employed around debates within the schools.

As well, to the extent that public education has been an object of study for right-wing academics, political correctness has been employed in their analysis (e.g., MacDonald 1992). However, such analysis is far removed from the on-the-ground struggles within schools, and 'political correctness' still fails to wield the same power here as it has in higher education.

References

Consultative Committee on the Education of Black Students in Toronto Schools. 1988. *The Education of Black Students in Toronto Schools.* Toronto: Toronto Board of Education

Foucault, M. 1980. *Power/Knowledge: Selected Interviews and Other Writings 1972–1977.* New York: Pantheon Books

Francis, M. 1984. 'Anti-Racist Teaching: General Principles' and 'Anti-Racist Teaching: Curricular Practices.' In *Challenging Racism.* London: All London Teachers Against Racism and Fascism

Goody, J., and H. Knight. 1985. 'Multicultural Education and Anti-Racist Teaching.' *English in Education* 19(3) (Autumn): 3–7

Hitner Starr Associates. 1985. *Race Relations Program Review.* Toronto: Toronto Board of Education

Lee, E. 1985. *Letters to Marcia, A Teachers Guide to Anti-Racist Education.* Toronto: Cross Cultural Communications Centre

McCaskell, T. 1988. *Facilitators Handbook, Multicultural/Multiracial Residential Camp for Secondary School Students.* Toronto: Toronto Board of Education, Office of the Advisor on Race Relations

– 'Anti-Racist and Anti-Homophobic Education.' Unpublished manuscript. Toronto: Centre for Lesbian and Gay Studies

MacDonald, Heather. 1992. 'The Sobol Report: Multiculturalism Triumphant' *The New Criterion* (Jan.)

Mukherjee, A. 1988. *From Racist to Anti-Racist Education, A Synoptic View.* Toronto: Toronto Board of Education, Equal Opportunity Office
Mullard, C. 1984. *Anti-Racist Education: The Three O's.* London: National Association for Multi-Racial Education
Ogbu, J. 1987. 'Variability in Minority School Performance: A Problem in Search of an Explanation.' *Anthropology and Education Quarterly* 18: 312–34
Shan, S., and Bailey, P. 1991. *Multiple Factors: Classroom Mathematics for Equality and Justice.* Stoke-on-Trent: Trentham Books
Solomon, P. 1992. *Black Resistance in High School, Forging a Separatist Culture.* Albany: State University of New York Press
Sub Committee on Race Relations. 1978. *Draft Report of the Sub Committee on Race Relations.* Toronto: Toronto Board of Education (May)
Thomas, B. 1984. 'Principles of Anti-Racist Education.' *Currents, Readings in Race Relations.* Toronto: Urban Alliance on Race Relations (Fall): 20–4
Toronto Board of Education, Minutes, 28 June 1990